PROVINCIAL RUSSIA

IN THE AGE OF

ENLIGHTENMENT

PROVINCIAL RUSSIA

IN THE AGE OF

ENLIGHTENMENT

The Memoir of a Priest's Son

DMITRII IVANOVICH ROSTISLAVOV

Translated and Edited by

Alexander M. Martin

NORTHERN

ILLINOIS

UNIVERSITY

PRESS

DeKalb

The frontispiece figure is from *Russkie deiateli v portretakh gravirovannykh akademikom Lavrentiem Seriakovym. Izdanie redaktsii zhurnala: "Russkaia Starina,"* 5 vols. (St. Petersburg: Tipografiia V. S. Balasheva, 1882–91), 2: 105.

Library of Congress Cataloging-in-Publication Data

Rostislavov, Dmitrii Ivanovich, 1809–1877.

[Zapiski. English]

Provincial Russia in the Age of Enlightenment : the memoir of a priest's son / Dmitrii Ivanovich Rostislavov ; translated, edited, and with an introduction by Alexander M. Martin.

p.   cm.

ISBN 0-87580-285-0 (alk. paper)

1. Riazan' (Riazanskaia oblast', Russia)—Social life and customs—19th century. 2. Rostislavov, Dmitrii Ivanovich, 1809–1877.

I. Martin, Alexander M. II. Title.

DK651.R495 R6713 2002

947'.33—dc21   2001044495

For my parents

Contents

List of Illustrations

FIGURES

DIAGRAM AND MAPS

Acknowledgments

• This project would not have been feasible without generous support and encouragement by a number of individuals and institutions.

I first read Rostislavov's *Zapiski,* and began preliminary work on the translation, while on leave from teaching thanks to a grant from the National Endowment for the Humanities. Once the translation was largely completed, a faculty development grant from Oglethorpe University gave me the opportunity to visit and do research in Riazan and other places connected with Rostislavov's life, while an invitation to lecture at the Third St. Petersburg International Summer School in the History of Ideas (hosted by the Russian Academy of Sciences and funded by the Open Society Institute) allowed me to work in the archives of St. Petersburg and Moscow.

Mary Lincoln and the late W. Bruce Lincoln gave their warm encouragement to the project, as did the readers for Northern Illinois University Press and my friends and colleagues of the Southeast Workshop in Russian History, who offered their comments on several draft chapters at our January 1999 meeting at Emory University. My work drew me into aspects of Russian social and cultural history outside my earlier area of expertise, and here I benefitted from the advice of Gregory Freeze, Laurie Manchester, the late Stephen L. Baehr, David Griffiths, and others whose help I acknowledge in my footnotes, as well as my colleagues at Oglethorpe (especially Ann Hall) who were always forthcoming with ideas and suggestions. Despite having worked on the translation for almost two years, I had no idea what Rostislavov actually looked like until Kelly O'Neill kindly obtained for me the portrait that is reproduced in this book, and I was able to design the maps for the book thanks to the assistance of the Oglethorpe University Network Services department.

I thank the Russian State Historical Archive (RGIA), the State Archive of the Russian Federation (GARF), and the Russian National Library for their assistance, as well as the staff of the Russian

Ethnographic Museum in St. Petersburg who kindly allowed me to use the photographs contained in this book and that I hope will be of value to readers who are newcomers to Russian social history. And I owe a special debt of thanks to the kind and helpful staff of the State Archive of Riazan Province (GARO), especially Dmitrii Filippov, who treated me as an honored guest and without whose invaluable assistance much of the archival research for this project would have been impossible.

My hope all along has been that this book would interest both the expert and the educated lay reader, so the opinion of such readers has been particularly important to me. Those who generously read the manuscript and offered their advice include my students at Oglethorpe—particularly Adrienne Lerner, Jennifer Entenmann, and Blake Stabler—and my mother, Gudrun Martin, whose reminiscences about rural Germany in the 1940s helped me make sense of Rostislavov's account of rural Russia a century earlier. Both of them taught me that, if our world has gained much by becoming affluent and modern and emancipated, there is also much that we have lost.

Finally, this book would not exist had my wife, Laurie, not had the idea of undertaking the project in the first place and been, as always, my best reader, sharpest critic, most supportive editor, and most patient listener, and I especially thank Jeff and Nicki for their patience at times when I seemed to spend more time with Rostislavov than with them.

Translator's Introduction

• The lead story of the St. Petersburg newspaper *Golos (The Voice)* on March 3, 1877, concerned the crisis brewing in the Balkans, which would lead within months to war between Russia and the Ottoman Empire, begin the unraveling of Russia's alliance with Germany and Austria-Hungary, and help set the stage for World War I. Another article foreshadowed the coming age of industrialism and mechanized warfare by reporting that Russia's artillery was experimenting with electric lights whose power equalled that of fourteen thousand candles. And, on page three, there was continuing coverage of the trial of fifty young men and women, most of them in their early twenties and ranging in social rank from prince to peasant, who had allegedly formed an illegal association aimed at overthrowing the monarchy and had disseminated seditious literature and fired shots from a revolver at a police officer who tried to arrest them. Four years later almost to the day, their comrades would kill the tsar, and forty years later, others like them would establish in Russia the world's first revolutionary Marxist government.

Perhaps without realizing it, the editors of *Golos* were observing the end of an era. Throughout the Western world, the forces of modernity and tradition had been locked in an inconclusive struggle for power ever since the late eighteenth century. After reaching a bloody climax on the battlefields of the 1850s and 1860s—in the Crimean War (which sparked the Great Reforms of the 1860s and 1870s in Russia), the American and Mexican civil wars, and the wars of German and Italian unification—the struggle ended in a lasting new synthesis of conservative and liberal forces embodied in the Kingdom of Italy (created in 1861), the Austro-Hungarian Dual Monarchy (created in 1867), the French Third Republic (in 1870), the German Empire (in 1871), the rise to power of Porfirio Díaz in Mexico (in 1876), the end of Reconstruction in the United States (in 1877), and the limited counterreforms of Alexander III in Russia (after 1881). Along with the old political conflicts, an entire traditional way of life seemed destined to fade into history, as American slavery and Russian serfdom were abolished, German guilds and the Church of England were stripped of their privileges, wealth and occupation came to replace inherited status as the key to social standing, and Germany, France, the United States, and—much more gradually—Russia followed Great Britain's earlier lead in making the breakthrough to industrialism. As *Golos*'s snapshot of Russia in early 1877 suggests, however, the reform era of the 1850s–1870s was giving way to new challenges and uncertainties: the aggressive nationalisms of Pan-Slavs and Pan-Germans, the revolutionary movements of socialists and anarchists, and the ominous amalgam of a jingoistic mass-circulation press, demagogic mass politics, and the emerging military-industrial complex.

Amidst these ominous if inchoate glimpses of a new world in the making, *Golos* noted the passing, in the provincial town of Riazan on February 18, 1877, of one Dmitrii Ivanovich Rostislavov, dead at sixty-seven and identified in the obituary as "a gifted and hard-working writer" on questions related to the Russian Orthodox Church. Born the same year as Abraham Lincoln and Charles Darwin—and within a decade of Charles Dickens, John Stuart Mill, Benito Juárez, and Karl Marx—Rostislavov had been in every respect a man of the era now coming to a close. The son of a mere village priest, he had a remarkable career as an educator and became an influential social critic in the era of the Great Reforms. His principal area of concern was the Russian clergy, but he shared the view, widely held among contemporaries in Russia and elsewhere, that it was essential more generally for the educated classes to gain a better understanding of the common people, because "the people" were the chief repository of national character and tradition, because their suffering deserved the sympathetic attention of the powerful, and because they embodied a way of life that might disappear with the modernization of society. Drawing on his childhood memories and on stories handed down in his family, Rostislavov wrote an account of life in his native region—the part of Riazan Province known as the Meshchora—in the late eighteenth and early nineteenth centuries. Part autobiography, part ethnographic investigation, and part sociological study, this panorama of provincial life introduces the reader to clerics and peasants, merchants and officials, Russians and Tatars, villagers and townspeople, with a focus that moves from folk beliefs and family life to farm work, drinking habits, education, the mores of the bureaucracy, and other topics. The present book is an abridged translation of that text. This introduction will first describe the region and society that form the setting for Rostislavov's account, and then discuss the life and times of the author himself.[1]

THE SETTING

Situated a hundred miles southeast of Moscow, the Meshchora region of Riazan Province *(guberniia)* lies within a large bend of the wide, navigable river Oka as it winds its way east toward the Volga. Surveys prepared by general staff officers found that Riazan Province—which took its name from its capital town, as did almost all Russian provinces and districts—consisted of two very unequal parts. South, west, and east of the great Oka bend, the land is more elevated, the soils are well drained, and in the mid-nineteenth century, grain agriculture flourished and population density was high. Across the Oka, however, lies the Meshchora, a marshy lowland with sandy soils and dense evergreen forests.[2]* The district *(uezd)* of Kasimov, the Delaware-size section of the Meshchora that was Rostislavov's home, had the most surface area, forests, and wastelands of any of the twelve districts that made up Riazan Province, but ranked at the bottom of the list for population density and acreage of farm land.[3]† Not surprisingly, the area was poorly suited to grain production or vegetable farming, had abundant lumber, game, mushrooms, and berries in its vast forests, and was infested with insects. The principal exception was—and still is—a narrow east-west strip of land that is slightly higher and drier, through which the main road passes, and along which most settlements in the Meshchora are situated. Like most of European Russia, the Meshchora has a continental climate: mid-nineteenth-century winters typically set in around the middle of October and lasted until early April, with lows around –20 degrees Réaumur (about –10 degrees Fahrenheit or –25 degrees Centigrade) that did not strike the general staff officers as particularly cold. Once the snow melted, the accompanying spring flooding subsided, and the mud dried into dust, a warm

---

* The region's name is probably related to the Riazanian regionalism *meshchernik,* which refers to "acidic soil covered with coniferous forests and unsuitable as meadowland or plowland." Please note: in the interest of reader convenience, this and other explanatory material is placed in *footnotes* at the bottom of the page. On the other hand, references to bibliographic and archival sources (including those relevant to the information contained in the footnotes) are placed in *endnotes* at the end of the book. To reduce confusion, *footnotes* are identified by stars and daggers, *endnotes* by numbers.

† At 54 inhabitants per square mile, population density in the 1840s was significantly higher in Kasimov District than in U.S. frontier areas (e.g., Ohio or Maine), but barely over half that of even sparsely settled European regions like northeastern Prussia.

Northern Districts of Riazan Province

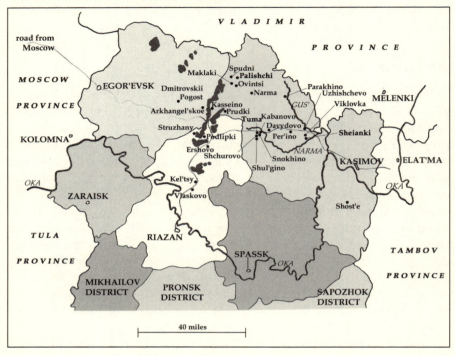

summer would prevail until mid-September, when the weather turned windy and wet in anticipation of the October frosts.[4]

The harsh conditions of premodern life—in nineteenth-century Russia, half of any given generation typically died before age ten,[5] and a highly precarious future awaited even those who lived to reach adolescence—combined with narrow horizons and a lack of education to produce a profoundly conservative way of life that was dominated by two interlocking institutions: the family and the community.[6] Most people lived on family farms where roles were assigned on the basis of sex and age. Men principally worked in the fields, and women labored in and around the house. Men were assumed to have authority over women, and older people over their juniors. Since rural Russians, unlike their American or West European contemporaries, typically lived in patrilineal extended families—i.e., adult sons continued living with their parents and brought their wives into their parents' households—a rural family was often a multigenerational structure with a complex chain of command in which the father was at the top, the youngest daughter-in-law at the

Plan of Tuma (1884)

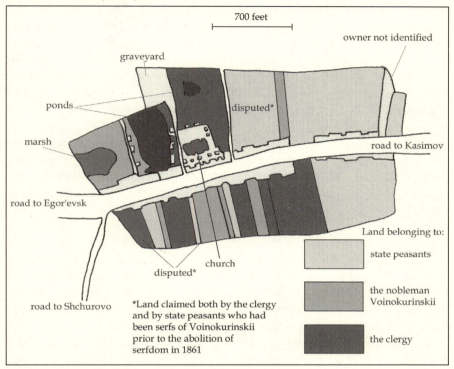

700 feet

owner not identified

graveyard

ponds

disputed*

marsh

road to Kasimov

road to Egor'evsk

church

disputed*

road to Shchurovo

*Land claimed both by the clergy
and by state peasants who had
been serfs of Voinokurinskii
prior to the abolition of
serfdom in 1861

Land belonging to:

state peasants

the nobleman
Voinokurinskii

the clergy

Map was based on surveys of 1772 and 1871. (Source: GARO, f. 892, op. 1, d. 230, l. 1)

bottom, and all others occupied various intermediate positions. It was a further Russian peculiarity that a village's land was managed in common and was redistributed among the village families every few years by the assembly of male heads of households, a powerful and more or less democratic institution that also determined each family's share of the village's tax burden and which family's sons would have to join the army when the government demanded recruits. Urban communities had similar assemblies that apportioned taxes and military obligations among their members. A map of Rostislavov's father's home community, the village of Tuma in Kasimov District, illustrates how this system worked: the village's agricultural land was permanently divided among the different communities that composed the village's population—in this case, state peasants, clergy, and the serfs of the local noble landlord—and those communities would, in turn, divide "their" land among their member households.

Within any given community, two separate systems of social identity uneasily coexisted. One system, created by local custom, sustained communal autarky but blurred the lines between social strata within individual communities. Since the solidarity, cohesion, and economic viability of family and community were paramount for everyone's survival, local society punished those who strayed from traditional norms of behavior but also shielded its members against outsiders. Thus, young men regarded as troublemakers were the first to be sent to the army; a community's attitude toward robbers was based on the threat they posed to that community itself; and, when an individual had offended the community, the response was either to punish and then reintegrate the offender or to eliminate him completely, but either way, the conflict was quickly resolved and communal harmony restored.

Geography encouraged this local communalism, for settlements were small and distances daunting. For example, the village of Palishchi, where Rostislavov spent his early childhood, had only twelve households and eighty inhabitants, yet it served as the regional center for settlements within a radius of twelve miles, because the district capital Kasimov—itself only a small town—was about sixty miles away.[7] Such distances hampered trade between town and country, while the short growing season and poor soils made it difficult for farmers and their landlords to live from agriculture alone. As a result, many peasant men supplemented farming with trade or seasonal labor in the towns, and the nobles adjusted to these circumstances by collecting cash rents (quitrent) from their serfs rather than demanding the compulsory agricultural labor (corvée) that was more common, and more profitable, in areas better suited to farming.[8]* Meanwhile, the urban population, in the absence of an easily accessible peasant market for their goods and services, often practiced agriculture in addition to trade or crafts. Provincial Russians were thus jacks-of-all-trades, at once farmers, traders, and artisans, who provided for most of their own needs and lived in a partly cashless economy where the distinction between town and country often had little meaning. That made it impossible for communities to pay their local clergy a salary, so the clerics supplemented the fees they charged for performing particular religious rites by farming land that belonged to the church.

---

* In Kasimov District around 1850, 64 percent of serfs paid only quitrent *(obrok)* while a mere 16 percent performed only corvée *(barshchina);* another 20 percent combined the two. By contrast, for Riazan Province as a whole—owing to the weight of the more agriculturally prosperous southern districts—the share of peasants on corvée reached 37 percent while the share on quitrent was only 38 percent.

The vagueness of occupational distinctions; the habits of local autonomy and self-sufficiency; the underdeveloped state of bureaucratic authority and of the road network, the book trade, money circulation, and other forces that might have given structure and unity to society; and the islandlike quality of the small settlements scattered among vast forests and marshes—all of these factors gave a medieval flavor to life in the Meshchora. To understand how the people there experienced and imagined their world, we need hardly look farther than Jacques Le Goff's account of the medieval West. Western Europe during the High Middle Ages, he points out, had "remained a collection, juxtaposed, of manors, castles, and towns arising out of the midst of stretches of land which were uncultivated and deserted." In that society, "the individual belonged first and foremost to his family. The family was a large, patriarchal or tribal one, directed by the head of the family. It stifled the individual, forcing him to submit to the collective ownership of property, collective responsibility, and collective action." The clearing settled by family and village was enclosed by the forest, a space that, both physically and symbolically, was the village's polar opposite—a world of freedom and riches, danger and mystery. "For the peasants and a mass of poor working people," Le Goff writes, the forest's economic resources were "a source of profit," but "the forest was also full of menace and imaginary or real dangers. It formed the disquieting horizon of the medieval world." "Hungry wolves, brigands, and robber-knights could suddenly spring out of its notorious dark depths," and "it was easy for the medieval imagination, drawing on an immemorial folklore, to turn these devouring wolves into monsters. [. . .] Thus, because they harbored terrors that were only too real, the forests became a world of marvelous and frightening legends."[9]

In the Meshchora around 1800, the general uniformity of living conditions and the insularity of rural life bred distinctive, typically premodern personality traits and habits of thought that one found among both women and men and at all levels of society. These included cleverness in practical things but naïve ignorance about scientific or intellectual matters, respect for manual dexterity rather than book learning, and slyness in manipulating or evading society's power structure but acceptance of its basic legitimacy. People were strongly attached to their social and geographic roots, harbored a deep, often superstitious religiosity, seldom engaged in psychological introspection or sensitivity, and exhibited a harsh and autocratic temper as well as a great ability to endure (and inflict) physical and emotional pain. They had a take-charge yet fatalistic view of life, preferred to eat, drink, and be merry today rather than save for a future that death might cut short at any moment, loved hospitality and gaudy display, and demanded respect for hierarchy but were indifferent to formal decorum. Rostislavov and other midcentury writers[10] were alternately appalled, amused, charmed, and bewildered by the spontaneity and lack of inhibition, the simple *joie de vivre* and unthinking cruelty, that earlier generations had seemed to exhibit in almost all facets of their life.

Thus, one system of social identity arose from local tradition and was organized around family and communal solidarity. In order to assert its own authority, support the church, and stimulate culture and trade, the government during the eighteenth century—in a fashion typical of early modern European states—strove to counteract these traditional social dynamics by dividing the population into a small number of clearly defined "estates" *(sosloviia),* thereby sharpening social distinctions *within* (but simultaneously strengthening the bonds *between*) villages and towns. The state's efforts in this area were seconded by particular social strata—nobles, clerics, and merchants— that sought to achieve and protect a privileged social status.[11] The estates had distinct legal rights and duties and were supposed to be hereditary, associated with particular occupations and ways of life, and endowed with limited powers of self-government. The core of this system was the selective exemption of particular estates from the onerous burdens that the government imposed on the population: a criminal-justice system whose principal penalties were brutal flogging and physical mutilation; decades-long compulsory military service; and the soul tax, a device whose implications were more than merely financial.* Beginning in the seventeenth century, the government had sought to tighten its control over society by minimizing the population's freedom to move across Russia's vast, poorly policed spaces. The soul tax and military conscription—both of which assessed a community's obligations on the basis of the number of inhabitants officially registered there, and refused to lower those quotas if the actual population was less—forced communities to become the government's allies in preventing their own members from moving away permanently and thereby escaping their share of the community's

---

* The soul tax was the principal form of direct taxation in Imperial Russia before the Great Reforms. How much a community had to pay was calculated by multiplying a fixed sum—three rubles per year during the period 1812–1839—by the number of male inhabitants ("souls") officially registered as members of that community at the last census *(reviziia).*

obligations. Subjection to the soul tax and conscription thus went hand in hand with the loss of freedom of movement. In addition, the state selectively granted particular estates the right to own serfs (by the late eighteenth century, only nobles had that privilege), elect officials to manage community affairs, and enjoy various symbolic markers of social status.

A clear social hierarchy existed under the terms of the law. The nobility *(dvorianstvo)*, whose already extensive privileges continually expanded in the eighteenth century but which remained open to social climbers from other estates, was at the top. The clergy likewise enjoyed immunity from the soul tax, military service, and corporal punishment by state officials, and tended increasingly to become a closed, self-governing, hereditary community; people sometimes left the clergy to join other estates, and the government periodically removed "excess" members of the estate for whom no ecclesiastical employment could be found, but hardly anyone from "outside" entered the clergy. The merchantry *(kupechestvo)* was likewise an increasingly privileged and exclusive group but remained "open" in both directions, with people both entering and leaving the estate. Beneath these three "privileged" estates stood the vast, "unprivileged" majority of the population, which was subject to corporal punishment, military conscription, and the soul tax: the townspeople *(meshchanstvo)*, state peasants, and serfs. The latter suffered the additional indignity of being the personal property of their noble masters.[12]* Rostislavov's account suggests the extent to which these distinctions permeated daily life. He usually mentions people's estate when first introducing them, lists them in the order of their estates' standing in society, and routinely, though sometimes ironically, refers to them as custom and law considered appropriate for their social status—the formal name and patronymic ("Anna Martynovna") for clergy and nobles, informal nicknames ("Grishka") for peasants, honorific titles ("His Honor," "His Grace," etc.) for officials and the more important clergy, and so on.

In practice, however, neither the principle of heredity nor the desired linkage between estate, occupation, and way of life could be fully maintained. Many nobles were too poor to own serfs, to receive a sophisticated education, or otherwise to cultivate a "noble" lifestyle,

---

* Throughout the text, the terms "merchant," "peasant," and "townsperson" (as well as "towns*man*" and so on) will be used exclusively to render legal estate identities. The population of Kasimov (town and district combined) in the 1840s included 296 nobles, 1,735 clergy, 996 "honored citizens" and merchants, 5,030 townspeople, 16,118 state peasants, and 89,654 serfs.

while anyone, of whatever social origin, who reached a certain rank in the army or bureaucracy was automatically ennobled. The "white" parish clergy (i.e., the priests and their assistants, as opposed to the "black" clergy of monks and nuns) was a hereditary estate, but since there was not enough ecclesiastical employment for all the sons of the clergy, some of them entered government service (where they might be ennobled) or the merchantry. Townspeople were supposed to engage in small-scale trade or crafts, but many were so poor that they worked instead as hired laborers or even farmers. The richest among them could enter the merchant estate, thereby gaining the merchants' coveted legal privileges and exemptions for as long as they could afford the high taxes that merchants owed; in practice, poorer merchants often sank back into the ranks of townspeople, while very rich ones were able to obtain noble status. Lastly, the vast majority of the population consisted of peasants, who might in turn be serfs (i.e., belong to a noble landlord) or state peasants (who were governed directly by state officials). Peasants, in theory, were supposed to live in villages and practice agriculture, but many were actually part-time craftsmen or worked seasonally as hired laborers in the towns. In the communities where Rostislavov grew up, the parish clergy, townspeople, and peasants lived in similar homes, did similar work, and resembled each other in most ways. Some of his relatives intermarried with peasants and became serfs, while others became townspeople and one even became a nobleman. Clergymen who needed farm hands could also circumvent the law and unofficially buy serfs, and it was not unknown (though it was illegal) for serfs to buy serfs of their own.

Alongside the "official" system of estates, local social structures persisted, sometimes even against the wishes of the regime. Thus, despite the opposition of both government and church hierarchy to precisely this practice,[13] the office of priest in the village of Tuma, held by Rostislavov's family as early as the 1720s, was passed down by them from father to son (or son-in-law) continually until at least the 1830s. Analogous, hereditary local power structures existed in the towns. In Kasimov and Riazan—the two largest towns in the region[14]*—a few merchant clans ruled society by dominating local business, making enormous fortunes through contracts with the imperial government (e.g., in the liquor trade and the construction of roads and bridges), providing employment and charity, supporting

---

* In the 1840s, Kasimov and Riazan had approximately 9,600 and 19,000 inhabitants, respectively, figures similar to those in 1840s Savannah, Georgia, or the German Baltic port of Kiel.

the church and (in the nineteenth century) the schools, getting elected to local office, intermarrying with other local families, and maintaining tight cohesion within their own clan. Local business, the church, elective office, local agencies of the imperial government, and the ties of blood, marriage, and friendship all combined to form a powerful, flexible, resilient social matrix. Dmitrii Filippov concludes from his study of the Kasimov merchantry that one can divide its history into distinct periods based on which merchant "dynasty" was in power at any given time. As the heads of one such dynasty pointed out in the late eighteenth century, when they were implicated in a corruption scandal,

> We are in control nowadays, and of the judges on the Kasimov courts, some are our blood relatives and belong to our clan, another is related to us by marriage, a third is a close acquaintance, and they are constantly visiting our home, we have a close friendship with them, and whatever we want done for our benefit, they will do for us.[15]

Government officials were sent by St. Petersburg to impose imperial control on this society, and the trappings of authority that surrounded them—their handsome uniforms with the characteristic gold embroidery, their impressive titles, arcane bureaucratic procedures and arrogant demeanor, and their vast arbitrary powers—might have been expected to cow the locals into submission. In practice, however, imperial power often proved ineffective, and the understaffed, poorly trained, and underpaid officials were instead drawn into the culture of personal relationships, mutual backscratching, and informal dealmaking by which traditional society governed itself. Thus, newly arrived Governor-General A. D. Balashov reported to Tsar Alexander I from Riazan in 1820:

> Your Majesty, your fatherly heart will shudder upon learning all the details of the conditions that prevail in the provinces. [. . .] Millions in taxes are not being collected. The police might as well not exist. In the offices of the administration, files pile up without end and are dealt with selectively and arbitrarily. The courts and judges are not respected and people suspect them of taking bribes. The litigiousness is horribly tiresome, and many make false denunciations. The best noblemen shun election [to district and provincial offices]. Official ranks and marks of distinction (ordena) are not properly esteemed. The salaries of government officials and clerks are minimal.[16]

By the mid-nineteenth century, conditions were gradually changing, at least in the more substantial towns. Thus, Riazan—the provincial capital—had no pavement, street lights, secular schools, theaters, restaurants, hotels, libraries, or bookstores before 1780; by 1860, it had all of these. As late as 1794, all but fourteen of the town's 798 houses were made of wood, many barely distinguishable from peasant huts. By the mid-nineteenth century, most of the town was still made of wood, but in addition there were impressive neoclassical mansions and government buildings, and in the 1860s the railroad revolutionized overland transportation. The merchantry—the elite of the non-noble population—remained in large part illiterate even by mid-century, but increasingly one found merchant sons with clean-shaven faces instead of the traditional Russian beard, daughters who wore European dress and played the piano, and generally a culture that was beginning to appreciate secularism, formal education, individualism, and civic activism at the expense of religion, narrowly practical training, tight family loyalties, and unquestioning obedience to the state.[17] Even in the villages, as Rostislavov describes, commercially produced cotton textiles were beginning to appear alongside traditional home-spun linen, tea was challenging vodka as the drink of choice, and at least some villagers were beginning to develop a literacy and sense of fashion and good manners that began to resemble those of the nobility, with profound implications for their own sense of personal dignity and social status. As one contemporary recalled, by the 1840s "the spirit of civilization" was making its appearance.[18]

Although the imperial regime actively fostered such changes, it did not wish to undermine a social order based on bureaucratic rule and on a system of distinct and unequal estates that competed for privileges that only the state could grant. The ecclesiastical education system, effectively under the control of both government officials and church hierarchs, exemplified this ambivalence. Beginning in the early eighteenth century, Russian Orthodox education had adopted Protestant and Catholic forms of organization and teaching, Latin as the principal language of instruction, and other features that helped turn the Orthodox clergy into a unique hybrid of European and Russian cultural practices.[19] While the clerical education system remained somewhat spotty and haphazard in the eighteenth century, the reign of Alexander I (1801–1825) saw a sustained effort to create two parallel empire-wide systems of education, one secular and designed for the laity, the other ecclesiastical and intended for the clergy. Ecclesiastical education was systematized by the reform of 1808–1814 that helped institutionalize a three-tiered structure: boys began in the lower church schools, attending first the two-year parish schools *(prikhodskie uchilishcha)* and then the four-year district schools *(uezdnye dukhovnye uchilishcha);* afterwards, many—including almost all who aspired to the priesthood rather than the humbler offices of deacon or sacristan—completed their education by spending six years at a seminary. A small elite would continue their education for four more years at an ecclesiastical academy, the church's equivalent of a university. The entire structure had about thirty-three thousand students in 1819 and almost twice that number by 1838. The system's quantitative importance is apparent when we consider that the church's secondary schools—the seminaries—enrolled more than ten thousand students in 1825, twice as many as the total for the secular secondary schools.[20]

Traumatized by the upheavals accompanying the French Revolution and the Napoleonic Wars, and searching for ways to unify the multiethnic Russian Empire, the government of Alexander I attempted, from 1815 to 1824—even as Rostislavov was beginning his education—to strengthen the bonds between state and people by building a shared culture of ecumenical spirituality and civic activism based on models derived from British Nonconformity, German pietism, and eighteenth-century Russian freemasonry.[21] A key element was that religion should henceforth emphasize an individual, nondenominational spirituality centered on reading the Bible, while deemphasizing the traditional role of the clergy and the ritual of Orthodoxy and other Christian denominations. The hope was that Russian subjects of all faiths, nationalities, and estates would find in such a spirituality an inspiration for hard work, self-discipline, personal rectitude, and social conscience that would lead rulers, officials, and subjects to become more supportive and respectful of each other. In order to achieve this goal, the state encouraged the spread of the Lancaster primary school system, which sought to circumvent teacher shortages by training older students to teach their juniors; the Bible was to be translated from Old Church Slavonic into modern Russian to make it accessible to the common believer; the Russian Bible Society, an offshoot of the London-based British and Foreign Bible Society, disseminated cheap Bibles in the various languages of the empire; philanthropic associations offered opportunities for the elite to help uplift the poor and downtrodden; and senior officials discussed plans for abolishing serfdom and turning Russia into a constitutional monarchy. These plans assumed, of course, that the nobles and the Orthodox hierarchy would abandon some of their claims to privileged status, that clergy and laypeople would agree to set aside denominational differences between Christian churches, that the Orthodox clergy would encourage Bible reading and other unprecedented forms of active participation by the laity, that state officials would allow groups such as the Bible Society an autonomous role in public life, and that the regime's critics would agree to channel their energies into these "authorized" activities. When none of these expectations seemed to be coming true by the early 1820s, the regime backed away from such ideas and reasserted the primacy of the traditional bureaucratic, ecclesiastical, and social hierarchy.

The ecclesiastical education system that emerged during this era embodied these conflicting impulses. Like education systems elsewhere in Europe, it aspired to train thoughtful, well-rounded citizens for a modern polity, yet retained the poorly qualified personnel, primitive material conditions, and harshly authoritarian pedagogical habits characteristic of early modern schools prior to the Enlightenment.[22] The church schools and seminaries taught an intellectually rigorous curriculum (much of it in Latin, and often too demanding for the students) in literature and composition, philosophy, theology, history, the classics, Old Church Slavonic, Greek, French, and German. However, rote learning was emphasized over independent thinking (in keeping with the tradition of viewing the Scriptures as the literal word of God), funding was inadequate, the teachers (especially those in the elementary-level church schools) were poorly trained, and relentless corporal punishment was regarded as a desirable method for purging boys' souls of moral corruption. As a result, the elite of ecclesiastical students obtained an excellent education but were traumatized by the experience.[23] The schools were both a breeding ground for social critics and an engine of social mobility in a society where literate people were scarce and many clerical sons were unable or unwilling to find employment in the clergy. The statesman Mikhail Speranskii (1772–1839), the literary critic Vissarion Belinskii (1811–1848), the radical journalist Nikolai Chernyshevskii (1828–1889), and the historians Afanasii Shchapov (1830–1876) and Vasilii Kliuchevskii (1841–1911) were all alumni of the ecclesiastical school system who resembled Rostislavov and each other in their intellectual sophistication and critical view of society

ROSTISLAVOV'S LIFE AND CAREER

Rostislavov's own family history bore witness to the transformative effects of education and cultural change. The family's roots in the

Dmitrii Ivanovich Rostislavov's Family Tree

Great-great-great-great-Grandfather, m. Great-great-great-great-Grandmother

Gerasim, m. Great-great-great-Grandmother
priest in Sheianki

Leontii Gerasimovich, sacristan in Sheianki, married to a peasant woman; descendants are serfs

Larion Gerasimovich, sacristan in Sheianki, died c. 1762

Nikifor, deacon in Elat'ma District

Anna Larionovna m.

Pelageia Nikiforovna, townswoman in Elat'ma

Mikhail, priest in Gus' (near Sheianki) m. Great-great-Grandmother

Kuz'ma Mikhailovich, a robber

Avdot'ia Mikhailovna, born c. 1742 m.

Martyn Larionovich, born c. 1762, sacristan in Sheianki; later priest in Tuma

Vasilii Larionovich, clerk in Melenki

Efim Vasil'evich, noble landowner

Vasilii Mart., born c. 1800, deacon in Prudki

Afim'ia Mart., born c. 1802, married to a deacon in Bylino (east of Tuma)

Ivan, priest in Tuma

Akim Vasil'ev, born c. 1732, m. Mar'ia, born c. 1728
priest in Tuma

Fekla Akimovna, born c. 1764 m.

Ivan Mart. (uncle), born c. 1797; priest in Palishchi; later priest in Struzhany; married, 1 child

Anna Martynovna, born c. 1785, married to Nikifor Mironovich, born c. 1781; priest in Tuma (his grandfather was the Tuma sacristan Andrei Andreevich)

Ivan ("Vania"), 1809–1819
6 other children

Nikita Arbekov, m. Grandmother
priest in Arkhangel'skoe

Ekaterina, born c. 1791 m.

Ivan Martynovich, born c. 1787; priest in Palishchi; later priest in Tuma

Stepan Nikitich, born c. 1794, priest in Podlipki; married, 4 children

daughters:
Natal'ia, born c. 1811
Elizaveta, born c. 1812
Mar'ia, born c. 1815
Aleksandra, born c. 1817
Evdokiia, born c. 1820

sons:
Aleksei, born c. 1818
Aleksandr, 1821–1889
Nikolai, 1823–1888

Dmitrii
1809–1877

Names given in this chart reflect the author's spellings, rather than spellings from archival sources (e.g., Ivan Martynovich = Ioann Martinov).

clergy of the Meshchora ran deep—most of his ancestors and relatives had occupied clerical positions in the region and married offspring of other clerical families. Like most villagers (irrespective of the estate to which they belonged), his father had only a first name and a patronymic, Ioann Martinov (John, son of Martin), but no surname; since seminary students were required to have a surname, he adopted the name Tumskii while he was a seminarian because he hailed from Tuma, but later in life he neither used that name nor bequeathed it to his children. Furthermore, in keeping with the importance of Old Church Slavonic (the archaic, Greek-influenced Slavic language used in the Orthodox prayers, liturgy, and Scriptures) among the clergy, he identified himself in official documents by the traditional Old Church Slavonic form of his name (Ioann Martinov) rather than the Russian vernacular equivalent (Ivan Martynov). However, in other ways, he and his wife were agents of cultural modernization in the countryside. Ioann Martinov appears to have been the first in his family to graduate from a seminary. He was a man of strong intellectual interests who had a rationalistic, scientific bent, and whose surviving seminary records support Rostislavov's account of his exceptional intelligence, scholarship, and rectitude.[24] Unlike most priests' daughters of her generation, his wife, Ekaterina Nikitina, was literate and took a critical view of the traditional village and clerical cultures that profoundly influenced her son. An unnamed contemporary later wrote that, "in private conversations, D.I. [Rostislavov] would often recall his mother, who, with her characteristic tender love, had pointed out to him the weaknesses of our rural clergy that hurt not only the clergy itself but also the society entrusted to its care. The mother's tender, spiritual conversations with her gifted son could not help manifesting themselves in the youth's intellectual abilities and had a deep impact on D.I.'s impressionable soul."[25]

Born on September 16, 1809, Rostislavov went through the usual clerical education in Kasimov and Riazan, graduated from the Riazan seminary in 1829 as the second best in his class of ninety-one, and was one of only three or four among that class to be chosen for an ecclesiastical academy.[26] He finished the St. Petersburg Ecclesiastical Academy in 1833 but remained there to become a professor of physics and mathematics—testimony to his outstanding intellectual gifts and interest in modern scientific thought. Success in the ecclesiastical education system had thus carried him from the provincial backwater where all his known relatives had lived since at least the early eighteenth century to the capital of the empire, one of Europe's great cities and a pulsating center of intellectual activity and cultural change. And he was not alone in what must have been a remarkable family, for at least two of his three brothers also attended the academy in St. Petersburg, and all three had sufficiently distinguished careers for their biographies to be included in one of Imperial Russia's greatest scholarly reference works, the multivolume *Russian Biographical Dictionary*.[27]* Rostislavov was an excellent and very popular teacher, so much so that the metropolitan of St. Petersburg supposedly complained to the rector of the academy that the students were receiving better training in mathematics and physics than in theology. Ill health forced him to retire in 1852, and he moved back to Riazan, where he settled near the seminary and took in and tutored young seminarians. He also began, in 1858, to give unpaid public lectures on mathematics and physics at the seminary and the club of the nobility *(dvorianskoe sobranie)*. Lastly, in his spare time, he wrote books and articles on the state of the clergy as well as his own autobiography.

A characteristic product of an elite ecclesiastical education, Rostislavov was fluent in French, German, and English in addition to Greek, Latin, and Old Church Slavonic. He was well read, but in contrast to many upper-class *literati* he was grounded in Russian folk and clerical traditions as well as in the classics and in modern European and Russian noble culture. Analytical and inquisitive, he displayed at the same time a strongly ascetic, moralistic streak, a distrust of vanity and elegance, and a determination to unmask evildoers (but also confess past sins of his own) that reflect the deeply religious character of a clerical upbringing. As Laurie Manchester's study of Russian priests' sons suggests, his view of life in general, and the clerical world and its educational institutions (the *bursa*) in particular, was shared by many others in the clerical milieu. Like they, he idealized his family and childhood, which was traumatically disrupted when he went to live and study at the church school. In his recollections as in those of his peers, "home represented heaven; school symbolized hell."[28] In contrast to the love and warmth of this lost Garden of Eden, the school seemed to offer only mindless rote learning and was a dog-eat-dog world of sadistic teachers, brutal hazing by older boys, savage class struggle between the sons of priests and those of sacristans, pervasive filth and corruption, and abject poverty. At the

---

* Nikolai Rostislavov (1823–1888) taught at the Kazan Ecclesiastical Seminary and went on to become a high-ranking official in the Marine Ministry. (He subsequently edited his brother Dmitrii's *Memoir* and arranged its publication.) The other brother, Aleksandr (1821–1889), became a senior figure at the Kaluga Ecclesiastical Seminary.

seminary, the intensity of these problems diminished, but Rostislavov still detected the same underlying flaws. Like many of his fellow seminarians, he found that this socialization trained students to become cruel and immoral, and molded them to such a degree that their highly distinctive manners, language, and value system impeded normal interaction with women, members of the secular estates, and anyone who had not shared the formative *bursa* experience.[29] (Rostislavov himself never married and never mentions a romantic relationship.) Proud of the inner strength that they derived from their suffering, yet also resentful toward the individuals and power structure responsible for their misery, and trained by the clergy and by Christian tradition to think in manichean terms of good and evil, they typically focus their accounts overwhelmingly on the dark side of *bursa* life.

Born and raised among villagers, Rostislavov passionately identified with the *narod* (the Russian common people, as opposed to the Europeanized nobility). He was proud to have worn their clothes and worked in their fields, he wrote elegaically of their life in harmony with nature, and he felt a deep love for their songs, customs, and expressions, great sympathy for their suffering at the hands of callous nobles and officials, and admiration for their skill, resilience, and stoicism in the face of life's hardships. Even when describing the shortcomings of their culture, his language is far more indulgent than when speaking of the government or the *bursa*. Reviewing his life experience from the vantage point of the intellectual sophistication and puritanical morals that he had internalized during his education, he could still discern much that was good in traditional rural Russia, but he also identified several powerful forces that conspired to perpetuate poverty and moral degradation.

One such force was the general primitiveness of rural life and mores, which shaped the lives of the "white" village clergy as well as the peasants to whom they ministered. Rostislavov vehemently denounced alcoholism, violence, filth, corruption, religious intolerance, unthinking traditionalism, and mindless waste of natural resources, all of which were prevalent in rural society and produced particularly baneful consequences in the perverted universe of the *bursa*. Physical squalor, he suggested, created moral squalor, and people who lacked the self-respect and sense of dignity that came from being sober, clean, polite, and restrained would also refuse to show respect for the dignity of others.

In Russia as in Europe and America, one part of the theoretical framework for these notions was provided by eighteenth-century Enlightenment ideas: that humans are fundamentally equal and should be treated accordingly; that society should use reason in order to achieve "progress" rather than cling to a supposedly divinely ordained tradition; that evil is caused by social conditions, not man's sinful nature; and that treating people cruelly in order to suppress sin is self-defeating because cruelty gives rise to the very vices it is intended to combat. The other source for his world view was a form of Christian ethics that stressed personal rectitude, an internalized individual spirituality, and the improvement of social conditions, in place of the older focus on strict adherence to ritual, tradition, and preparing people's souls for the afterlife. While these Enlightenment and religious notions were becoming commonplace among the elite, they were only slowly trickling down to the non-noble classes and, as Rostislavov describes, could be profoundly unsettling to people accustomed to a strict religious and sociocultural orthodoxy.

In Russia as in France or the German states (though not in Great Britain or the United States), the military provided one model for realizing these values in daily life, and even Rostislavov—despite his intensely antiauthoritarian instincts—had a grudging respect for the spirit of efficiency, neatness, discipline, and pride encouraged by army culture, in contrast to the slovenliness and false humility that seemed to be *de rigueur* at ecclesiastical educational institutions.[30] The other social group in Western Europe and North America that modeled the new values in everyday life was the bourgeoisie, i.e., the class of professionals, academics, and entrepreneurs who subscribed to the modern ideals of order, rationality, hard work, thrift, personal honesty, and self-restraint, but did so in a resolutely civilian and usually politically liberal spirit, and with the proud awareness of being an affluent social class that deservedly towered above the common people.

In Russia, no self-conscious class analogous to the bourgeoisie had yet developed by midcentury. Indeed, the merchants in Rostislavov's story are distinctly premodern figures who are uneducated, earn their fortunes by managing liquor sales for the government rather than through genuine entrepreneurship, and aspire ultimately to become noble. It is telling that Riazan's premier merchant and self-made man, the stunningly rich G.V. Riumin, had his portrait painted for posterity in the bemedalled uniform of the provincial official he became, not in the austere black suit of a self-confident European bourgeois, for his proudest accomplishment had been to cease being a merchant at all and acquire a rank in government service.[31] As a state councillor—a class-five rank in the fourteen-level Table of Ranks that governed all official titles and positions—he and his immediate family benefitted from hereditary noble status and all of its attendant rights and immunities, and also enjoyed a host of lesser privileges that were nonetheless highly gratifying in so status-conscious a society. For example, under an official nomenclature of titles that was translated from seventeenth-century German models and that covered state officials, military officers, and the clergy,[32] Riumin's class-five rank gave him the right to be addressed by others as "Your High Born" *(Vashe Vysokorodie)*—not quite as flattering as the "Your Excellency" *(Vashe Prevoskhoditel'stvo)* to which officials in classes four and three were entitled, yet (oddly) preferable to the "Your High *Well-Born*" *(Vashe Vysokoblagorodie)* used for humbler ranks in classes eight through six. Envelopes addressed to him would carry the title "gracious lord" *(milostivomu gosudariu)* before his name; again, that was less than the "*most* gracious lord" *(milostiveishemu gosudariu)* reserved for counts, princes, and barons, but far more desirable than the simple "my lord" *(gosudariu moemu)* used for officials of lower rank. Anyone writing to him would be expected to sign as "your most obedient servant" *(pokorneishii sluga);* higher-ranking individuals, of course, were entitled to "your *very* most obedient servant" *(vsepokorneishii sluga)* or even, if they were particularly aristocratic, "your very most humble and very most devoted servant" *(vsenizhaishii i vsepredanneishii sluga)*, but those lower in the hierarchy had to content themselves with a mere "your obedient servant" *(pokornyi sluga)*.[33] The right to carry a sword, the livery one's servants might wear, where one was seated at formal dinners and the order in which one was served, the number of horses one might hitch to his carriage—these and other highly visible signs of a family's status were directly dependent on one's standing in the Table of Ranks. Only well into the nineteenth century did a new system of values, capable of competing effectively with the combined attraction of noble status and government service rank, begin to penetrate Russia's embryonic bourgeoisie.

Rather than the bourgeoisie, the principal carrier of the new Enlightenment values outside of the government, nobility, and military was the intelligentsia, a legally undefined yet increasingly self-conscious social group that included the (as yet relatively few) people who were educated, interested in public issues, open to modern ideas, and inclined to be critical of the autocratic, estate-based sociopolitical order. Like Rostislavov, many of them were of humble social background and tended to identify emotionally with the poor and downtrodden. As a result, they generally shared the Western liberal bourgeoisie's attachment to due process of law and to orderly government, personal honesty, the work ethic, education, and scientific rationality, as well as its opposition to hereditary privilege, but not its commitment to private property and capitalist economics, its pursuit of refinement in manners and lifestyle, and its belief that gross socioeconomic inequalities were part of the natural order of things.[34] Many among the intelligentsia were convinced that the progress of Russian society required not only that the elite provide enlightened leadership to the benighted masses, but first and foremost that the elite itself recognize the moral dignity, cultural achievements, and socioeconomic rights of the common people.

The cultural primitiveness of rural society thus appears, in Rostislavov's account, as one cause of Russian society's woes; a second was the power structure of the regime, in the form of police officers, serf owners, local officials, and even church-school teachers. Their role in society reflected the baneful interaction of two forces that might be harmless in isolation but became calamitous when acting together. On the one hand, ever since the early eighteenth century, the imperial regime had been conceived by its masters as a rigid chain of command through which the rulers and their agents would transform society. As Rostislavov's chapter on Governor-General Balashov suggests, the officials' intentions might be laudable, but the authoritarianism and brutality of their methods ensured that they were often out of touch with everyday realities and unaware when their orders were inappropriate or counterproductive. Up and down the official hierarchy, superiors expected uncritical obedience to any and all orders. Such an attitude toward power became particularly damaging at the bottom of the hierarchy, where officials were poorly trained and supervised, ill-paid, understaffed, and overwhelmed by the difficulty of governing a population that neither comprehended nor sympathized with their mission. As Rostislavov's account makes clear, villagers might cooperate with the police or take independent action against troublemakers if they believed their communities to be directly threatened (usually by outsiders), but they had no general desire to uphold "the law." Teachers in the church schools, whose conduct Rostislavov implicitly likens to that of officials, likewise faced the impossible task of providing a sophisticated humanistic education to hordes of coarse, ignorant, brutal village boys who usually lacked all interest in intellectual matters. To make matters worse, the police and teachers themselves were unsophisticated men who shared the lower classes' inclination to think of power in terms of personal relationships rather than the systematic implementation of formal rules. However, unlike the leaders of a typical village community, they often had little incentive to cultivate lasting relationships with the populations under their power. Hence, they combined the worst of both worlds. Themselves bullied and oppressed by their superiors, they would do the same to the population, unrestrained by either the communal loyalties of the villagers or the bureaucratic ethos prescribed by the imperial regime.

The third factor that Rostislavov held responsible for the woes of society, or at least of the clergy, were the monks or "black" clergy, to whom Orthodox canon law reserved all the senior ecclesiastical offices (bishop, archbishop, metropolitan) that ruled the lives of the "white" clergy who staffed the churches of Russia's villages and towns. In his eyes, the black clergy were steeped in a reactionary monastic ethic that emphasized the appearance rather than the substance of piety, regarded filth, pain, squalor, and phony humility as proof of godliness, condemned intellectual progress or creative thinking as a deviation from the true faith, and denied the white clergy the autonomy, funding, and proper education they required if they were to live decent lives themselves and carry out what Rostislavov believed to be the clergy's primary mission: to improve the moral and cultural conditions of village life. While monks might be well suited to the task of preserving church tradition and upholding religious orthodoxy, Rostislavov considered them remote from the daily life of the people and hence unequal to the task of providing secular moral leadership for society—the role traditionally claimed by the state and to which, more recently, the intelligentsia as well as some in the clergy had begun to aspire. As he wrote (five months before his death) in a letter to someone who evidently shared his views on the black clergy, "Let us hope that this structure, which is 'blackened' by its very name, will be destroyed by the united efforts of those who comprehend the full extent of its moral 'blackness'; in truth, it has survived only by force of inertia and because [the authorities] prevent those people from approaching it who have in their hands the battering rams needed to destroy what is old and decrepit."[35]

The black clergy, he held, maintained their power to the detriment of genuine religiosity, a point he saw vividly illustrated in the linguistic issues debated in the church. Traditionally, the ecclesiastical language of the Russian Orthodox Church was Old Church Slavonic, a language only distantly related to Russian and poorly understood by average Russian speakers—a situation roughly analogous to that of Italian- or Spanish-speaking Catholics and the use of Latin in the Roman Catholic Church, and which heightened the clergy's role as sole interpreters of the faith but also created the risk that parishioners would recite prayers and hear the liturgy without understanding what they meant. During the eighteenth century, a modern Russian literary vernacular emerged that was increasingly free from Old Church Slavonic and Greek influences and that employed the "civil" alphabet, a modernized, simplified, less Greek-looking version of the "ecclesiastical" alphabet used to write Old Church Slavonic. The Orthodox Church, however, remained little affected by these changes. By the time Rostislavov attended the church school and seminary in the 1810s and 1820s, the 1815–1824 reform movement associated with Tsar Alexander I had begun to challenge many aspects of church tradition. The episode ended, however, with the victory of conservative senior members of the black clergy who defended the primacy of Old Church Slavonic and hence the dominance of the clergy over the laity and, more generally, the primacy of authority and tradition over the ideals of participation and reform. Rostislavov, on the contrary, advocated an education based on the Russian vernacular, the "civil" alphabet, scientific and humanistic rather than theological studies, and a pedagogy that encouraged independent thinking.[36] His rejection of the clerical linguistic traditions extended to names as well, so that, in his *Memoir,* he Russianizes his ancestors' Greek or Old Church Slavonic given names: Ioann and Martin are rendered as Ivan and Martyn, Evdokiia becomes Avdot'ia, Ioakim and Ilarion become Akim and Larion, Stefan becomes Stepan, and so on.*

After the long reign of Nicholas I (1825–1855), during which Russia had remained authoritarian and agrarian while its rivals in Northwestern Europe underwent liberal reforms and industrialization, educated Russians hoped that their new tsar, Alexander II (who reigned from 1855 to 1881), would undertake sweeping reforms of all that seemed stale, oppressive, and reactionary in Russian society. And they were not disappointed. In a burst of reform, fundamental aspects of the sociopolitical order were transformed, including legislation to abolish serfdom and quasi-lifetime military service, democratize local government, and create a modern judiciary. More generally, significant steps

---

* Similarly, he sometimes modernizes their patronymics. Traditionally, lower-class Russians lacked surnames and instead used their father's given name (the patronymic) with the ending –v, or –va for women. By contrast, those who did have surnames—first the higher classes, later everyone—added the endings –vich or –vna to their patronymic. Rostislavov often adopts this usage, for example by referring to his father as "Ivan Martynovich" instead of "Ioann Martinov."

were taken toward dismantling the entire social order that had been based on hereditary estate distinctions.[37] Given the commitment of educated public opinion to legality, individual rights, scientific rationality, and modern Russian culture, the entire complex of issues associated with the structure of the clergy, the church schools, and Old Church Slavonic was bound to revive. In the heady atmosphere of the late 1850s to the 1870s, when the press enjoyed unprecedented freedom to criticize social ills, the problems of ecclesiastical education and other aspects of clerical life indeed became the subject of searing exposés, most famously Ioann S. Belliustin's *Description of the Clergy in Rural Russia* and Nikolai G. Pomialovskii's *Seminary Sketches.*[38]

Rostislavov was asked as early as 1859, by a senior official in the Holy Synod (the governing body of the Orthodox Church), to draft a memorandum containing ideas for reforming the church education system. The finished text, however, was apparently too polemical for the Synod's taste, and publishing it in Russia was impossible for censorship reasons. Instead, Rostislavov sent it to the historian and journalist Mikhail P. Pogodin, who had earlier encouraged Belliustin to write his *Description* and who arranged to have Rostislavov's work published anonymously in Germany. This publication was followed, within a few years, by other, similarly voluminous, meticulously researched, and aggressively polemical works on the white and black clergy and on the wealth of the black clergy. It is also during these years, in the mid to late 1860s, that he apparently began writing his reminiscences.[39]

Not surprisingly, his opinions aroused controversy. Some contemporaries' views on Rostislavov's writings have come down to us thanks to the Third Section of His Imperial Majesty's Own Chancellery—the secret police. They freely opened citizens' private mail and made copies of interesting passages that, written in elegant cursive and accompanied by helpful explanatory notes, were submitted to senior officials and survive to this day in Russian archives. In a letter about Rostislavov's book on the white and black clergy, an unidentified priest in St. Petersburg described to his correspondent, a monk in Moscow, the complex interaction of reformist and conservative, secular and ecclesiastical, forces involved in the issue:

> I have read this book, and I admit that I have never even heard anything more furious about the despotic rule of our higher clergy. Although this book has been banned, it is being disseminated in Russia in huge numbers. Laypeople, who don't like us anyway, will stop going

to church altogether after reading this book. The Synod tracked down the author (rumored to be Rostislavov, who lives in Riazan) and wanted to have him taken to court and convicted of libel, but the secular authorities wouldn't let them touch him. Instead, it seems that [the secular authorities] have had the book sent to all senior clergy—"Take a look at this, and shape up where you have to." Trying to deal with this book by just remaining silent or ignoring it would give the enemy additional fuel for his fury, nor can you answer it with eloquence alone because many of its facts are irrefutable.[40]

Rostislavov had sympathizers in high places—the police noted in their accompanying report that his book had "fallen into the hands of prominent individuals" and "most had read Rostislavov's book attentively"—and could feel reasonably secure in the face of attacks from the black clergy: "I am very calm," he confided to his brother Nikolai (and, perhaps unbeknownst to him, the police). "I don't know why, but I am sure that the black crowd will find it difficult to do anything to me, I mean, anything big, because just spending a few months as a prisoner in a fortress or jail is hardly a terrible disaster!" In the end, he not only suffered no ill consequences—though he was ordered to stop giving public lectures on physics because he was suspected of "godlessness and Protestant sympathies"—but his books were even officially included among the materials reviewed by the commission that worked out the reform of the ecclesiastical school system in the late 1860s. These reforms did address some of the most urgent concerns raised by Rostislavov and other writers on clerical issues: the curriculum was changed to stress Russian authors rather than the classics, corporal punishment was banned, as was the system of appointing student elders who could abuse other students, and rote learning was deemphasized. It was a sign of the changing times that the complete Bible now appeared in a Russian translation.[41]

It was in this atmosphere, in the 1860s–1870s, that Rostislavov wrote his *Memoir*. He was convinced, like Victorian social critics across Europe and America, that the moral and physical squalor of the world of his childhood must give way to a new culture of cleanliness, sobriety, good manners, rationality, self-restraint, rule of law, and respect for oneself and for others. In much of the Western world during the 1850s–1870s, including the Russia of the Great Reforms, this dream seemed for a time destined to be fulfilled. It is from that perspective that Rostislavov, in his *Memoir,* contemplated the distant days of his childhood. Gazing back across a half-century divide, recording events whose meaning he had been pondering for fifty years, he was struck by how alien the world of his childhood appeared in light of the direction in which society now seemed at last to be moving. Partly, the *Memoir*—which was published after his death and which he may not have had time to complete—is the nostalgic reminiscence of an aging man. It is also an old fighter's parting salvo at forces and institutions that he had hated and combatted throughout his adult life. And partly, it is an effort to make sense of the long road that he—the professor of mathematics and physics—and his family had traveled since the time when his unschooled grandparents had believed that owls were embodiments of the Evil One and that thunder was caused by the flaming chariot of the Prophet Elijah chasing demons in the clouds.

. . .

The text on which this edition is based is "Zapiski D. I. Rostislavova, professora SPb. dukhovnoi akademii. † 18-go fevralia 1877 g.," which appeared in installments in the journal *Russkaia Starina,* beginning in January 1880 and concluding in the June 1895 issue. The entire text is 690 pages long and consists of forty-four chapters. The challenge was to pare it down to a length that would be publishable today and interesting to the modern reader. The task was facilitated by Rostislavov's focus on describing different facets of society rather than on the story of his own life. As a result, it was possible to translate some chapters and leave out others without disrupting the flow of the narrative.[42]

Nineteen chapters of the original (1–13, 23–25, 39–40, 44) focus on the author's family and on life in villages and towns; the remainder deal with the ecclesiastical education system. The process of selecting and editing chapters for translation was guided by the belief that the modern reader will be more interested in an overview of different social strata than an in-depth study of the *bursa.* Therefore, only two complete chapters, and brief excerpts from several others, on the church-school system were translated in order to convey a sense of Rostislavov's arguments, whereas all the chapters on family, village, and town life are included in the present edition.

Each individual chapter constitutes a coherent whole that the translation seeks to preserve. However, Rostislavov's habit of digressing, giving very detailed descriptions of places and events, and offering multiple anecdotes to support a single point, occasionally made it advisable to delete passages. In the translation, passages that I have simply deleted are marked by ellipses within brackets: [. . .]; if, however, the deleted passage contained information important to the flow of the narrative, I have briefly summarized it in my own words and placed the summary in brackets.

In most cases, I have used footnotes to provide additional information that might help the reader understand the text. (All the footnotes are mine.) However, it was sometimes preferable to include explanations in the text itself. In those cases, the explanation appears indented in brackets and is preceded by the words "Translator's Note." In either case, the additional explanations have one of two purposes: to clarify vocabulary or concepts that might otherwise be opaque to the modern reader; or to introduce information, based on printed primary sources and archival documents, that can assist the reader in evaluating Rostislavov's statements and enhance the book's value as a primary source on Russian social history.

Rostislavov's style is conversational and idiomatic, and consciously seeks to render the distinctive vocabulary and levels of speech of different social groups. I have tried to reproduce this in the translation on the basis of present-day American usage, rather than attempt to recreate mid-nineteenth-century English usage, in the hope of making Rostislavov's prose sound as idiomatic and pungent to modern readers as it was to his Russian contemporaries. He also wrote quickly and, apparently, with little editing, so that words and phrases are occasionally repeated several times in quick succession; that, too, I have tried to preserve. On the other hand, I have taken the liberty to break up or rearrange the lengthy sentences and paragraphs that were standard in the nineteenth century but seem stylistically awkward today. In the interest of clarity, I have generally converted Russian weights and measures into inches, feet, yards, and pounds. This choice was made easier by the fact that most of the Russian units convert smoothly into American units of measurement (though not into metric units)—for instance, one *sazhen* is equal to seven feet, and one *pud* is thirty-six pounds—and that Rostislavov's numbers are, in most cases, only imprecise estimates anyway. However, I have not converted the principal unit for measuring distances, the *verst* (equal to 1,060 meters), since it is almost the same as one kilometer and the reader will have little difficulty understanding distances expressed in versts.

All dates are based on the Julian calendar that was in force in Russia until 1918, under which dates in the nineteenth century were twelve days behind the Gregorian calendar used in the West, i.e., September 1 in Russia was September 13 in Western Europe.

The photographs accompanying the text date from the twentieth century and hence are not contemporaneous with Rostislavov's narrative. However, by showing important sites and scenes of traditional rural life in his home region, they do evoke the vanished world in which that narrative takes place.

NOTES

1. On the history of autobiography as a genre in Russia, see the introduction to Toby W. Clyman and Judith Vowles, eds., *Russia Through Women's Eyes: Autobiographies from Tsarist Russia* (New Haven: Yale University Press, 1996).

2. Vladimir I. Dal', *Tolkovyi slovar' zhivogo velikorusskogo iazyka*, 4 vols. (Moscow and St. Petersburg: Tovarishchestvo M.O. Vol'f, 1903–9; reprint, Moscow: Izdatel'skaia gruppa "Progress," "Univers," 1994), 2:845.

3. "Population: 1790–1990" (U.S. Census Bureau Chart); Thomas Nipperdey, *Deutsche Geschichte 1800–1866: Bürgerwelt und starker Staat* (Munich: Verlag C.H. Beck, 1987), 105.

4. *Voenno-statisticheskoe obozrenie Rossiiskoi Imperii. Izdavaemoe po Vysochaishemu poveleniiu pri 1-m Otdelenii Departamenta General'nago Shtaba*, tom 6, chast' 3, *Riazanskaia guberniia* (St. Petersburg: V Tipografii Departamenta General'nago Shtaba, 1848), 7, 14, 23–24, 30, tables 1, 5; M. Baranovich, *Materialy dlia geografii i statistiki Rossii, sobrannye ofitserami general'nago shtaba: Riazanskaia guberniia* (St. Petersburg: Tipografiia Tovarishchestva "Obshchestvennaia Pol'za," 1860), 28–29, 31, 32, 64–65, 98–100, 127, 134–35.

5. *Rossiia: Entsiklopedicheskii slovar'* (Leningrad: Lenizdat, 1992), 100.

6. For a description and analysis of village society, see Christine D. Worobec, *Peasant Russia: Family and Community in the Post-Emancipation Period* (DeKalb: Northern Illinois University Press, 1995).

7. Baranovich, 458–79; *Rospisanie gorodskikh i sel'skikh prikhodov, tserkvei i prichtov Riazanskoi eparkhii* (n.p., n.d.), no pagination.

8. I. P. Popov, E. S. Stepanova, E. G. Tarabrin, and Iu. F. Fulin, *Dva veka riazanskoi istorii (XVIII v.–mart 1917 g.)* (Riazan: Riazanskoe otdelenie Sovetskogo fonda kul'tury, 1991), 23–24.

9. Jacques Le Goff, *Medieval Civilization*, trans. Julia Barrow (Oxford: Basil Blackwell, 1988), 131–33, 280.

10. Perhaps the best-known example is Sergei Aksakov, *A Russian Gentleman* (Oxford: Oxford University Press, 1994).

11. Boris N. Mironov, *Sotsial'naia istoriia Rossii perioda Imperii (XVIII–nachalo XX v.): Genezis lichnosti, demokraticheskoi sem'i, grazhdanskogo obshchestva i pravovogo gosudarstva*, 2 vols. (St. Petersburg: Izdatel'stvo "Dmitrii Bulanin," 1999), 1:98–102; Gregory L. Freeze, *The Russian Levites: Parish Clergy in the Eighteenth Century* (Cambridge: Harvard University Press, 1977), 3, 32–33, 185–210.

12. *Voenno-statisticheskoe obozrenie*, table 3.

13. Freeze, *Russian Levites*, 190.

14. *Voenno-statisticheskoe obozrenie*, table 3; Campbell Gibson, "Population of the 100 Largest Cities and Other Urban Places in the United States: 1790 to 1990" (U.S. Census Bureau, Population Division Working Paper No. 27), table 4; Nipperdey, 113.

15. D. Iu. Filippov, "'Epokhi kupecheskikh dinastii' v zhizni provintsial'nogo goroda XVIII–XIX vekov," in *III Konferentsiia "Goroda Podmoskov'ia v istorii rossiiskogo predprinimatel'stva i kul'tury" (Serpukhov. 3–4 dekabria 1999 g. Doklady, soobshcheniia, tezisy)"* (Serpukhov, 1999), 51–54. The quotation is by I. P. and D. P. Polezhaev. See also D. Iu. Filippov, "Kupechestvo goroda Kasimova kontsa XVIII–nachala XX v.," Avtoreferat dissertatsii na soiskanie uchenoi stepeni kandidata istoricheskikh nauk (Voronezh, 1998).

16. P. V. Akul'shin, "Riazanskii general-gubernator A. D. Balashov (reformatorskie plany Aleksandra I i Riazanskii krai)," in *Iz proshlogo i nastoiashchego Riazanskogo kraia. Sbornik nauchnykh trudov* (Riazan, 1995), 17–25 (the quotation is on 20–21).

17. Irina G. Kusova, *Riazanskoe kupechestvo: Ocherki istorii XVI–nachala XX veka* (Riazan: "Mart," 1996), 70–71, 85–86, 89, 96, 101–2, 108–9, 111–13, 117–21, 123.

18. A. V. Antonov, cited in Kusova, 113.

19. Mironov, *Sotsial'naia istoriia*, 1:102; Freeze, *Russian Levites*, 79–96, 102.

20. B. V. Titlinov, *Dukhovnaia shkola v Rossii v XIX stoletii*, 2 vols. (Vilna: Tipografiia "Russkii Pochin," 1908–9), 1:104, passim; Nicholas V. Riasanovsky, *A History of Russia*, 3rd ed. (New York: Oxford University Press, 1977), 387. On the ecclesiastical education system in general, see Gregory L. Freeze, *The Parish Clergy in Nineteenth-Century Russia: Crisis, Reform, Counter-Reform* (Princeton: Princeton University Press, 1983), 102–25.

21. See, for example: the introduction to Elena A. Vishlenkova, *Dukhovnaia shkola v Rossii v pervoi chetverti XIX veka* (Kazan': Izdatel'stvo Kazanskogo Universiteta, 1998); Raffaella Faggionato, "From a Society of the Enlightened to the Enlightenment of Society: The Russian Bible Society and Rosicrucianism in the Age of Alexander I," *Slavonic and East European Review* 79 (July 2001); Alexander M. Martin, *Romantics, Reformers, Reactionaries: Russian Conservative Thought and Politics in the Reign of Alexander I* (DeKalb: Northern Illinois University Press, 1997), ch. 6 and 7.

22. Richard van Dülmen, *Kultur und Alltag in der Frühen Neuzeit*, 3 vols. (Munich: Verlag C.H. Beck, 1999), 3:168–88.

23. Laurie Manchester, "Secular Ascetics: The Mentality of Orthodox Clergymen's Sons in Late Imperial Russia" (Ph.D. diss., Columbia University, 1995), ch. 4; Freeze, *Parish Clergy*, 133–39.

24. Rossiiskii Gosudarstvennyi Istoricheskii Arkhiv (RGIA) (Russian State Historical Archive), *f.* 802 (Komissiia dukhovnykh uchilishch), *op.* 1, *d.* 138, *ll.* 18, 96, 98 *ob.*

25. "D. I. Rostislavov (po povodu 30 letiia so dnia konchiny)," *S.-Peterburgskiia Vedomosti,* 18 February 1907, 3.

26. Gosudarstvennyi Arkhiv Riazanskoi Oblasti (GARO) (State Archive of Riazan Province), *f.* 1280 (Riazanskaia dukhovnaia seminariia), *op.* 1, *d.* 80, *l.* 1 *ob* – 2; *Bibliograficheskii slovar' pisatelei, uchenykh i khudozhnikov, urozhentsev (preimushchestvenno) Riazanskoi gubernii,* eds. I. V. Dobroliubov, S. D. Iakhontov (Riazan: Gubernskaia Tipografiia, 1910; reprint, Riazan: Izdatel'stvo Riazanskogo gosudarstvennogo pedagogicheskogo universiteta, 1995), 211.

27. *Biograficheskii slovar' studentov pervykh XXVIII–mi kursov S.-Peterburgskoi Dukhovnoi Akademii: 1814–1869 gg. (K 100–letiiu S.-Peterburgskoi Dukhovnoi Akademii)* (St. Petersburg: Tipografiia I.V. Leont'eva, 1907), 413–15; *Russkii biograficheskii slovar',* ed. A.A. Polovtsov, 25 vols. (St. Petersburg: 1896–1911; reprint, New York: Kraus, 1962), 17: 165–69.

28. Manchester, 265; Freeze, *Russian Levites,* 97.

29. Manchester, 400–12.

30. For example, see his description of a military school, in "Peterburgskaia dukhovnaia akademiia pri grafe Protasove 1836–1855 gg.," *Vestnik Evropy,* July 1883, 121–87; August 1883, 581–611; September 1883, 200–248; the military school is described in the July issue, 157–62.

31. Kusova, 76, 85.

32. Leonid E. Shepelev, *Chinovnyi mir Rossii. XVIII–nachalo XX v.* (St. Petersburg: "Iskusstvo-SPB," 1999), 174; van Dülmen, 2:192–93.

33. August Wilhelm Tappe, *Neue theoretisch-praktische Russische Sprachlehre für Deutsche,* 2nd ed. (St. Petersburg: in der deutschen Hauptschule zu St. Petri; Riga: bei Hartmann, Meinshausen, Deubner und Treuy, 1812), 252–54.

34. On the mentality of the intelligentsia, see Abbott Gleason, *Young Russia: The Genesis of Russian Radicalism in the 1860s* (New York: Viking Press, 1980).

35. *Shchukinskii Sbornik,* vyp. 5 (Moscow: Tovarishchestvo tipografii A.I. Mamontova, 1906), 502, letter to N.V. Sakharov.

36. D. I. Rostislavov, *Nachal'naia algebra* (Moscow: Tipografiia Gacheva i Komp., 1868), v.

37. Mironov, *Sotsial'naia istoriia,* 1:141. See also the discussion of the reforms in Freeze, *Parish Clergy.*

38. In English, see: I. S. Belliustin, *Description of the Clergy in Rural Russia: The Memoir of a Nineteenth-Century Parish Priest,* translated and with an interpretive essay by Gregory L. Freeze (Ithaca: Cornell University Press, 1985); N. G. Pomyalovsky, *Seminary Sketches,* translated and with an introduction and notes by Alfred Kuhn (Ithaca: Cornell University Press, 1973).

39. Belliustin, 38. *Russkii biograficheskii slovar',* 17: 166. The works in question are *Ob ustroistve dukhovnykh uchilishch v Rossii,* 2 vols. (Leipzig, 1863); *O pravoslavnom belom i chornom dukhovenstve v Rossii,* 2 vols. (Leipzig,

1866); *Opyt izsledovaniia ob imushchestvakh i dokhodakh nashikh monastyrei* (St. Petersburg: Tipografiia Morskago Ministerstva, 1876).

40. Gosudarstvennyi Arkhiv Rossiiskoi Federatsii (GARF) (State Archive of the Russian Federation), *f.* 1395 (III otdelenie "sobstvennoi ego imperatorskogo velichestva" kantseliarii [sekretnyi arkhiv]), *op.* 1, *d.* 1419, *ll.* 6, 6 *ob,* letter from "ierei I. P." to Andrei Nikitich Polisadov, 20 October 1866.

41. Ibid., *ll.* 2, 4, letter from Rostislavov to his brother (19 October 1866); *Biograficheskii slovar' studentov,* 413; Manchester, 264, 280, 305, 356.

42. The following information identifies the passages that are included in this translation. The Preface was taken from *Russkaia Starina* (RS) 27 (January–April 1880): 4–6; Chapter 1—RS 27: 7–10, 14–20; 2—RS 27: 21–32, 34–38; 3—RS 27: 549–57; 4—RS 27: 557–58, 562–63, 567–72; 5—RS 27: 681–84, 689–94; 6—RS 27: 696–704; 7—RS 28 (May–August 1880): 35–53, 58–62, 65–68; 8—RS 28: 179–86; 9—RS 28: 186–95, 203–6; 10—RS 28: 209–11, 213–17; 11—RS 28: 385–90, 397–98, 402, 406–8; 12—RS 33 (January–March 1882): 68–70, 75–85; 13—RS 33: 263–69, 287–90; 14—RS 34 (April–June 1882): 585–605, 607–14; RS 42 (April–June 1884): 495–96; 15—RS 42: 496–504; RS 43 (July–September 1884): 305–6; 16—RS 33: 666, 668–70; RS 56 (October–December 1887): 445–47, 449–50, 454–56, 460, 465; 17—RS 59 (July–September 1888): 63–88 (the pagination skips directly from 63 to 78); 18—RS 76 (October–December 1892): 528–37; 19—RS 82: (December 1894): 53–66; 20—RS 82: 67–76; 21—RS 83 (June 1895): 58–60.

PROVINCIAL RUSSIA

IN THE AGE OF

ENLIGHTENMENT

My Goals and Intentions
in Writing My *Memoir*

• In my entire life, I have not occupied high administrative office, gained great renown for my scholarly or literary works, or succeeded in acquiring a large fortune. In fact, I have actually had very few dealings with rich men, scholars and officials, or aristocrats, and I have played no noteworthy role or had any particular significance among my contemporaries. Therefore, the events of my life cannot hold any interest for posterity, and my biography, if limited to those events alone, would be quite useless—at most, my kin and a few friends and acquaintances would read it with a bit of curiosity. But, by living a good long time in this world, I could not help coming into contact and even conflict with people of all stations. I had the opportunity to observe my contemporaries and could not avoid knowing their customs, prejudices, superstitions, weaknesses, and so on. When I was unable to see something for myself, I could obtain information from others. I was particularly familiar with the condition of the peasants, the clergy, and the educational institutions of the church, for I was born in a village and lived there until the age of ten, so I grew up and played with peasant children, and even after entering school I spent three months a year in my father's house and took part in all aspects of farm work. Later on, when I was in service and then in retirement, I was mainly an urban resident, but even at that time no Chinese Wall separated me from the village. Some peasants were my acquaintances, and many more came to me for advice about their affairs; in addition, my relatives, most of whom belonged to the clerical estate, lived in villages, and I even had a few relatives among peasants and townspeople. As for the educational institutions of the church and both the white and black clergy, I can say without exaggeration or boastfulness that I knew them thoroughly—as the son of a priest, as a pupil of the lower church schools and the seminary, and as a student and teacher at the ecclesiastical academy. The majority of my relatives, schoolmates, and friends belonged to the clergy. Even among the people who occupied episcopal sees in the 1850s and 1860s, I knew more than half by sight.

Of course, neither I nor my relatives and acquaintances were political actors who decided the fate of the Russian tsardom. Of course, neither my name and deeds, nor theirs, will go down in history. But then again, it is generally accepted nowadays that history consists not only of monarchs, generals, and ministers, but that it must also deal with the human reality of nations, and I have known the human reality of the Russian nation very well, so my biographical memoirs, which deal with that reality, should not be without interest for posterity. In particular, the future historian of the Orthodox Church in Russia will find in them many facts and observations to show that the church, which the theologians teach is sustained by the direct intervention of Providence, is very often undermined by men, especially those individuals who think they are the Savior's representatives and the Apostles' successors but who in fact do great harm to the Christian religion and live in ways that contradict its moral teachings. In order to assist the historians of the future in this regard, I will select from my life and the life of my contemporaries the facts that are most representative of my times.

My thought had been not to speak of myself at all and have my memoirs consist of separate chapters, one of which might talk about, say, the peasants, another about the schools, etc., which in fact is what in many places I have decided to do. However, I abandoned that plan owing to the following consideration. Accounts of the prejudices, beliefs, customs, weaknesses, actions, and flaws of the people of any era produce, in my opinion, a stronger impression when the narrator himself is a participant in the story than when he describes them as an outside observer. As a person involved in the events, he will bring greater emotional energy to his task in the former case than in the latter. The reader likewise will have more confidence in the truthfulness of what he reads when he sees that it is told by one who either participated in the events described or personally experienced their effect, for an eyewitness, by Baumeister's logic,[1]* is preferable to one who relies on what he has been told. I have in-

---

* Friedrich Christian Baumeister (1709–1785), a German scholar and author of widely read textbooks on the ideas of Christian Wolff, eighteenth-century Germany's premier philosopher. Rostislavov thought him a scholastic and considered his textbook (used in Russian seminaries) "worthless."

cluded the actual events of my life in the *Memoir*, not because they concern myself in particular, but because they convey the character of the time in which I lived. I humbly ask that they be seen as facts that are more or less revealing of the life of my contemporaries.

Most likely, many will find my descriptions too explicit at times, especially where I discuss corporal punishment. True, my account of that is not only explicit, but, frankly, sometimes quite distasteful. But what else can I do? After all, our future descendants need to know what we, their ancestors, went through. If the reader were to hear from me only that we were punished cruelly and often, he would have no conception of the repulsive particulars and rituals that took place on those occasions, and he therefore would have a far from accurate understanding of the character of our times and would be at a loss to explain the gross behavior that distinguished us. The reader will see that, in those descriptions, I have not been particularly lenient toward myself, either.

My Family Background

• As I noted in my introduction, by ancestry I do not belong to the aristocracy. On my father's side, my great-great-grandfather and his father were priests in the village of Sheianki, in the Kasimov District of Riazan Province.[2]* However, my great-grandfather Larion Gerasimovich rose no higher than the rank of sacristan in that village, perhaps because he died very young.† He left three children: a daughter Anna and two sons, Vasilii and six-month-old Martyn, my grandfather. They lived with their mother, my great-grandmother Avdot'ia Mikhailovna,‡ in the home and under the authority of their uncle Leontii Gerasimovich, who was also a sacristan in Sheianki.

Leontii Gerasimovich had a bold character and a wild streak, as we can see from his wedding. He had his eyes set on a peasant girl from the hamlet of Viklovka, near the village of Sheianki, but her family were rich peasants and did not want to become his in-laws.§ Undeterred by that obstacle, Leontii Gerasimovich first talked his fellow village clergy into agreeing to wed him, then set off secretly at night to her hamlet and took his fiancée with him directly to the church.

---

* Sheianki's Church of the Mother of God of Kazan served a parish that included both Sheianki itself and a dozen smaller communities within a radius of four miles, and contained a total in 1816 of 355 households and 1,354 male inhabitants. This many households officially entitled the parish church to three "staffs" of clergymen, i.e., 3 priests, 2 deacons, and 6 sacristans.

† The term *sacristan* covers various clerical offices *(prichetnik, d'iachok, zvonar', ponomar')* whose holders are not ordained—unlike the priest, who heads the clergy of a given parish, or the deacon who assists him—so they cannot perform the liturgy or administer the sacraments. Instead, they assist the ordained clergy by singing, lighting the candles in church, ringing the bells, etc.

‡ Larion Gerasimovich died around 1762. Rostislavov's great-grandmother (who is listed in the census as Evdokiia Mikhailova—here and elsewhere in the footnotes, names are spelled as they appear in the census records) was born around 1742 and was the daughter of a priest from the village of Gus' (a short distance east of Sheianki).

§ A "village" *(selo)* was usually a farm community with administrative offices or a parish church that served both its own needs and those of the nearby "hamlets" *(derevnia)*, smaller settlements that lacked such institutions.

In the meantime, the abduction was soon discovered and a pursuit was mounted. As soon as he reached the village, the abductor started arranging the wedding. They were about to perform the sacrament when they found out that the pursuers were already in the village. Decisive measures needed to be taken. The church was at once locked from within and the wedding ceremony began. The pursuers pounded on the door and even tried to break it down, but in vain. The ceremony ended, the door was opened, and the peasants ran into the church with the father of the bride in the lead. Then the young couple threw themselves at his and his wife's feet and asked for their blessing while the clergy began arguing with her father and mother to forgive the young couple: "Look, you can't undo their wedding—'what God has united let no man put asunder.'" The old people began shouting and arguing, but little by little they calmed down and finally set off with the young couple to celebrate the wedding. When he would reminisce about it, the venerable Leontii Gerasimovich liked to say that "the devil himself was amazed at the way I got married."

But the angels were probably not protecting the young couple, or at least they refused to assist the growth of their children's intellectual abilities. None of Leontii Gerasimovich's descendants were able to enter the clerical estate. Instead, they settled in the hamlet of Viklovka among their uncles, grandfathers, cousins, and so on, and later, when the government carried out a census, they were somehow registered as serfs of the noble landlord who owned the hamlet. That is why we had very many peasant relatives in Viklovka; I myself later stayed over with my father at the house of one of them, Ivan Vasil'evich, on the way to Kasimov. But my grandfather, and his sister and brother, were more fortunate than their cousins. His sister Anna was given in marriage to a deacon by the name of Nikifor in the Elat'ma District of Tambov Province; though his brother Vasilii did not finish the seminary, he did receive some education and became a clerk in the town of Melenki in Vladimir Province. One of his sons, Efim Vasil'evich, became district treasurer in Vladimir and was later a noble landowner in that same province.

My grandfather had learned reading, writing, and choral singing while he was still a child, and he even knew how to read ecclesiastical sheet music, so in time he was able to take over the post of sacristan after the death of the uncle who had raised him. Until then, however, he had to bear many hardships and earn his crust of bread with great labor. Once he was grown up, he worked as hard as any industrious peasant. His particular specialty—which was typical of the entire area at the time—was that he would both harvest and buy the sapwood of linden trees, which is used to weave bast shoes, and take it to Moscow, even when he was already a sacristan. Most likely, he was known in the area as a good householder and hence a good marriage prospect, because Akim, the rich priest of the village of Tuma Nikolaevskaia, agreed to give him his daughter in marriage.[3]*

After my grandfather had served for about ten years as sacristan in the village of Sheianki, his father-in-law died. The parishioners and clergy of Tuma gave my grandfather a "letter of support," that is, written statements that they wished to have him as their priest. Grandfather took the letter of support and his own petition and went to Vladimir to see Prelate Ieronim,[4]† because both Sheianki and Tuma then belonged to the diocese of Vladimir. It may be interesting to know what sort of "fatherly" relationship a prelate of that time had with the clerics who were his subordinates. All who needed to see him came into the "petition room" (*podacha*), that is, the room where the prelate received petitioners. Ieronim usually took a seat on the sofa in the petition room, called in the petitioners one by one and heard them out, and most often pronounced or wrote down his decisions or "resolutions" on the spot. Many came to present complaints against each other, while others were summoned because they had done something bad that His Grace had somehow found out about. The punishments in these cases varied, of course: the culprits might receive a more or less stern reprimand, be made to perform menial labor in the prelate's residence, or be sent off to a monastery, but very often they would also be punished physically, right there in the petition room, in front of everyone, for the edification of the others. "Well, aren't you a troublemaker," or "aren't you litigious" or "a good-for-nothing," His Grace would exclaim. "Watch, I'll teach you a lesson. Hey!" he would add, speaking to his servants, "bring me the lash!" [The servants would flog the culprit, whom the other clerics had to hold down, while the bishop watched.]

My grandfather himself was almost thus entertained by the prelate. There were plenty of claimants for the position of priest in Tuma, but

---

* The bride, Fekla Akimovna, was born around 1764. Her father Ioakim (Akim) Vasil'ev, born around 1732, was priest in Tuma and was married to Mar'ia Ivanova, born around 1728 and herself the daughter of a priest in Tuma.

† Ieronim (Farmakovskii) (1732–1783), bishop of Vladimir from 1770 on. Rostislavov may be mistaken in identifying the bishop as Ieronim, since Ieronim died in 1783 and Rostislavov's grandfather did not become priest in Tuma until 1792.

Grandfather was the only one to present a letter of support, and he also excelled in reading and singing during an on-the-spot examination. For some reason, the prelate did not want to offer the position to Grandfather, but to a different claimant. Of course, Grandfather asserted his rights. On the first day, nothing was decided, and he was ordered to come back the next day. When they were gathered again, the prelate began urging Grandfather to withdraw his petition and promised to give him a different, better position somewhere else, but Grandfather stood firm and pointed out that he had a letter of support from the parishioners, that the deceased priest had been his father-in-law, and that he read and sang better than the others. In defending his rights, Grandfather got carried away and said something that Ieronim found insulting. "Well, aren't you something!" His Grace shouted. "All right, I'll tame you—withdraw your petition, or I'll have you flogged for rudeness." Grandfather would not yield, so His Grace called for the lash and ordered him to undress and lie down. Grandfather undressed, but, standing in his shirt, he said: "Your Grace! You can flog me all you please, but I will keep saying that the position belongs to me. As Your Grace wishes, but I will continue saying the same thing even after you flog me, and the parish will take my side." Whether His Grace had intended only to scare the obstinate petitioner, or whether he was taken aback by his boldness—in any case, he did not flog him, and instead ordered him to get dressed and offered him the priest's position.[5]*

This bold priest, then, was the father of my father, although actually my father was born when Grandfather was still sacristan in the village of Sheianki. My father, Ivan Martynovich, was originally the priest of the village of Palishchi in the Kasimov District of Riazan Province. He belonged to the category of priests who at the time were called "learned," that is, who had completed the entire course of studies taught at the ecclesiastical seminaries of the time. [. . .]

At the end of the eighteenth and even the beginning of the nineteenth century, most ordained clergy and sacristans, and especially their wives, were reluctant to send their children to the seminary "to study," and the children themselves regarded the seminary studies as "torture." Various reasons account for this negative attitude toward a

---

* The church of St. Nicholas the Miracle-Worker in Tuma (hence the name Tuma *Nikolaevskaia*) ministered to a large number of hamlets divided among three separate parishes, with a total in 1816 of 559 households and 2,083 male inhabitants; it therefore had 3 priests and a corresponding number of deacons and sacristans. By the 1850s, Tuma itself had 44 households with 554 inhabitants, very impressive numbers by local standards. Martyn Larionovich was appointed priest there in 1792, when he was about 30 years old.

seminary education. The primary factor may have been the ignorance that prevailed at the time among the clergy. However, it cannot be said that the seminary education of the time was appealing even for people who did not lack all education. The principal subject of study in the seminaries was Latin, for it was the language of the textbooks not only for philosophy and theology, but even for philology. These disciplines, virtually the only ones taught in the seminaries, could be called models of scholasticism and consisted almost exclusively of "definitions," "postulates," and "negations"—i.e., the definition of the various objects of a discipline (for example, in philology, the definition of every trope, every figure, and so on), followed by statements, or more often actually short little sentences, that expressed this or that verity (as they used to say), and finally objections to that verity, accompanied by the refutation of those objections. All of this was presented in Latin, in a dry and lifeless manner, and in relation to subjects that were not only abstract but actually nonexistent, whereas the historical, physical, natural, and mathematical sciences were held in utter disdain.

How could anyone at all enjoy this sort of learning? People studied this against their will. Of course, some people took to it because they felt a need to show that "we are learned people," but most could see neither practical nor intellectual use in it and feared it as though it were the forced labor of a serf, or torture. In addition, the educators of those times were not noted for their gentle and humane methods. The most harsh and even cruel forms of corporal punishment were all too common. Canes from birch or willow branches were considered inadequate, so in every seminary administration office, there always hung several two- or three-tailed leather lashes. When needed, these lashes were brought to the classrooms, and in experienced and strong hands, they covered the undressed parts of the body with scars that sometimes remained visible for weeks after the operation. [. . .] Lastly, stipends, especially those for students studying at state expense, were utterly inadequate, and sometimes they would literally go hungry. [. . .]

But it is already clear that the children of the clergy did not have much cause to go happily to the seminary and continue and complete their education there. My grandfather [. . .] told me himself that they used to send the land police* to catch the churchmen, that is, the children of the ordained clergy,† who were then bound or

---

* "Land" *(zemskii)* institutions (the land police, land court, and land captain) had jurisdiction over all areas of a district not legally part of a town.

† I.e., priests and deacons.

even put into irons and sent under guard to the place where the seminary was located. Obviously, such measures were inappropriate for ten- to fifteen-year-old children, but grown-up fellows as well, even married ones, were "drafted to become scholars." As a result, Grandfather would say, such a conscript of seminary learning might be seen off not only by a wailing mother and sisters but even by a wife with a baby in her arms. In light of this, it is only natural to expect that many of these conscripts tried to save themselves by fleeing. In Vozdvizhenskii's *History of the Riazan Hierarchy*[6] one often encounters these words: under such and such prelate, so many were studying at the seminary and so many were fugitives. The fugitives sometimes numbered in the dozens and were almost equal in numbers to those who were studying. My grandfather would sometimes actually boast about having avoided the seminary, but on the other hand he was forced many times to flee from his village into the forest or to some hamlet and spend several days there while waiting for the withdrawal of the land police who had come to "catch" him "to make him go study." Then, as later, the officers of the land police liked to ride with little bells attached to their horses, so that as soon as the sound of the bell from the field reached them in the village, all the churchmen who were fugitives from seminary learning would rush to find shelter in cozy places where they would be impossible to find. Many others besides the land police officers would ride with little bells, so that such alarms sometimes turned out to be unnecessary. My grandfather told me how, once, a relative of his so scared him with his bell that it took them a long time to find my grandfather, and the relative almost left again without seeing him. [. . .]

[Father, however, did attend the seminary.] My father was among the top students of his class.[7*] Probably because the seminary studies did not satisfy his intellectual curiosity, he decided, two years before the end of his seminary education, to enter the medical academy. My grandfather and my grandmother Fekla Akimovna, just like almost the entire clergy at that time, felt that the calling of clergyman was the best one for their sons. They were motivated of course by the conviction that the clerical calling was superior to other, secular

---

* When he graduated from the Riazan seminary in 1808, he was, according to the school records that survive today, one of the 7 youngest students in his class of 79. He was one of only 5 whose overall academic performance was rated "good," while 69 others were merely "not too bad," "not bad," or "not bad at all," and the only one whose conduct was "honorable," whereas 62 of his classmates were only "not bad" or "not suspect." Also, out of a group of 48 students, he was the best in Hebrew and was tied for first place in Greek.

offices and occupations, but also by the desire to have their sons nearby so they could go more often to see them and, consequently, drink with them. [. . .] Besides, then and even still in my time, the medical academy aroused horror and disgust in many members of the clergy because the students had to deal with anatomy and operations, or, as they said at the time, "cut up the living and the dead." When my grandfather found out that his son, my father, intended to enter the medical academy, he became extremely angry, decided to go to Riazan, and boasted to Grandmother that he would "beat that nonsense out of Vaniusha's head" (that is what he called my father until his death, even though Father was a respected archpriest[8*] and known almost throughout the diocese). To carry out his threat, Grandfather even took along a lash to "beat the nonsense out of Vaniusha's head." By the standards of the time, such methods were considered not only acceptable but also especially reliable and easy.

Only, Grandfather either had no intention of actually making good on his threat and was merely posturing and blustering in front of Grandmother and the other villagers, or perhaps he changed his mind on the road to Riazan—in any case, once he had arrived in Riazan, Grandfather started acting completely differently from what he had said in Tuma to Grandmother, who had begged him to be gentle with their son. [. . .] Grandfather forgot all about his parental rights and the threats uttered in Tuma, he began to cry and embrace his son, he even was ready to bow and would in fact have bowed if my father had not stopped him, he started to beg and implore him not to go to the medical academy, and so on and so forth. My late father had a firm character and absolutely no desire at that time to become a priest, but when he saw his father's tears and heard that, in Tuma, his mother was also weeping ceaselessly and imagining with horror how he would "cut up living people and dead ones"—my father could not bear it, and gave up his cherished dream of being a doctor. Grandfather was delighted, but when he returned home he still at first told Grandmother and the other villagers, "I let him have it, my Vaniusha, I beat the nonsense out of his head." The truth came out only when my dad came to Tuma at the end of the semester and told Grandmother everything. However, Grandfather did not become angry about that, and I myself later often heard him say, "So, what was I supposed to do? I knew that the lash wouldn't do any good in this sit-

---

* Archpriest was a largely honorific title that was usually held by no more than about a dozen clerics in a given diocese. Substantively, archpriests had the same function as priests.

uation, but at home I couldn't tell them right away that I had to beg in order to talk him into it—I couldn't embarrass myself like that." However, Grandfather was afraid that his Vaniusha might again have the idea of going to the medical academy, so he started looking for both a position and a bride for him, found both, and persuaded Vaniusha to petition the prelate to give him the position of priest in the village of Palishchi. The prelate agreed, and during the summer vacation, one year before graduating from the seminary, my dad was married[9]* and ordained as priest, after which he still went to class for an entire year. [. . .]

---

* He married Ekaterina Nikitina (three years his junior), the daughter of the priest of Arkhangel'skoe, a community of 14 households and 75 inhabitants (in the 1850s) and located about twenty miles northwest of Tuma.

CHAPTER TWO

The Village of Palishchi
and Its Environs

•   When my father obtained the position of priest in the village of
Palishchi, he also bought the house that his predecessor had owned.
However, since he had to live and study in Riazan for most of the year,
he was in Palishchi only during vacations, and even then he scarcely
spent all his time there. My mother, for her part, spent the entire year
with my grandfather in Tuma, which is why I was born in that village.
When my father returned from Riazan in October 1809, my parents
moved to Palishchi for good and settled into their own home and
household. In this chapter, I will describe both my and their life in
Palishchi not only on the basis of what I was able to find out from others when I was already grown up, but also my own impressions and observations. Of course, those were a child's impressions and observations, but I tried to verify their accuracy or inaccuracy once I was old
enough to form a judgment about them that was no longer childish.

The first childhood memories that are clearly fixed in my memory
date from the fourth and fifth year of my life. In particular, two events
from that time left a vivid impression in my mind: my vaccination
against smallpox and the death of the Palishchi priest Vasilii. The first
event took place before I turned four. Smallpox at the time could be
called a terrible scourge of the Russian people, which not only disfig-
ured but also killed a huge number of children and adults. However,
ignorance and the prevailing prejudices led the mass of the people to
regard smallpox vaccinations as either impious or terribly dangerous.
In the villages and hamlets, most mothers never voluntarily agreed to
bring their children to a medical assistant or even to a physician to be
vaccinated, and if they did decide to go, it was after extensive urging
and even coercion, and, of course, amidst weeping and wailing. The
priests were given orders to make every effort to encourage vaccina-

tions with religious arguments. [. . .] In addition, the priests were likewise virtually ordered by imperial edict to set an example for their
parishioners by allowing their own children to be vaccinated.

I do not know whether it was by coincidence or in response to the
governmental instructions I just mentioned, but my vaccination and
that of my two sisters was public, indeed almost a ceremony. It was
Sunday, and many village women and men had gathered in the log
cabin *(izba)* where we lived. [. . .] Some of the women had started crying even before the operation. Most likely I felt shy because I was
confused by the whole situation, for when the medical attendant
started rolling up my right sleeve, someone said about me, "He's
scared and wants to cry." To help me be brave, my dad answered,
"Come on, I know he's not scared and would never cry—he's not a
little girl." These words aroused my ambition and, as I recall today, I
pressed my lips together, held back the tears that were about to flow,
and gathered up all my courage, so that I neither screamed nor
cried, which of course won me praise from all sides. On the other
hand, of course, my sisters (Natal'ia was two years younger than I,
and Elizaveta was still an infant) did cry and fight back against the
danger threatening them, so they had to be restrained. [. . .]

The death of Father Vasilii occurred soon after our vaccination
and impressed me by its tragic character. Father Vasilii was already an
old man with gray hair and a beard and a somewhat stooped figure.
To be honest, for some reason I was afraid of him. Like our third
priest, Evdokim, he was a drinker.[10*] My father, although thirty or
forty or even more years younger than they, was a "learned man," i.e.,
a seminary graduate, so he held a higher rank in our church; as they
used to say, he was its "senior priest." The old men were probably not
very happy to be thus humiliated in their old age, and did not look
kindly upon me; that must be why I was afraid of them.

Once, Father Vasilii had to go for some reason to the village of Ovintsi (six *versts†* from Palishchi) and there, as was his habit, he got
thoroughly drunk. He was returning home by himself and must have
fallen off his sleigh, lacked the strength to catch up with his horse,
and was left in an open field. His horse came home alone, but they
apparently did not notice its return right away and so did not start
looking for him until the next day. They found the old man frozen to

---

* Like Tuma, Palishchi served 3 parishes—with a total in 1816 of 392 households and 1,523 male
inhabitants—and therefore had 3 sets of clergymen.

† One verst equals 1,060 meters and is almost identical to a kilometer (0.6 miles).

death. I remember, the sun was already setting but it was still fairly light out, when people in our cabin started saying that Father Vasilii was being brought back. I was standing on a bench by one of the windows facing the street and saw a horse harnessed to the kind of sledge that is called a "wood-sledge." On it lay Father Vasilii, covered with a bast mat, and at the end of the sledge stood a peasant holding the reins. They were going at a fairly fast trot. I was frightened, of course, for I had heard often enough that death was always a terrible thing and dead people were fearsome beings, but that drunkards who had frozen to death were even more terrible because their souls were not received anywhere, so they were given up to the devil or left to wander the earth and haunt people.

As a child, I liked the village of Palishchi very much, as almost everyone likes the places where he spent his childhood. Actually, though, the village deserved no particular praise with regard to its location. It was completely surrounded by woods, and I can still remember that it was impossible to see any of the neighboring hamlets. The clergy of Palishchi finally grew tired of this isolation and decided to clear a large section of the forest in the direction of the hamlet of Spudni. At the beginning of the summer, they cut down several *desiatiny** of woods, including even construction-quality trees, and left them to dry out during the hot months. Then, one Sunday in September, they set fire to all the wood. [. . .] While the adults were busy kindling the wood and ensuring that the fire did not spread beyond the intended area, we children were delighted at this unaccustomed spectacle. [. . .] It remained smoky for a few more days, but finally the fires died down, that is, everything had burned, and now we could see all the way to Spudni.

Around the village, at a greater or lesser distance, there were marshes on all sides, so that the site could be called an island in a sea of marshes. This made riding to other villages very difficult in the summer, and doubled or even tripled the time needed for travel. [. . .] For travelers on foot during the summer, logs were laid out in the marshes; they were arrayed just about any which way, some trimmed, others not, now two or three next to each other, now just one. I actually suppose that the village could be called an island that was not only surrounded on all sides by marshes, but that had marshes beneath it as well, as we can see from the following incident. [. . .] A man was working on sinking a well when he began shouting in fright for people to pull him up

---

* One desiatina is 2.7 acres.

as quickly as possible. Back on the surface, he recounted in terror that he had almost fallen through the earth. At first, people laughed at him, but then one bold fellow decided to go down to the bottom of the well. As it turned out, it really was unstable and quivered when you struck it hard. [. . .] [From a hole in the bottom of the well] there flowed a not very thick mud and foul-smelling water. They handed him long poles, but those sank easily into the mud beneath and did not touch firm ground. The villagers then got cold feet because they were afraid their entire village might fall through the earth, perhaps into "Tartarary," that is, into Tartarus, Hell, so they filled up the well. You can see from my description how right the archbishop of Riazan, Feofilakt, was about Palishchi when he said that "that village is in the middle of nowhere, in the marshes." In that village, amidst those marshes, lived the clergy for three parishes: three priests, two deacons, and six sacristans, in addition to three townsmen, namely the Galkin family (distant relatives of ours), one Il'ia, and one Silushka, and also the daughter of Father Vasilii who had frozen to death.

Owing to its marshy, damp, and wooded location, the village was filled with awful numbers of mosquitoes during the summer. In that regard, Palishchi was almost like the shores and surface of the Mississippi, where people wear iron netting to escape the mosquitoes. The villagers of Palishchi resorted to no such sophisticated devices. Instead, sometimes several times a day and invariably in the evenings, they would kindle clay pots filled with manure, which filled the rooms with an acrid smoke that the mosquitoes disliked and that made them leave through the open door. Then they would usually close the door and lie down to sleep in the smoky, stinking room.[11]* I don't think that we burned much manure, but instead we would "fumigate," that is, we would fill the cabin with smoke by burning damp wood. However, my late father made use of a new technique that he had discovered. Mosquitoes do not fly very high off the ground, and the bell tower of our village church was very tall; no mosquito ever flew that high. That is why, after dinner, my father would take a pillow and the requisite clothing and head for the bell tower, right beneath the bells, where he would sleep all night. "Now, that's a nice place," he would say, "not one fly, not one mosquito."

---

* The Frenchman Frédéric Le Play, on a trip to the Urals in 1844, observed that peasants protected themselves against mosquitoes by going to their fields with a pot of dried mushrooms that gave off a thick smoke while burning, and that a fire fueled with manure and rotten wood burned continually at the windward side of the village to keep insects away.

However, the inhabitants of our village and the nearby hamlets had other unpleasant neighbors from the animal kingdom who were bigger than mosquitoes—wolves, eagle owls, and bears. There were lots and lots of wolves in the woods around our village. In the summer, they presented no danger to people, although domestic animals often paid with their hides. In the winter, however, people had to take precautions against the wolves who frequently roamed in entire companies and liked to chase after a man, even if he was driving a horse-drawn sleigh. The roads were so narrow, and the snow so deep, that the wolves could not overtake a horse, but hunger forced them to attempt bold stunts. If they caught up to the sleigh, they sometimes tried to make a leap and become uninvited companions in the sleigh. However, since the wolf needed to pause for a few moments to make the leap, the horse had time to move on and the leap did not help the wolf get onto the sleigh. In a different maneuver, the wolf would seize the rear end of the sleigh with its teeth, dig its heels into the snow, and try to stop the horse. Of course, that maneuver also failed. [. . .] In any case, I cannot remember a single instance of any villager or parishioner of Palishchi getting eaten by wolves. However, when dogs and other animals ran into the street or out of the village in winter, especially at night, their boldness often did not go unpunished, because at night the wolves came right into the villages. [. . .] In many villages during the winter, almost all the dogs that were not on a chain ended up one way or another falling prey to wolves.

The wolves terrified most of the villagers of Palishchi not only with their attacks on them and their domestic animals, but also with their "concerts." It is well known that, when the frost is too severe and especially if they are hungry in addition, wolves begin to howl. The sound of their howling really is scary, and every wolf can vary the tone and modulation of its voice, so you might hear one or especially two such singers and think that an entire, large chorus had gathered. [. . .] I remember one time when a performer from the woods wanted to entertain us with his singing right outside our windows. [. . .] My father was not at home, so only the women and children were by the fire in the cabin. I remember how frightened everyone was, how most ran for the stove, the high sleeping bench, as though the wolf had already climbed through the window. I had been sitting on a bench by the wall, but now I also jumped up and ran along it to the icon corner,* and there I

---

* Traditionally, every Russian cabin had a corner *(perednii ugol)* in its main room where sacred religious images (icons) were prominently displayed.

took refuge. I will not even discuss the screaming that we felt was needed to defend ourselves against the attacks of our adversary, even though he had no intention of climbing in to where we were. The performer soon fell silent, and we gradually recovered from our fright.

The eagle owl is actually not at all dangerous to man, but superstitious villagers feared its visits to Palishchi almost more than the wolf's. Like the owl and the bat, the eagle owl is a nocturnal bird.[12]* That already makes it suspect in the eyes of superstitious people, because daytime and light are thought to belong to God, whereas nighttime and darkness are, of course, ruled by the Evil One, who also loves to do his mischief then, especially before midnight. It follows logically that nocturnal birds in general are not creatures of God, but creations of the devil. In addition, the front of both the eagle owl's and the owl's head looks a little like a human face—clearly, if this distorted human appearance was not actually the devil's own, then at least these must be his favorite animals, into which he might even change himself when necessary.

When I was already at the [St. Petersburg Ecclesiastical] academy, and my father lived in Tuma, an incident occurred in our house in his absence that frightened everybody. An owl had somehow flown into our vestibule† and could not find its way out. Somebody went out into the vestibule, saw its gleaming eyes, and reported it in the cabin. An entire expedition set out to investigate. The sight of a bird whose muzzle looked like a human face astonished them all and even terrified a few, but someone was bold enough to seize the owl and carry it into the cabin. Luckily, there was in the cabin a fairly large cage, where the prisoner was at once confined. Everyone stood around and tried to figure out what sort of creature this was. Father and Mother were not home at the time, so the commander, so to speak, was grandmother Fekla Akimovna, who had lost her eyesight a few years earlier. Of those who were present and able to see, none had ever seen an owl before. Naturally, everyone looked to Grandmother to resolve the question, and in describing the bird's exterior they made it seem even scarier than it actually appeared. The old woman, who knew little about natural history but fancied herself an

---

* Two and a half feet tall, and with an impressive wingspan of five and a half feet, the eagle owl—the largest of all owl species—is nearly twice as large as the common European tawny owl.

† The vestibule *(seni),* whose purpose it is to keep the weather and mud out of the cabin, is a small room located between the entrance and the main area of the house.

expert in demonology, determined that it had to be a little devil, and the others agreed. Grandmother at once gave the order to make the sign of the cross over the cage from all sides, because everyone believed that the devil would not dare come out in a direction where it had been made. They started making the sign, and when they were sure that there was nowhere left for the Evil One to slip through, they left the cage until morning, when they were going to turn over the captured devil to the proper authorities. In the morning, however, some good person explained that the supposed devil was actually an owl.

The eagle owl frightened the villagers not only with its looks, but also with its voice. It is true that its wild, doleful, vaguely human-sounding screech can scare a superstitious person. In addition, the eagle owl likes to give its concerts at night, and sometimes it flies up to the bell tower of village churches for that purpose. Imagine the commotion in the village when suddenly, in the dead of night, the wild and terrifying screech of an eagle owl resounds from the bell tower. Superstitious people are not only petrified with horror during the concert, but for a long time after they will wait in agony for some misfortune to occur, because village logic had it that the screech of an eagle owl, especially from the bell tower, foretells a fire or some other evil, and if something of that nature were to occur, though it be a few weeks, months, or even a year later, the eagle owl will be considered the culprit as well as the prophet of the misfortune. In Palishchi, the screech of the eagle owl was heard exceedingly often, and once an eagle owl even decided to choose the bell tower as its permanent home. My father tried to convince the villagers that they should expect no more misfortune from the screech of an eagle owl than from that of any other animal, but their convictions remained firm. Even in my father's home, just about everybody except he thought the eagle owl was, if not the devil himself, then a creature very close to him, and so they were terrified when they heard its screech from the bell tower. I, too, when I saw all the frightened faces, would retreat into a corner and sit and wait for some terrible disaster. In the woods, the nocturnal screech of the eagle owl was even more frightening, because it was amplified and multiplied by echoes. It was exactly as though someone were laughing and some-one else were answering with the same laugh a few seconds later. Obviously, only "wood goblins" could call to each other like that in the forest. That is why almost everyone thought that the forests around Palishchi were full of wood goblins.

The bear—or, as people call him, Mishka or Mikhail Ivanovich*—is an individual who prefers a lonely, reclusive life, so, except when necessary, he avoids showing himself to human eyes. Around Palishchi, however, encounters with him were not rare. [. . .] I don't know why, but, as I heard as a child, people believed that when Misha seized a person, he would usually crush him underneath himself with the head facing backward and then roll up his clothes almost like on a boy who is about to be caned, and then he would mainly, or at least to start out, eat those soft parts of the body where the blows of the cane fall. I even remember that, in one instance, a peasant was rescued from a bear who had already eaten one of his hips. The wounds were somehow healed and the man lived, but from then on he always sat leaning to one side. [. . .]

Another folk belief held that Misha did not like to use women, particularly young ones, for his table. Instead, if he captured one, he would take her to his lair and live domestically with his captive. When he went hunting, he would block the entrance to his lair so the captive could not escape, and when he returned, he would bring her lunch or dinner. People said, and with utter conviction, that children were actually born of such civil marriages,† that the wife was sometimes very pleased with the caresses of her shaggy husband and did not want to leave him, and that she would pine for life in the forest even after returning to her previous village and family. Not only the peasants believed these sorts of tales, but most of the clergy did as well. [. . .]

[The most renowned bear hunter in the area was a man named Trofim.] I should point out that Trofim descended from a lineage whose members were remarkable for their longevity and their almost bearlike strength. He lived with an old man, his uncle's father.‡ My father knew him from 1809 until 1817 and loved to talk with him. When asked how many years old he was, the old man would usually answer, "Truth is, I don't know, Father, but it sure is an awful lot. For instance, I can remember when the *strel'tsy* mutinied, when Tsar Petr Alekseevich locked up his sister Sof'ia Alekseevna in a convent," and so on.§ When asked about events that had occurred during his lifetime, the old man would give answers that were quite original:

---

* Mishka and Misha are both nicknames for Mikhail (Michael).

† I.e., marriages not sanctioned by the church.

‡ An "uncle" in Russian can be either a brother or a cousin of one's parent, so "his uncle's father" does not necessarily mean the same thing as "his grandfather."

§ In a coup in 1689, the young tsar Peter I (Petr Alekseevich) overthrew his half-sister, the regent Sof'ia, sent her to a convent, and took power himself. Troops known as *strel'tsy* (musketeers) later mutinied against Peter in 1698.

"So," my father might ask, "did this or that event occur a long time ago?"

"Oh no, Father, that happened recently, under our mother Ekaterina Alekseevna" (that is, Catherine II).*

That is what he would answer even for events that had occurred at the beginning of her reign, fifty and more years earlier. When discussing events from the reign of Empress Elizabeth, the old man would say, "Now, that was quite a while back, under our mother Elizaveta Petrovna." He had a remarkable memory and his description of events was accurate and to the point. He had high regard for Peter I but especially loved Sof'ia Alekseevna. He still lived for several years after my father left Palishchi and must have been around a hundred and fifty years old when he died. Despite his extreme old age, he still had all his teeth, and only his eyes began to fail him about ten or fifteen years before he died. [. . .]

While the forests that surrounded Palishchi were not without danger for people because of the wolves and bears, they were also made attractive, at least in the summertime, by the gifts of the plant kingdom. Of course, the trees in the field did not bear tasty, edible fruit; fir and pine cones, and sometimes acorns and rowanberries, were almost the only fruits of the trees in the woods around Palishchi. On the other hand, there were many different sorts of berries. Within a few hundred sazhens,† to say nothing of larger distances, one could find wild strawberries, blueberries, bog bilberries, and especially raspberries, mountain cranberries, and cranberries. We children would run by ourselves into the woods and eat our fill of berries before coming back home; on some days we would go out on several such expeditions. Our elders would go to gather as many berries as they could to bring home for the whole family. The wild strawberries and bog bilberries would be eaten almost at once or the next day. The raspberries and blueberries were partly eaten, partly dried and stored for the winter or as filling for pies, or they would pour hot water over them in place of tea leaves to make a sudorific‡ or a remedy for diarrhea; thrifty and hospitable hosts would prepare a liqueur

---

* Catherine II reigned from 1762 to 1796. Elizabeth, mentioned in the following paragraph, reigned from 1741 to 1761. The common people often referred to monarchs as "father" (*batiushka*) or "mother" (*matushka*) rather than the more official "His (Her) Majesty," and used the traditional first name and patronymic ("Ekaterina Alekseevna") instead of the Europeanized form that included the first name and number ("Catherine II").

† One *sazhen* is seven feet.

‡ A sudorific causes a person to sweat and is used to combat fevers.

from raspberries and blueberries and serve these liqueurs only to particularly honored guests. [. . .]

One could hardly find a place where mushrooms grew in greater abundance than in Palishchi. There was everything—edible boletus, orange-cap boletus, milk-agaric, saffron milk-cap (the forest and meadow sorts), shaggy boletus, granulated boletus, and so on and so forth. In the summer, we had meals made from mushrooms almost every day; during the season when there was work to be done in the fields, the children were sent to gather them. For the winter we would stock up on large quantities of dried edible boletus and "black" mushrooms. Milk-agaric and saffron milk-cap were steeped in water, as were mountain cranberries, and boiling water was poured over orange-cap boletus, after which they were stored in glass jars. Hard though mushrooms might be on the digestion, on fast days* they were the villagers' favorite treat, both as a relish in cabbage soup and pies and even as a separate dish.

Lastly, during the summer, we children would seek out other plants for ourselves in the fields and woods. [. . .] In the woods, we would especially gather pine buds at the beginning of the warm season, when they had not yet turned to wood. Our favorite treat was pine sap. It was obtained in the early spring by stripping off the pine tree's bark, beneath which a somewhat hardened sap was forming the pine's new outer layer. We scraped this sap off in ribbons and took it home, where it was regarded as a great delicacy; however, you had to eat it quickly, or else it would soon turn into something like wood. The adults did not lag behind the little children in this pursuit. The children generally removed only the bark that was near the ground. Of course, often that was enough to kill the trees. The adults, however, acted more decisively than the children: they would usually select a construction-quality tree, cut it down completely, and remove the bark. It was a good thing if the wood was at least used for firewood or some other purpose, but usually it was left to rot in the place where it had been cut down. In those cases, the villagers and even the clergy acted like savages who might cut down a tree to pick its fruit. Not surprisingly, there is by now a shortage not only of construction-quality timber, but even of firewood, in places where I still remember there being impassable, almost primeval forests.

---

* Every Wednesday and Friday, as well as during four longer periods of the year (the longest of which was the six weeks of Lent, followed by the week before Easter), the Orthodox were to fast by abstaining from meat, dairy products, and sex. Other days were known as "meat days."

CHAPTER THREE

A Village Household

[The typical villager's home was a rectangular cabin whose narrow front side faced the street. It was usually divided into two sections connected by a large clay or brick stove—located in a corner at the back of the cabin—used to prepare food and to heat the cabin and on which people could sleep in cold weather. The smaller section of the cabin (the *chulan*) served as a kitchen, while the larger one faced the street and was used for all other purposes. The left corner of the wall facing the street, diagonally across from the stove, was the cleanest and most carefully kept spot in the house, where the sacred icons were displayed.[13] In the summer, the master and mistress of the house often slept in a clean, unheated storage building adjacent to the cabin (the annex or *gornitsa*), but in cold weather the entire family would sleep on the benches that lined the wall of the cabin, on the stove, or even on the floor. "White" cabins had a chimney, but in the more primitive (and common) "black" cabins, there was no chimney and the smoke was expected to escape through the door— as a result, such homes were often filled with smoke, with serious consequences for the inhabitants' health. They were also poorly ventilated, and the combination of smoke and human and animal odors fouled the air. Owing to the difficulty of obtaining window glass and of lighting the interior, the cabin was also generally quite dark.]

• When my father was still a seminarian, he was friendly with a noble landlord family, the Ivanov brothers, who lived in the hamlet of Snokhino in the parish of Tuma, especially one of the brothers, Aleksei Vasil'evich.[14]* He acquired ways and habits from them that were alien to the clergy, and even became familiar with the ideas of eighteenth-

---

* Another brother, Petr Vasil'evich, appears in the 1816 records as an ensign in the Imperial Guards who owned 172 male serfs in Snokhino near Tuma.

century French liberalism that had spread in Russia. At least, I heard from him more than once that he had read translations of several works by Voltaire, such as *Candide,* that he had borrowed from Aleksei Ivanov.* Also, among the seminarians of my father's generation, liberal and even atheistic ideas circulated at least occasionally. For example, he told me about one of his classmates who went out onto the porch when storm clouds were gathering, bared his chest, faced the sky, and shouted, "Well, if you (i.e., God) really exist, then smite me." In addition, as I noted earlier, the fact that Father had decided to go to the medical academy was proof that he did not much like the life of the clergy. Once he had become a priest, I think, he became pious without being sanctimonious or fanatical, and both when I was a child and when I was an adult as well as when he was old and when he died, I saw many instances of his sincere Christian sentiments. For all that, however, among the village clergy of his time, from 1809 on and later, he seemed a progressive, a man of advanced ideas.

However, in external matters, both the prevailing customs and his financial resources compelled him to act almost exactly like all the other clerics. In Palishchi, as I said earlier, he bought and moved into his predecessor's house. The house consisted of only one heated room, the cabin—a "white" cabin of course, with "red" windows†— while past the vestibule, as custom prescribed, there was an unheated annex. That remained the situation almost until I turned five, when they finally made the annex heatable and equipped it with a so-called Dutch stove,‡ the first of its kind in the village of Palishchi. Yet, even after that, our entire family spent most of its time in the cabin. Only Father and Mother would usually sleep in the annex, which is also where honored guests were received.

But otherwise, day and night, everyone would both sit and lie, eat lunch and dinner, work and relax, and so on, in the cabin. Even in extraordinary circumstances, when we small children should have been taken out of the cabin, they kept us inside. For example, my mother gave birth to one of her daughters—Mar'ia or Aleksandra, I can't remember which—on the stove in the cabin. I was sitting on the bench in the icon corner during that time and simply could not understand why suddenly blood started flowing from the stove, a baby was carried away, and so on. Also, following village custom, domestic

---

* Rostislavov's father's school records indicate that he knew Greek and Hebrew, but apparently no modern languages, so he probably was unable to read contemporary foreign authors in the original.

† "Red" ("i.e., beautiful") windows were large windows with glass panes.

‡ This kind of stove was used for heating, not food preparation.

animals were carried, driven, or admitted into our cabin. Not only did the cow eat her feed here, but the piglets would spend several days with their mama, as did the lambs, calves, geese, and so on. We children especially liked the lambs, and somewhat also the piglets, with whom we would actually play games, but we were terribly afraid of the geese because they are very nasty when they are hatching their chicks and so we children got to know their bills.

We also [like the other villagers] mostly used torches* for lighting at night. Only on special occasions, when we had honored guests or Father needed to write something, was a tallow candle lit. At the time I did not notice whether the air was good or bad; I only remember that, for ventilation, they would occasionally open the stove pipe and even briefly open the door a little, but they had never even heard of a *fortochka.*† The floor also was not very clean, especially because large numbers of peasant men and women would come into the cabin, above all on Sundays and holidays. But I daresay that our cabin, despite these inauspicious circumstances, was much cleaner and neater than any peasant cabin. Sometimes we would come home not only from a [peasant] hamlet but even from some sacristan's or deacon's house and would find that our cabin was, as we put it, almost like a respectable parlor. To keep the cabin clean, or at least prevent it from being too filthy all the time, the floors and benches were washed. (I forgot to mention that the cabin contained no chairs, armchairs, etc. Instead, benches were attached to the wall, and there were an additional two or three [freestanding] benches. For the annex however, once it was made heatable, we bought up to a dozen chairs.) The most energetic cleaning occurred before Christmas, Easter, and the Holidays of Christ: Whitsunday, the Prophet Elijah (July 20), and the Protection of the Virgin (October 1); then we would mostly cover the ground with fresh straw, in which we loved to play and roll around. In addition, we often cleaned the floors on Saturdays.

Of course, there were not many servants in my father's house, especially at the time when he had just started his family. Generally there was a "workwoman," a simple peasant villager who did most of the menial chores. They also would hire a peasant who was not particularly able or smart, called a "workman," to look after the horse, plow the field, mow hay, chop wood, and so on. However, it seems

---

* These torches *(luchiny)* were long, inch-thick strips of dried birch wood that produced large amounts of fumes and soot when lit.

† A section of the window that can be opened separately for ventilation and that is common in more affluent Russian houses.

that we did not always have a workman during the winters when I was a child. Later, as the number of children began to grow, Father invited his cousin Pelageia Nikiforovna, the daughter of Grandfather's sister Anna, from the town of Elat'ma, and she became nanny and governess to us. Lastly, when I was four or five, Father decided to have so called "bought people." To explain this term, I would like to remind the reader that, during the time of which I write, serfdom was in full force. In imitation of the noble landlords, the clergy, merchants, so-called personal nobles,* and sometimes even townspeople and state peasants also wished to have serfs as their servants. However, the laws did not permit them to enserf anyone or, as they said at the time, "register serfs in their own name." Of course, they found a way to circumvent the law. A noble landlord would sell one or another of his serfs to a priest, a merchant, and so on, but for census purposes the sold person remained his former master's property. However, the master gave his word not to take possession of him. Of course, fraud was always possible. To protect himself against that risk, the buyer would make a contract in which the seller, making use of the rights granted him by the law, ostensibly gave a peasant man or woman into his service for a more or less clearly defined period of time. The contract would be periodically renewed, but often even that formality was not observed; the one would sell and the other would buy and take away the purchased human merchandise and at once treat it like a noble master. In some cases, such merchandise was even recognized in the official census records.

Following this custom, my father bought from his close acquaintance Karl Vasil'evich Kronstein, the landlord of the hamlet of Uzhishchevo (also in Kasimov District), an already elderly woman named Praskov'ia and two grandchildren of hers, the seven-to-ten-year-old girls Tat'iana and Natal'ia. I remember when they were brought to us. I was sitting at the table by the icon corner. The woman went off to the kitchen, and the girls sat down on the sleeping loft in the back of the cabin and looked around with timid curiosity. The woman was a stupid, lazy peasant and a great gossip. The older sister, Tat'iana, was an intelligent girl, quick on the uptake and eager to lend a hand, whereas the younger one, Natal'ia, in many ways resembled her grandmother. On winter evenings, when she was "sitting at the hackle," that is, spinning flax into thread, or doing

---

* "Personal" nobles had noble status but, unlike hereditary nobles, were unable to bequeath that status to their children.

some other work, she would always doze; sometimes she would do that even during the day.

In addition to the "bought people," we almost always, as I said earlier, had a male worker. Thus, just about until I left for Petersburg, we had four servants. Even so, my father and mother—like all members of the clergy—did not "like to sit with their arms folded," as the saying goes, especially where the household and field work in Palishchi was concerned. As mistress of the house, my mother not only looked after the preparation of the food, but it would be more accurate to say that she herself prepared it with the assistance of the servants. Only when she grew old and her health failed did she occasionally decline to do this. When we lived in Palishchi, she would move the earthenware and cast-iron pots in and out of the oven, clean the beef and the fish, knead and roll loaves of bread, and so on and so forth; in a word, she fulfilled all the duties of a cook. She would even carry water from the well in a tub. When I was already a professor and once was spending my vacation at my parents' house, I saw my mother and her workwoman carry a tub to the well to get water. I could not let her carry a full tub of water from the well to the kitchen, so I went over to them, lifted up the tub, and carried it with the help of the workwoman, but my late mother only very reluctantly accepted that. Furthermore, she was not exempted from looking after the farm animals. I often saw her carrying hay to the cattle shed, preparing feed in the cabin, milking the cows, and carrying slops to the pigs. Once the bought girls were a bit older, however, she rarely did those chores anymore. She even washed the crockery herself at least occasionally, as well as the floors in the cabin and the annex. As for the so-called women's tasks, my late mother was a great expert at those and, I think, greatly enjoyed them. In the fall and winter, she would spend a great deal of time sitting at the hackle and spinning, and during the summer, she would weave and then bleach coarse linen herself, and even sew linens.* In a word, until her daughters started helping her, she alone made all the coarse linen that was needed for herself, for Father, and for the children, and she still had plenty of coarse linen in reserve. Also, I forgot to mention that she would wash dirty clothes in lye and clean them, and even in the winter she would take them to the river.

My father was also busy with domestic cares. When necessary, he would himself harness and unhitch the horse, grease the wheels of the

---

* The term "linens" *(bel'e)* covers clothing as well as sheets, towels, tablecloths, and so on that are made from linen *(kholst)*.

cart, and at least sometimes, I think, go out for firewood, but he particularly liked going into the forest himself to cut down construction-quality trees and bring them home; this he would do even when he was already a district superintendent* and quite advanced in years. In emergencies he would also help out with the farm animals. There were many marshy areas around Palishchi where our livestock, especially the cows, would get mired, so that in the evenings, and sometimes even at night, they had to be sought after and then pulled out of the mud; when that happened, Father worked harder than just about anyone else. But some of his greatest worries were occasioned by the swine. In Palishchi, the swine he had were of a very large breed. In the summer, when they roamed free on the pasture, they did not like coming home and instead made their home in the woods, which is even where they would bring forth their young. After a long period of living free, they would almost revert to being wild, and even when the weather turned cold they would not always return home on their own with their offspring. [As a result, returning the swine to the farm was difficult and dangerous work.]

The clergy of those times and their families were even less free from work in the fields and kitchen gardens than from chores and worries in the household. Even now, in 1870, it is the rare village priest who lives "like a gentleman," as they say, and who does not work in his kitchen garden or field, or who can turn over all those jobs to his workers while keeping for himself only the labor of supervising them. The deacons and sacristans personally do the plowing and mowing, spread the manure, thresh, and so on and so forth; in a word, in the summer, they and their families are indistinguishable in this respect from the peasants. The actual priests, of course, don't all plow or mow hay, but it is the rare priest who does not thresh, rake hay, or do other not too difficult physical chores. Among their wives and children, especially the unmarried daughters, there are by now many who are said to have "white hands," that is, who do no agricultural work at all. However, during my childhood, the sacristan, the deacon, and the priest all worked almost like the peasant, and they did not allow the others in their household to "sit with their arms folded." My parents were in the same position. It is true that, as far as I can remember, Father hardly ever took up the scythe or the plow, and Mother rarely used the sickle, but they did not exempt themselves from any of the other chores, including threshing

---

* A district superintendent *(blagochinnyi)* is a priest responsible for supervising a district composed of several parishes.

and taking manure from the courtyard out to the fields. My late mother was a great expert at "standing on haystacks" and stacking the hay in such a way that the stacks were straight and did not lean to one side, and Father, at least in Palishchi, would at such times almost always himself pass the hay with his pitchfork, which was very hard work.

My parents were often busy with work in the household and the fields, and the relief provided by servants—particularly during my first years—was far from adequate, so I and the sisters who were born soon after me were not looked after very much.[15]* My late mother herself told me more than once that, when I could still barely stand on my own legs, she would go out to the fields to work all day and leave me by myself in the cabin, lock the cabin and the gates [to the farm yard], and leave the children under the sole supervision of our very mean mongrel. She would seat me on the floor and open up the box with the copper coins, which I loved to take out, lay out on the hem of my shirt, and then put back in the box. To make sure that I did not go hungry, they set out some food close to me, which I ate depending on my appetite. My late mother would add that, when she returned in the evening, she would often find me asleep on the floor. Once there were more of us children and we were a little older, somebody would stay at home with us, and sometimes they would take some of us to the field and meadows, where we were free to run around and pick flowers. But even when we stayed at home, we gave our legs little rest, and I, being a boy, often went off into the woods with others my age to either eat berries or simply walk around and have a good time. We didn't give any thought to the wolves; it is remarkable that, despite the vastness of the forest, as far as I can recollect we always found our way home to the village.

We were not especially spoiled with regard to clothing, either. As a child I never owned a single shirt of calico or any other cotton fabric—all my linens were made from homemade flaxen linen that had been spun, woven, and bleached by my mother. For long johns (*podshtanniki*), a special sort of homemade linen was used that was called "heavy." That was a striped fabric made partly from white thread and partly from thread that was dyed dark blue. This fabric [. . .] was unusually dense, thick, and hence strong. Long johns sewn from this fabric would at first, as we used to say, "stand like a picket" and even seemed

---

* The 1816 census, taken just before the family moved away from Palishchi, recorded that the priest Ioann Martinov, 28, and his wife Ekaterina Nikitina, 24, had four children: Dmitrii, 6; Natal'ia, 4; Elizaveta, 3; and one-year-old Mariia. In the next census, conducted in 1834, the following children were added: Aleksandra, 17; Aleksei, 16; Evdokiia, 14; Aleksandr, 12; and Nikolai, 10.

quite hard to our certainly not effete bodies. "Heavy" long johns were not worn everywhere in Riazan Province and were a distinctive attribute of the people who lived in the region called the Meshchora.

During the summer we boys walked around freely in these linens. We wore no caps and put on shoes only for special occasions, for example, when we went to church for mass* on holidays, but the rest of the time when it was warm, or rather when it was not cold, I also went barefoot and lightly outfitted. In truth, we did not like boots, either, because they hampered us in running quickly and freely. It is true that we would prick our feet, not only when we walked in the forest but also when we ran in the street, but we were afraid that we would not be allowed to run around with an injured foot, so we almost always kept silent if our legs were pricked, cut, or otherwise hurt, until it became obvious that we were going lame. We also had on our legs a sickness of the calves called "red spots." It came from the fact that dirt, heat, or rubbing against our long johns caused the skin on our calves to become chapped, which produced an extremely unpleasant itch and sometimes pain. The skin on our completely unprotected necks would also turn dark and sunburnt and often develop "rashes," a sort of inflammation of the skin. Even in the winter, my boots and my sisters' shoes had little work to do, for we would almost always sit barefoot in the cabin, and they did not often let us out into the street. Besides, I will not conceal that in Palishchi I also wore bast shoes,† and even preferred them to boots. For that reason, at the beginning of the spring, as soon as a sufficient little area in the street was clear of snow and they let us out of the house, we boys would both sit and play without our shoes on. We even enjoyed walking barefoot in the remaining snow. Colds were unknown to us, or at least we did not fear them. Once, at Easter, when our fathers were touring the parish with icons and our mothers were sitting at home, a whole group of us, none more than eight or nine years old, went off to the forest, which was covered in water that was not very deep and at the bottom of which was still a layer of ice that had not yet melted. We took off our long johns and lifted up our shirts to avoid getting them wet, and walked through this water, on the ice, with bare feet. Of course, our feet were not warm, but walking through the woods, almost waist deep in the water—at no price did we want to deny ourselves that pleasure.

---

* Orthodoxy provides for a cycle of four religious services: vespers (after sunset), the all-night vigil, matins (before sunrise), and mass (during the day).

† Cheap, traditional peasant footwear.

CHAPTER FOUR

Corporal Punishment at Home

• In the period that I am describing, in the villages and even the towns of the Russian tsardom, no one knew about the humane ideas on which people today consider it necessary to base their attitude toward children and which hold that gentle methods should be used to teach children not to be naughty. People then were no less benevolent than now, but they believed that a child benefitted from treatment that was not only stern but downright harsh. "One who's been beaten* is worth two who haven't," or "You won't make something out of children with kindness alone," and other such sayings were then regarded as axioms. Nowadays, opinions are rapidly changing on how to treat children both in school and at home; in another fifty years, or even earlier, people will not even have heard stories about the system of child rearing that prevailed in the first half of the nineteenth century in Russia, especially among the lower classes and the clergy. For that reason I would like to discuss in greater detail the correctional measures that were then used, at home and in school, on children and adults. Describing these measures is, of course, not very pleasant, and will also not give any pleasure to the reader. It will, in fact, sometimes be disgusting and somewhat unseemly. But, as I already said in my preface, posterity needs to know what was done with us. For now I will talk about child rearing at home; later, in other places, I will talk about school and about correctional and punitive laws.

It was rare to scold or admonish children in order to make them stop being naughty. When the punishment was merely verbal, people were not usually very delicate in their choice of words: not only adults, but even little children were told that "you're a fool," "an animal," "a lowlife," "a son of a bitch," "a good-for-nothing," "disgusting,"

---

* I.e., one who has the maturity and inner strength that come from being beaten. As English-speaking contemporaries put it, "spare the rod and spoil the child."

and other nice things like that. They also did not usually like to make you stand in the corner, get on your knees, wear a dunce cap, or other such things; instead, in most cases children, both boys and girls, were subjected to corporal punishment. [The first response of angry and impatient adults was to slap children or tear at their hair. It was also common to use birch rods, and clergymen often used leather lashes with two or three tails.]

It sounds absurd, but the rod and the lash were, so to speak, among the civilized correctional measures and were used in hamlets and villages by the clergy, landowners, merchants, etc. The peasants, on the other hand, did not all make use of them and instead punished their children with whatever happened to be at hand. That might be a stick, even a very thick one, a rope, or a leather strap, even in the form of reins or a horse whip, etc.—the culprit's body had to absorb it all. Sometimes the blows also fell any which way and on any body part, and there was not enough patience to make the culprit undress first. One who was striking another's bare body with a rod or lash could see the effects of his blows, and was hence likely to relent sooner than a peasant who was pummeling someone on the shoulders, the back, and so on with a rope or stick and who could not see, through the other person's shirt, the bruises that were appearing on his body. For that reason, it may have been more rare for peasant children than for children of the other estates to be flogged in the actual sense of the word, with all the preliminary preparations and rituals, but they did get beaten, pummeled, and even maimed.

The age at which children were subjected to corporal punishment by their parents depended entirely on the arbitrary will and personal character of the latter. Even now, there is a section of the code of laws of the Russian Empire that gives parents the right to subject their children to domestic corrective punishment, and in this case no age limit at all is indicated when they lose that right. When I was a child, it would have been considered tantamount to freethinking* for someone to say that a father or mother could not flog even quite grown-up children for misbehaving. It was customary to see entering marriage or reaching the age of majority as a license, as it were, that released a child from the rod and the lash. At that point, he or she would have children of his or her own and have the right to flog them. Among the peasantry, however, even grown children were

---

* Freethinkers formed their ideas independently of tradition or authority, particularly in religious matters. Russian conservatives thus designated anyone whose ideas they considered dangerously radical.

beaten, had their hair torn, were slapped in the face, and so on. Also, until they were married or were eighteen to twenty years old, no sons or daughters could consider themselves entirely safe from a flogging if their father or mother wanted it, and public opinion in the hamlet or village was unconditionally on the side of the parental authority. I know of many cases when not only quite grown-up sons were flogged, but also unmarried daughters, and often in a revolting manner.

[For example, in Tuma, a townsman's sixteen-to-eighteen-year-old daughter had flirted with a young man. To punish her, her father tied her to a post in the courtyard, stripped her below the waist, and beat her bloody with rods while the villagers watched through cracks in the fence. Another father, a sacristan, would make his son undress completely and likewise tie him to a post and flog him with rods if he misbehaved. Other fathers treated their sons similarly.]

Grown-up daughters, even married ones, likewise experienced the admonition of the parental rod. One such case involved the wife of G. S. D——ii, my classmate from the academy. His wife was the daughter of the archpriest of St. Isaac's Cathedral in St. Petersburg. As she was beautiful and had seen around her many who at least complimented her beauty, if they did not truly worship it, she very much wished to have for a husband not some awkward and clumsy academy student, but one of the Imperial Guards officers with whom she loved to dance.* Meanwhile, fate arranged things differently. Her father was sick at the time after almost losing consciousness from a rush of blood to his brain, so the family was instead commanded by his wife E. V., whom people called "a baba's baba" and "a really mean baba."† She had been able to obtain a priest's position for her daughter in the School of Commerce, that is, not for her daughter to be priest but for her daughter's future husband; that honor went to D——ii. I have to say that he was not especially easygoing and relaxed, and his fiancée, who was in love with the epaulets on the officers' uniforms, did not want to get married, but her mother would not hear of it.

---

* These officers were drawn from elite families, and many went on to hold top positions in the army and the government. Marrying a handsome, elegant Guards officer was probably the dream of many a lower-class girl, whom such a marriage—unlikely though it was—would have catapulted into a world of material wealth, cultural refinement, and great social prestige.

† *Baba* is a colloquial term for a peasant wife. The stereotypical baba is a hard woman, shrewd, uneducated, unsentimental, despotic, gruffly affectionate, fiercely protective of her family, and deeply conservative in her habits and values—the polar opposite of the stereotypical aristocratic Guards officer.

The daughter bowed to necessity, but said, "Mama, I'll marry D——ii as you wish, but ma'am, I'm not going to love him as you would like." Mama answered, "Just go ahead, go ahead, and you'll see what happens later." They got married. I was at the wedding: the entire evening, the bride paid attention only to the officers and other nimble dancers, and did not even want to look at her husband. When he got up his courage and decided to compliment her engagement ring, she took it off and threw it onto the floor, claiming that it hurt her finger. She was determined to display the same unfriendly and downright unapproachable character during the following days as well, in a word, she would have nothing to do with her husband. One day, his mother-in-law said to him, "Why're you always sitting at home like this? Go somewhere, visit your friends, have fun." So he went to visit our mutual friend Smiriagin, who was then instructor at the St. Petersburg seminary, and tearfully told him about his woes. "Oh God, I don't know what to do," the unhappy husband said more than once. The two friends parted, but when they met again two days later, Smiriagin found his former interlocutor in a most cheerful disposition. "What happened to you?" Smiriagin asked, "you seem to be in seventh heaven!" "Wouldn't you know," D——ii replied, "my wife started being nice to me the very day I saw you. I'm overjoyed, but to be honest, I have no idea what could have caused such a change in her."

The explanation was actually quite simple. The mother had seen her daughter's coldness and outright contempt toward her husband. "What is this, Masha," the old woman said on more than one occasion, "this is how you treat G. S.? Come on, he's your husband. Enough of this nonsense. Start liking him." "I already told you, ma'am," her daughter would answer, "I can't and won't love him." To which her mama would answer, "Enough already, what's there to talk about? I'm telling you, start liking him, or you'd better watch out, because I'm your mother." But the daughter would not obey her mama's words. So, on the same day as she sent her son-in-law to see his friends, the mother made sure to be at home alone in the evening with her daughter and the maid. Then she approached her daughter and told her, "Masha, since you've refused to stop your foolishness, I'm going to teach you some sense. Hey," she called to the maid, "bring me what you've prepared." The maid appeared with the rod, and the proud beauty who had dreamed of being a Guards officer's wife was painfully flogged. "Now look," the mother added, "start liking him, or else—you know me, I'll flog you again." [. . .] After that, husband and wife lived in perfect harmony. [. . .]

There is no reason to hide the fact that, as they used to say, the rods and lashes went for walks on me, too. I, too, have sat on a bench or cowered in a corner while watching them take down the lash from the wall, or tear a twig from the broom and strip it of its leaves. I have seen them come to me, and then felt them take me by the shoulder, pull me from the bench and so on . . . I, too, have squirmed in all directions and struggled to free my head when it was wedged between someone else's legs . . . all that happened, and not rarely . . . the same thing also happened to my sisters. However, I seem to have gotten it the most often, because I was very naughty and mischievous, and I was not very diligent in my studies and even fairly lazy. Naturally, I had to pay for all that with my body. But we did not suffer cruel punishments from our father and mother. When we needed to be flogged, they did not tie us to the benches or even make us lie down on the benches or on the floor, and they never made anyone hold anyone else by the arms and legs. Whoever was punishing us would also hold us, and when you use that method, the flogging is not too painful. Only after I entered school did I become acquainted with being held during a flogging or being tied to the benches. Before that, I was flogged quite painfully only three times. [. . .]

Aside from those three instances, I cannot remember my parents inflicting painful punishment on me before I entered school. They loved me and so were lenient with me, especially Mother. On the other hand, our relative Pelageia, the townswoman from Elat'ma who lived with us (as I mentioned earlier), treated me exceedingly cruelly in their absence. When Mother and Father were away, she was entirely the mistress and commander in the house, and she did not hold back with the rods and the lash, nor did she spare our bodies. I was terribly afraid of her. When I was already forty-five years old, we met in Father's house and she herself talked about how she had punished me cruelly and often. Luckily for me, Pelageia was sent back to Elat'ma soon after we acquired the "bought people." We, and particularly I, could then breathe freely.

The fairly strict upbringing I had as a child, and even Pelageia's cruelty, do not seem to have had a negative effect on me. I was not someone who was frightened and cowed, I remained independent in my character and way of thinking, and perhaps I was bolder and more self-reliant than I would have needed to be for my well-being, for succeeding in my service career, or for obtaining the favor of superiors. As I already said, my parents loved me, although Father was cold and sometimes even severe when at first I performed poorly at the church school. However, after I had, as they say, "made it" in the world, they were at times even excessively indulgent with me. With the frequent mischief I caused, they could have been sterner with me.

Since I remained independent and self-reliant in my thinking and character, I was very bold and free in my relations with peasants, the clergy, my teachers and mentors, and especially my peers; with the latter I was almost always the main organizer of our games, the center of the conversation, and so on. However, for a long time, a very long time actually, I remained extremely shy around nobles and around women or adolescent girls, even those of the clerical estate.

The former, at least, I think I can explain. In the parish of Palishchi, when I was growing up, there lived only the one landowning noblewoman in the hamlet of Ovintsi. [. . .] My parents were welcome guests at that noblewoman's house. They would take me with them, but I didn't like it there. The lady had no small children, so there was no one to play with, and I would sit, and actually be told to sit, on a chair somewhere. Even later on, I would find reasons not to go visit the lady. When she would come to visit us with her widowed daughter, I rarely sat with them in the annex, for I didn't like to put on shoes, get dressed up, and sit quietly, and besides, people at the time did not see any need for children to sit together with honored guests. Subsequently, when I heard how the landowners oppressed the peasants, I began to hate the lords and ladies and regarded them all as evil people.

However, I don't really understand why I avoided opportunities to talk and even sit together with women and adolescent girls, even those of the clerical estate, even relatives. But that is how it was. I was already about six, if not older, when my aunt and godmother Anna Martynovna came to visit us. She loved me very much and wanted to kiss me right away. I was sitting at the table by the icon corner. I guessed her intention when she came up to the table from one side and stretched out her arms to hug and kiss me, so I stood up on the bench, ran quickly along the other side of the table, jumped onto the floor, and then climbed onto the stove, settled myself there and refused to climb down again for any reason. Later, of course, I didn't do things like that anymore, but almost always, actually until I was quite mature in years, I felt awkward and uncomfortable around women and girls. Could it be that my mind was influenced by ascetic ideas that women were temptresses? Truly, I don't know.

CHAPTER FIVE

My Early Education

• Children today have acquired great intellectual curiosity and find much pleasure not only in toys, but also in looking at all sorts of drawings that give them a greater familiarity with many things than we, today's old people, received in school. Today, the occasional boy can already read before he turns five or even four, who knows, maybe even write, and by six he will be able to write a letter. No, when I was a child, at least among the village clergy, nobody even dreamed of such a rapid development of one's curiosity and of other abilities and inclinations of the mind. Until we were six, sometimes even seven, we were permitted only to eat, sleep, run around, and frolic in all sorts of ways; only when we were being wild at inappropriate times, or disturbed the others who were grown up, were we ordered to sit still. If that time may be called happy when you have no lessons, duties, cares, fears, and so on, then children in the old days were very happy folk, at least until they were made to sit down with their books. For me, that happy time lasted a little over five years and ended in the sixth year of my life. So, how did they teach us? Most likely, in fifty or especially a hundred years, there will be many people who will refuse to believe that such a method ever existed, and indeed was considered almost sacred, as the one by which we were taught to read. I talked about it in my book on the structure of the church schools, but not in full detail. Here I will deal with it more extensively.

The mass of the clergy will probably never really care about the true, correct development of people's intellectual faculties. Under the pretext of upholding moral and religious ideas, they will forever seek, so to speak, to "clip the wings" of an inquisitive mind, and restrain and virtually kill the intellectual curiosity that is so characteristic of our nature. It is through observations over the entire course of my life that I have arrived at these sad thoughts, and I am filled with them now that I am about to describe the method for teaching literacy that prevailed during my childhood.

Every literate Russian knows that we have two forms of reading and printing, the "ecclesiastical" and the "civil."* Anyone who is even a little dispassionate and perceptive can see that the latter is simpler than the former. The ecclesiastical, for no reason, uses the letters *ksi* and *psi, zelo* and *ius,* as well as the letter *on,* which is often placed before *u* but is not pronounced. Finally, it would seem obvious that it would be better to have a single form of print and reading, and the simpler and easier one at that. But just try writing nowadays that it is time to introduce a single form of print and reading in Russia, i.e., that it is time to print the ecclesiastical books and the Bible in civil letters and use them in that form during religious services! Well, that would arouse such a hue and cry as though the entire universe were in danger. Such a proposal would be regarded as blasphemy, an assault on the sanctity of religion and the inviolability of Orthodoxy, and the one making the proposal would be called an atheist and a cursed unbeliever. Furthermore, the most basic principle of rationality requires starting any activity at the easiest level, which means that teaching children to read should start with civil books. [However, the church hierarchy even now, in 1868, demands that all children, even those from nonclerical families, be taught to read first the ecclesiastical letters.] Tell them that the ecclesiastical alphabet is much harder than the civil, and they will answer, "Let the children learn to work and be patient. It's good for them; the kingdom of heaven suffereth violence, and the violent take it by force."† Tell them that the ecclesiastical books are unintelligible even to adults, that a child who learns by them becomes accustomed to reading without understanding, worse yet—to misinterpreting what he reads as he sees fit, and that this obstructs and distorts his intellectual faculties rather than fostering them, and they will answer, "Why think? It's enough to have faith. So what if a boy doesn't understand what he's read? At least he's being reverential toward the objects of worship of the church." You will never get anywhere with that crowd. They think that their Cyrillic, i.e., reading in ecclesiastical print, is the only key to salvation in the life to come and to well-being in this life on earth.

---

* See Translator's Introduction, p. xxxv

† Matthew 11:12 ("And from the days of John the Baptist until now, the kingdom of heaven suffereth violence, and the violent take it by force"). In this passage, Jesus emphasizes the spiritual intensity and effort ("violence") required for gaining admittance to the Kingdom of Heaven.

If that was how people reasoned when I was already approaching sixty, what sorts of progressive ideas about teaching reading could there have been during my childhood, especially in the heads of members of the village clergy? They "believed and professed verily" that the ecclesiastic Cyrillic alphabet is the surest path to salvation and the easiest, actually almost the only way, to teach reading. Since, at that time, they or those who had learned to read by their method—townspeople, discharged soldiers, lackeys, old and mostly schismatic* peasant women—were almost the only teachers of reading, it followed that the children of peasants, urban residents, the clergy and even provincial nobles began learning to read with Cyrillic. There were exceedingly few apostates from this method. I will describe it.

[Teaching children to read consisted of three stages. In the first stage, they would learn to recognize the ecclesiastical letters and memorize their pointlessly cumbersome names (*az* for *a, buki* for *b, vedi* for *v, glagol* for *g*, etc.). Then they would learn consonant-vowel combinations by unthinking memorization: *b* + *a* was to be pronounced *bukiazba* because *buki* + *az* = "*ba*"; *v* + *a* was *vediazva;* etc.

In the second stage, they would learn to read longer words drawn from the ecclesiastical vocabulary (archangel, divinity, and so on) and were even required, absurdly, to recite the names of the sixteen different punctuation signs and Old Church Slavonic accent marks—none of which, of course, are actually pronounced when one reads a text. Students who failed to learn in this mind-numbing and senselessly difficult way suffered brutal, traumatic corporal punishment.

In the third stage, rather than read texts that might engage their interest, the pupils were required to read prayers and psalms whose archaic vocabulary and profound meanings they were too immature to grasp. Again, less successful students were subjected to verbal insults and physical violence. As a result of these methods, education was generally regarded as akin to torture.]

During my childhood, many clergymen, townspeople, and even rich peasants and so on saw a need to teach reading not only to their sons, but also to their daughters, and given the shortage of female

---

* After the seventeenth-century schism that split the Russian Orthodox Church, those who rejected the church hierarchy's authority and teachings were known as Old Believers or "schismatics." They typically belonged to the lower classes, were archconservative in religious (and hence linguistic) matters, and because they could not rely on spiritual guidance from the official clergy, many learned to read religious texts on their own.

teachers, they would send both to the same male educator. Of course, the girls were almost always punished by the same method as the boys, and in front of everyone. There was no question of feeling sorry for each other. All only felt sorry for themselves. On the other hand, they were always prepared and gladly undertook to help the teacher flog one of the others, or at least they would follow the flogging with a kind of cheerful curiosity and try to position themselves so they could see the parts of the body on which the rod or lash fell. But the boys especially liked it when girls were flogged, and what they liked was precisely the aspect that should have inspired revulsion. "It's fun," those chivalrous youngsters would say, "to watch them flog girls. They're all naked from the heels up to their back; only, it's hard to hold on to their legs because your hands slip." On the other hand, the boys considered it the ultimate humiliation when the teacher flogged them and made the girls hold them, especially by the head. In that case, the one who had been flogged was usually taunted and told that "just now, or yesterday, your head was under a girl's skirt." In the eighteenth and early nineteenth centuries, especially in Little Russia,* the custom was almost held sacred (it had not been abandoned everywhere even when I was a child) that, on Saturdays, all students without exception were to be flogged according to a special ritual, a kind of pious reminder to honor the holidays [. . .] With the method I have described, the students did not quickly acquire literacy even in its ecclesiastical form. Some were never able to take the hurdle of the alphabet, and others stopped with the syllables, but even those who took on the Book of Hours and the Psalter†—that is, the more gifted ones—did not finish them quickly. Many sat over them for three, four years and even longer, and even the most gifted were made to spend no fewer than two years on them.

I beg your pardon, dear reader, for drawing your attention at such length to the "ecclesiastical" method of teaching people to read. I wanted to persuade you to be lenient with us, your ancestors, as well as with those who came before us. Who knows, you might reproach us for lacking intellectual curiosity, for not being educated at a level comparable to other nations of our time, for having had among us so few who were literate and even fewer learned and truly educated people. Have mercy on us and our ancestors! After all, to feel an inclination and attraction for learning, when for us it began with the *az* and

---

* I.e., central Ukraine.

† Books containing psalms and prayers.

the *buki*, the *bukiazba* and the *vediazva*, the *zvatel'tso* and the *erok*,* the Book of Hours and the Psalter—well, I suppose it was hard for us. All the endless slapping, pinching, shoving, and beating with rods and two- and three-tailed lashes was even less likely to make us want to learn. Not many of us were able to endure all these hardships, but even those who somehow did endure them, would later, as we shall see, end up encountering even more obstacles to developing and sustaining their intellectual curiosity. [Yet the church seeks even now to perpetuate this system.]

It is now time to turn to my own schooling. My father, who was busy with his priestly duties and household cares, did not have the opportunity to teach me to read himself. Therefore, I would certainly have been sent to study with some freelance educator, some sacristan or soldier, perhaps even in another village, and there, most likely, I would have undergone all the details of the method I have described, even the regular reminders of the Sabbath day, had not my mother, to my great fortune, been an exception among the priests' wives of the time. She could read both the ecclesiastical and the civil print very well and took on the duty of teaching me, and then my oldest sisters, to read. My parents were pious people, so they began my schooling with a prayer. This took place in the winter of 1814–1815, when, in addition to all of us, there lived in our cabin the priest Fedor Eneidov, who had just arrived in Palishchi to replace Father Vasilii (the one who had frozen to death) and had not yet been able to build himself a house. As I remember today, in the evening they lit wax candles by the icons. Father Fedor put on a stole,† under which I was made to stand, and jointly with my father he began to perform the brief service called "beginning one's schooling." I did not understand the service, or listen to it, but I was very concerned about my position under the stole, from where I could not help looking out to exchange glances with my sisters. From that evening on, my scholarly and literary activities began. Of course, they began teaching me according to the Cyrillic alphabet, the ecclesiastical print, starting with *az* and *buki* and so on. I don't blame my parents for that, because at the time in the backwoods of Kasimov District, they could not even imagine that anyone could be taught differently, much less the son of a priest. [This home schooling was utterly dull, devoid of intellectual stimulation, and filled with corporal punishment, and learning to read in this manner took three long years.]

---

* Accent marks used in Old Church Slavonic.

† A strip of material that the clergy wear over their shoulders for certain ritual purposes.

CHAPTER SIX

My Family Moves to Tuma

• In Palishchi there were two churches, both of them wooden, and despite the minimal cost of firewood at that time, neither of them had a stove, so that it was unbearably cold in them in the wintertime. But that was, so to speak, in fashion. In the entire northern half of Kasimov District, and in the neighboring villages of Riazan and Egor'evsk districts, all the churches without exception were wooden and unheated; only in Gusevskii Pogost were there churches that were made of stone and also heated. In their famous wisdom, our pious ancestors were somehow unable to grasp that one should not make the Orthodox Christians freeze in church, and that even the fire of the most ardent prayers will not warm the sinful body at twenty or thirty degrees below freezing. Then again, even the Cathedral of the Assumption in Moscow* became heatable only in the middle of the nineteenth century. Is it surprising, then, that in a place such as Palishchi both wooden churches were unheated?

My father ventured to undertake something unheard of—he set out to persuade the parishioners to build a church that would be not only heatable but also made of stone. For that purpose, a number of "rallies" (really, just traditional Russian village assemblies) were held. Father's main adversary was Mr. Novosil'tsev's bailiff,† the peasant Spitsyn from the hamlet of Malakhova, an old man of about seventy if not more, with a little gray beard and a malicious look in his face and eyes, but a perky, vigorous, smart old man. Until my father arrived in Palishchi, Spitsyn had been *the* authority, not only on his estate but throughout the parish; he had even given orders to the clergy, who, truth be told, were stupider than he. My father significantly weakened Spitsyn's authority with his intelligence and by giving instructions

---

* The cathedral in the Kremlin where the tsars were crowned.

† A bailiff was a peasant appointed by the landlord to oversee serf communities on his estate.

independently of him. Naturally, Spitsyn did not like his rival and opposed him wherever he could. He also did this when the question of building a new church was discussed. It was indeed a bold undertaking. The parishioners would need to take their carts to go for iron, feldspar, and lime to the Gus' factory, the village of Maleevo, and other places eighty to ninety versts away.* In addition, large amounts of money were needed to pay the workers and so on, and the church had virtually no reserve capital.

The popular assemblies were unusually lively, even stormy. One in particular made a strong impression on me. It took place in the street not far from our house. I was not allowed into the street, for fear that I might get trampled, so I watched the scene through the open window. The commotion was terrible. My father, supported especially by the bailiffs of the hamlets of Spudni and Ovintsi, was carrying on an animated, noisy dispute with Spitsyn, while the people were wavering between the two adversaries. Finally, I saw Spitsyn quickly push his way out of the crowd, sit down on a log that was lying on the ground, and rest his left elbow on his leg and his bowed head on the palm of his hand. It was obvious that he felt defeated and did not know what to do. Meanwhile, the commotion had subsided, and finally Spitsyn also got up. My father was victorious, and the parishioners had agreed to build a stone, heatable church. I must give Spitsyn his due, though, because later, when the construction of the church had begun, he raised no obstacles and, without ever procrastinating, sent the required number of carts from the estate that he managed.

Equipped with a letter from the parishioners and the clergy of his parish, my father set out for Riazan to obtain authorization to build a new stone church and close down one—the smaller—of the wooden ones. In Riazan, the prelate at the time was Feofilakt, who later became exarch of Georgia.[16]† My father was a bold man and quite independent of character, so his demeanor attracted the attention of the prelate who met in other clergymen only humble admirers of his own greatness. When he heard that my father intended to be the builder of a stone church, he told him, "My goodness, young priest! You sure are

---

* The Gus' factory, located in present-day Gus' Zheleznyi, was a large metal-working plant owned by the wealthy Batashev family.

† I.e., head of the Orthodox Church in Georgia (in the Caucasus). The son of a sacristan from Arkhangel'sk Province, Feofilakt (Fedor Gavrilovich Rusanov, 1765–1820) was one of the most influential Russian Orthodox clergymen of his time and a key figure in the reform of the ecclesiastical education system under Alexander I. He was made archbishop of Riazan in March, 1809, and became exarch of Georgia in 1817.

bold! Do you realize how difficult it is to build a new stone church?" and so on. But when my father, who may have been a bit miffed at the prelate's tone, animatedly and clearly laid out his ideas, he very favorably impressed the prelate, and after receiving the blessing to build the church he was also told that "I won't forget about you. We have to get you out of there and into a more distinguished position."

After my father returned from Riazan, construction on the church began. I especially remember when they laid the foundation and then when they deconsecrated one of the wooden churches. The solemn religious procession, the fluttering banners, the many icons, the large gathering of people, the magnificent vestments of the entire clergy of the church, the solemn pealing of the bells, the powerful voices chanting the prayers in the open air—all of that made a deep impression on me. Especially solemn were the minutes when, filled with deep reverence, all the people fell to their knees and in that position listened to the prayer that my father read with a powerful voice. The deconsecration of the old church also strongly affected me, but in a different way. In churches that are to be closed, they solemnly perform the liturgy for the last time, then celebrate a service, and after that, in conclusion, they remove from the altar and the credence table all the holy objects: the chalice, the paten, the Gospel, the reliquary, and so on,* even the fabric that covered it on all sides, so that there remained, so to speak, only its naked wooden skeleton, consisting of a few squared beams and boards, and finally they remove even the skeleton. All of this is emotionally affecting to the people, and in Palishchi, in this case, both the clergy and many of the parishioners wept. Of course, we children who were watching all this also could not help crying.

A few days later, another scene took place, but this time only in the presence of the country folk and various workmen. According to the existing customs and apparently even statutes, the lumber from a wooden church may be used only for a new church, but under no circumstances for any residential, secular structures. If using the lumber from the old church for a new one is not possible or desired, then it is used to fire the bricks with which a church is to be built. In Palishchi, the latter use was made. To do that, however, the church needed to be torn down. They started with the cupola: they tore the wood siding from its neck, cut down the supports that held it up, and

---

* The credence table holds the objects required for the Eucharist, including the paten (the metal plate on which the host is placed) and the chalice (for the wine).

attached to it one end of a rope while several dozen people took the other end. When the signal was given they pulled at the rope. The cupola was probably still not fully detached from its foundation, so it remained immobile for several seconds, but finally it began to rock slightly, and then quickly, with all its bulk, it crashed to the ground. I don't know why, but I, who was standing very far from the church, was tremendously affected by this fall. I felt sorry for the cupola, and then even sorrier looking at the church, which, without its cupola, seemed like a strange sort of building.

However, my father was not able to complete the construction of the church in Palishchi which he had initiated. Archbishop Feofilakt had not forgotten him. In 1816 my father's brother, also named Ivan Martynovich, graduated from the Riazan seminary. My grandfather, Martyn Larionovich, the priest of Tuma, was a little over fifty at the time. By then he had decided to pass on his position as priest to his second son. Two health problems impelled him to do this, a hernia and lower-back pain. Both arose from the fact that, in his youth, my grandfather had been too hard-working a man and had not spared his energies, especially when he was a sacristan in Sheianki, where he had hardly worked less than any peasant. His hernia and lower-back pains occasionally caused him extreme suffering. Despite his tough and unbending character, and even though he was certainly no mollycoddle and was accustomed and able to suffer emotional and physical pain in silence, he nonetheless sometimes had to scream from the pain of his hernia and his lower back. It seems to have been this circumstance that forced him to think about passing on his position to one of his sons and thereby assure some bread for his family, which included his wife, mother, son, and daughter.[17]* Grandfather probably feared difficulties in carrying out his plan. Tuma Nikolaevskaia was considered an excellent, wealthy village, and the inheritability of positions in the clerical estate at that time had not yet become fully established. Grandfather therefore took my father with him to Riazan, on the assumption that, if the prelate refused to appoint his second son to his position, he would ask him to allow my father, who was already a deserving and highly regarded priest, to move to Tuma, and allow my uncle Ivan Martynovich to become priest in Palishchi.

---

* The 1816 census lists him as "priest Martin Ilarionov, age 53," whose household also included his wife Fekla Akimovna, 51, and their three children: Ivan, 19, and Vasilii, 16, both currently receiving an ecclesiastical education in Riazan, and Efim'ia, 13. Martyn and Fekla appear again in the 1834 census, which also listed Vasilii as deacon in Prudki, a short distance west of Tuma.

Grandfather and my uncle appeared before His Grace with their most humble petition. His Grace read it, paused at the words "Ivan Martynov," repeated these words out loud a few times, and asked my grandfather, "What, don't you have another son Ivan Martynov who is a priest somewhere over toward Vladimir, past the marshes?" Grandfather replied that he did. Then the prelate said, "All right, I permit you to give your position to your son, only not this one (pointing to my uncle), but the one from Palishchi, and this young one can take over his brother's position. Send for your older son as soon as possible." "He is already here, Your Grace," my grandfather answered. "Then bring him to me right away," the prelate answered. My father, who was waiting for the prelate's decision on Grandfather's petition, was walking around by the cathedral, not far from the prelate's residence. Grandfather, together with my father and my uncle, at once drew up a new petition, and they all went together to the prelate. "See," His Grace said when he saw my father, "I haven't forgotten about you. You've been out in the middle of nowhere long enough. Go to Tuma, that's where I need you." The concern was that Tuma was a village with three parishes and the center for thirteen to fifteen villages that formed a single ecclesiastical district. The district superintendent at the time was also a priest in Tuma, Nikifor Mironov, who was my uncle through his wife, the same aunt and godmother with whom, as I said earlier, I did not want to exchange kisses.[18]* Father Nikifor was an extremely goodhearted man, but exceedingly weak and not very bright. The prelate had long wanted to replace him with a more energetic district superintendent. That is why my father was transferred to Tuma; in Palishchi he could not be district superintendent, because the village really was "in the middle of nowhere, past the marshes," and would have been seventy versts from some villages in the ecclesiastical district.

Even though Tuma was decidedly superior to Palishchi in almost all respects, my father and especially my mother were extremely reluctant to leave. I never spoke about this with them, but I suspect that they had many causes not to wish for the move that they were offered. Grandfather was a man of hard character, as independent and persistent as one could imagine. Of course, he was an excellent farmer (by the standard of the time) and worked better than any workman, but

* The 1816 census listed the priest Nikifor Mironov, 35, as living in Tuma with his wife Anna Martynova, 31, their son Ivan, 7 (he died three years later), and their four daughters aged 2 to 11. At least one more son and daughter were born in the following years, and the family was still living in Tuma at the time of the 1834 census.

he liked it when no one got in his way and all unquestioningly carried out his instructions. My father knew his own father and knew that, even once he was retired, he would not allow the new owner to take charge of the farm activities. In addition, Grandfather's mother [Avdot'ia Mikhailovna], my great-grandmother, whom Grandfather fully resembled in his character, was still alive. Also still alive was Grandfather's wife [Fekla Akimovna], who of course was a good-hearted woman, but fully under her husband's command. Consequently, when my mother moved to Tuma, though by rights the real mistress of the house, she would find above her another two older mistresses who, one could expect, would not want to take second place in the home. In addition, Grandfather still had a third son Vasilii, who was studying hard at the district ecclesiastical school, and then there was his fourteen- or fifteen-year-old daughter Afim'ia. Both of them needed to be supported, and the daughter also had to be given in marriage* by my parents who already had five children of their own. It was probably for these reasons that, when my father had returned to Palishchi after being appointed priest of Tuma, he and my mother were not cheerful at all, and Mother often even wept.

Even though the instruction to move was given in October, if not September, 1816, we stayed in Palishchi the entire winter. Every Saturday, my father would set out for Tuma, while my uncle, who had been ordained as priest and was living with Grandfather, would go to Palishchi.[19†] The two brothers would meet on the way, exchange greetings, talk, and then continue on their way. On Mondays, the reverse movement occurred. It made sense that my parents did not want to move to Tuma for the winter. They already had five children, three bought female servants, and the two of them, ten people in all, in their household. Grandfather's household consisted of another five people, not counting the workman. But Grandfather lived entirely the old-fashioned way, and during the winter he used only the cabin as a residence, while the annex was unheated. There was also another cabin, but it was rented by an innkeeper who operated a coaching inn.‡ Thus, if we had moved from Palishchi to Tuma for the winter, a single cabin would have had to accommodate fifteen or sixteen people.

---

* I.e., she would require a trousseau.

† Tuma and Palishchi are about thirty miles apart. The census records of 1834 report that Ioann Martinov (Rostislavov's uncle), 36, had by then moved from Palishchi to become priest in the nearby village of Struzhany where he was living with his wife Evdokiia Alekseeva, 33. Apparently they had only one child, a 13-year-old son named Petr, then attending the Kasimov church school.

‡ A coaching inn offered shelter and food, both fairly rudimentary, for travelers and their horses.

However, over the course of the winter, especially in 1817, my father began little by little to transport his property to Tuma, both on his horse and with the help of his other acquaintances who lent him their horses for the purpose. Finally, I think at the end of the sixth week of Lent,* we definitively moved to Tuma. I remember how the clergy of Palishchi gathered in our house, how they celebrated a brief religious service to see us off, how my mother wept bitterly, and how even my father had tears in his eyes. After completing all the preliminary rituals we went out into the courtyard, where there was almost an entire wagon train, I think eight or ten carts. They seated us in a sleigh, wrapped us in our sheepskin coats because it was still winter, and finally we set out on our trip. We went slowly through the entire village. Just about all the villagers, young and old, came to see us off. Mother, with whom I sat in the same sleigh, exchanged bows with everyone and bade them farewell; I did not see Father, for he sat in a different sleigh. Toward evening we arrived in Tuma and were greeted by Grandfather's family. In Palishchi I was still a little child, but I came to Tuma as an older boy who already understood a few things, wished to understand even more, and grew up there until the age of twenty.

To conclude this chapter, I would like to make a few remarks about the role that copper coins played at that time, if not in the entire Russian tsardom, then at least among the villagers of the provinces around Moscow.

[Translator's Note: The Russian currency, then as now, was the ruble (1 ruble = 100 kopecks). Around 1800, Russia used four different kinds of money: copper coins for the smallest denominations (under 10 kopecks), silver for larger denominations (up to 1 ruble), gold for still larger ones (up to 10 rubles), and paper bills for the largest (up to 100 rubles).

Between these types of money there existed a fluctuating exchange rate similar to what exists today between the currencies of different countries. On one hand, the shifting market value of different metals could make a coin's metal content more or less valuable than its face value. On the other hand, paper rubles tended to lose value over time as the government (and counterfeiters) printed more of them; 4 paper rubles were worth only about 1 silver ruble by 1812—at the nadir of the Napoleonic Wars—when the government printed vast quantities to cover its military expenditures, and the exchange rate did not

---

* I.e., just before Palm Sunday (March 18, 1817).

change much in the following years. Furthermore, since coins and bills of any given denomination were often in short supply, the value of money was affected by considerations of convenience—small coins were more useful for daily purchases, and bills for larger transactions. As a result, for example, an item valued at 100 paper rubles would cost about 25 silver rubles; however, if payment was effected in paper rubles, the buyer was charged the full 100 but received a discount of about 20 percent (depending on the face value and physical condition of the bill) and hence actually paid 80 paper rubles. Similarly, at a time when a 1-ruble coin was worth 3.60–3.80 paper rubles, 1 ruble in smaller coins was worth 4 paper rubles.

A few examples may put the ruble's value into perspective. A loaf of bread cost several kopecks, and a cheap book under 1 paper ruble. From 1812 until 1839, the soul tax (the amount villagers had to pay annually for every male inhabitant) was 3 paper rubles, while the annual dues that serfs owed their noble lord were several times that figure. A rural priest in the 1770s is thought to have had an annual cash income of about 50-60 rubles. However, villagers lived in a rural subsistence economy where cash was rarely used. An affluent lifestyle in Moscow, on the other hand, with a few servants, a horse-drawn carriage, fine foods, foreign clothes and books, and so on, cost at least 2,000 paper rubles a year for a family around 1800.[20]]

Copper five-, two-, one-, half-, and quarter-kopeck coins (there were even one-eighth-kopeck coins) were almost the only coins around at the end of our time in Palishchi and when we first lived in Tuma. Silver rubles and fifty-kopeck coins, and especially gold five- and ten-ruble pieces were rarities, and even small silver coins and paper money were rarely seen in circulation. Consequently, when the clergy returned home after making the rounds of the parish on patronal* or other festivals, they would bring home large amounts of copper. The pockets of the priests' cassocks, strong and large though they were, could not always hold all the day's takings; they also needed to bring along little bags that some sacristan would carry, sometimes even over his shoulder. So it is no surprise that, when they came home to divide up the money, a very large heap of copper would be spread onto the table in the priest's house from bags and pockets. They would begin to count it, separate little stacks of five-, two- and one-kopeck pieces would be made, these

---

* A church's patronal festival is the day of the saint to whom the church is dedicated.

would be formed into rows and even pyramids, and after dividing them up people would take them home. There, especially in the homes of priests, the money would be put away in bags of [coins whose value was equivalent to] twenty-five paper rubles each and locked up in a chest, or sometimes they would be kept somewhere in the storeroom in the shape of a woodpile or in triangular stacks.

When the government ordered that taxes be paid to the treasury in paper rubles,[21]* the peasants were forced to obtain them, in exchange for their copper money, from affluent people who of course did not miss the opportunity to profit by taking a little surcharge. Thus, a measure that was supposed to restore the state's credit had the effect of burdening the peasants. Soon after we moved to Tuma, silver and gold coins began to appear, but the copper ones were still "at large" and in my father's chests I still saw many bags of them.

Shrewd people at the time could more than double the value of their copper coins. A *pud*† of copper coins had a face value of only sixteen rubles, yet the market price of the copper was forty paper rubles. Consequently, one needed only to melt down the five-kopeck pieces, two-kopeck pieces and so on, and already you had a profit of almost 150 percent. Many coppersmiths, particularly bell founders, samovar makers from Tula,‡ and so on took advantage of this. For this, of course, the government prosecuted the culprits who fell into its hands and flogged them with the knout,§ exiled them to hard labor, and so on, but the exceedingly high profits would nonetheless make people risk these dangers. Finally, the government decided to take the old coins out of circulation and replace them with newer, cheaper ones. Orders were given for the old coins to be brought to the district treasury departments, where they were exchanged for paper money. At that point, many buyers appeared who paid not only the going rate but even a little above it; evidently, the buyers were agents of those manufacturers who hoped to use the copper for various products and make a profit for themselves. Rumor had it at the time that the copper coins collected from many rich villagers—even peasants—filled entire carts, so that a wagon train had to be sent to exchange them at the treasury. It was said that some peasant in Murom District declared that he had accumulated 80,000 paper

---

* The government did this in 1812 in an unsuccessful attempt to restore the paper ruble's value by reducing the quantity in circulation.

† One pud equals thirty-six pounds.

‡ A town located south of Moscow and famous for its metal-working industry.

§ A type of whip used to punish convicted criminals.

rubles' worth and was requesting instructions on what he should do with these thousands. People said that the government itself, at its own expense, transported his entire 180,000 pounds of copper coins to someplace by boat on the Oka River. Of course, it was not taking a loss, since all this copper, minted into new coins, was worth up to 200,000 rubles.

However, it would seem that another peasant proceeded very cleverly even before the new coins were issued. He gathered his copper treasure in a sturdy storage shed by the threshing floor, where of course he also posted a watchman. Ostensibly to prevent thieves from attempting to cut through the walls of the shed, the peasant surrounded it with large stacks of firewood. One summer night however, when there was a powerful storm, "suddenly the firewood and the shed caught on fire." Everything was so well prepared that the fire quickly spread to the building. The people came running; the owner exhibited utter despair—there lay all his wealth, it was too late to put out the fire, and there was not even any need to do so because there was no serious threat to the hamlet. The copper, of course, had melted and mostly sunk into the ground. However, the "ruined" owner gathered up the hardened clumps and became twice as rich. As was proper, he shared the money with the authorities whose investigation showed that the fire had been caused by lightning against the will and wishes of the owner and that it had not been detected early because the watchman had taken refuge from the rain in the cabin and there had fallen asleep; in the end, "they all came away looking almost like saints."

CHAPTER SEVEN

Outlaws and Law Enforcement

• Those of us who had pursued some sort of studies and who came from Tuma used to enjoy searching for the etymological meaning of that name, and we discovered that, in Russian, only the word *tumak* might have the same etymological root as Tuma. *Tumak* was the term commonly used for the strongest blow that one person could inflict on another, so "to give a *tumak*" has virtually the same meaning as "to beat to death." I don't know which of the two words, Tuma or *tumak,* should be considered the root from which the other is derived, or whether perhaps they have a shared root in the language of some long-ago Finnish tribe.* But it has to be said that, not long before I was born, the similarity between Tuma and *tumak* was more than just etymological. As late as the reign of Catherine II,† Tuma was, in the popular expression, a robber village, or at least a haven for robbers.

I heard many times from my grandfather Martyn that the robbers who plied their trade in or around Tuma mostly came from the local clergy. Under Catherine, many churchmen—specifically, adult sons of the clergy who had been neither educated nor registered anywhere— were supposed to enter the military estate.‡ That did not appeal to them, but they needed to live somewhere and carry on some kind of

---

* Many Finnish tribes had lived in medieval Russia but were later absorbed by the Slavic Russians.

† 1762–1796.

‡ Until 1793, the lower ranks of the Russian army consisted of men who were drafted for life; after that, until 1874, they were required to serve 25 years. Owing to the hardships of military life and the length of the term of service, conscription was feared and hated by the population. Upon entering the army, a conscript—until then a peasant, townsman, etc.—legally left the social estate of his birth and became a member of the military estate. He retained that new status even after he was discharged, and his wife and children acquired it as well. Since there were not enough positions as sacristans, priests, etc., for all the young men from clerical families, the government sought to draft "surplus" clergymen into the army and, because they were often literate, into the bureaucracy; as Rostislavov mentions elsewhere, one of his relatives became a government official. Many conscripts deserted and became outlaws.

trade. Their relatives, acquaintances, and even fathers and brothers were in Tuma, and the village was located on a well-maintained road, so the profit was also nice—why look for a different refuge? At first they may have lived openly in their homes, but when the police started coming after them, they needed to hide out in basements, drying barns, outdoor cellars,* in haylofts, and so on, or even make dugouts in the neighboring woods.

One of those nice fellows from the clerical estate who engaged in robbery around Tuma was actually our kinsman Kuz'ma Mikhailovich, the brother of grandfather Martyn's mother Avdot'ia Mikhailovna. When the order went out under Catherine II for all churchmen who had no ecclesiastical position to be enlisted as soldiers, Kuz'ma Mikhailovich ran away with two men named Ivan Grigor'ev and Samoilo. They roamed the forests around Tuma and kept watch over the main road and other people's granaries and larders.† My kinsman had a bitter enemy, Aleksei, the father of deacon Fedot of Paralino, who threatened to catch him. Kuz'ma Mikhailovich got cold feet, abandoned his comrade, and ran away to Saratov‡ under the alias of townsman Petr Kondrat'ev. Since he had a good voice, he was taken into the prelate's choir, then he was made a deacon, and ultimately he became a priest. [. . .]

In the village of Arkhangel'skoe, Egor'evsk District, as late as 1809, a tragic incident occurred. The priest there was my mother's father Nikita. He was a kind and easygoing man, beloved by his parishioners and certainly no bully. However, the deacon who served with him (and whose name I have since forgotten) was a man of unusually violent character whose criminal ways were later continued by his descendants. One holiday in September 1809, while Father Nikita was sitting at his window with some of the villagers, the deacon's sister—who was already very much a grown woman—became a little too exuberant, started dancing and humming various things, and generally behaved quite inappropriately. When she was doing her rollicking dance steps in front of Grandfather, the old man said to her, "What

---

* The basement (*podpol'e*) was located beneath the cabin, while the drying barn (*ovin*) was a separate building used to dry sheaves of grain before threshing. An outdoor cellar (*pogreb*) was a low wooden structure whose floor was below ground level and where beer and other goods were kept cool during the warm months.

† A granary (*ambar*) is a structure whose floor is typically above ground level, to keep out moisture and vermin, and where grain is stored after it is dried and threshed. A larder (*kladovaia*) was a room or annex used for storage.

‡ A town on the Volga, 370 miles from the Meshchora.

are you doing, stupid? Are you out of your mind? I should give you a good whack with my stick," and indeed he struck her lightly with the staff he had in his hands. The deacon's sister took offense at both the scolding and the blow, started screaming, and ran to complain to her dear brother. Without much thinking, the latter picked up one of the [seven-foot-long, three-inch-thick wooden "hooks"] that are generally used to support the roofs of cabins, awnings, sheds, and so on. [. . .] Armed with such a hook, the deacon came running to Grandfather and screamed, "You worthless bum *(shelygan)* (an insult for priests), what did you strike my sister for?" Although Grandfather knew the deacon's rabid character, he never suspected that he would make use of a hook with which you could have killed a bear, so he replied to him, "Why don't you teach your sister a lesson? Come on, how could she just start dancing and carrying on like that here!" "Well, aren't you a worthless bum! How dare you say that? Here, I'll teach *you* a lesson." With that, he struck Grandfather on the temple with his hook. Grandfather passed out and died that same night. The deacon initially fled to the nearby woods, but later turned himself in and was, of course, exiled to Siberia.*

Now, by your leave, we will look at what the sacristans were like during the time I am describing. Let us choose the sacristan of the village of Tuma Nikolaevskaia, Andrei Andreevich, the grandfather of Nikifor Mironov (the priest of Tuma to whom my aunt Anna Martynovna was married). The venerable Andrei Andreevich was the terror, or better, the tyrant of his family and would beat his wife and two sons with whatever happened to be at hand. Even at that time it would have been difficult to find a peasant who treated his family less humanely, but people who did not belong to his family also caught it from him. I will describe a few of his exploits.

His wife lived under his iron fist and kept "quieter than water and lower than grass," endured all his beatings with the lash, reins, logs, pickets, and so on, and even so failed to please him. It seems that the venerable sacristan intended to marry another who was younger. But, despite all the beatings the old woman was alive, so Andrei Andreevich decided to "finish her off." Once, during the agricultural working season, a large haystack needed to be made. Andrei Andreevich was very tender with his wife and ordered her to stand on the stack while he passed the hay to her with a pitchfork. When they were almost

---

* Deportation to Siberia for resettlement or forced labor, often preceded by flogging, was the standard punishment for people convicted of serious crimes in Imperial Russia.

finished, he sent his children off to a different job and stayed behind alone with his wife. The stack was done, so his wife needed to come back down to the ground. For that, a long rope was usually thrown over the stack. The person standing on the haystack would take one end of it, and a robust man would hold onto the middle and slowly lower the hay stacker. The rope was thrown, and the wife took one end and said, "Hold on tight, Andrei Andreevich!" "I am," he answered. But his wife had barely begun to lower herself when her spouse let go of the rope and she fell to the ground from a height of over fourteen feet. He, meanwhile, took his pitchfork and his rake and headed home as though nothing had happened. The poor woman could not get up or even crawl on all fours. The children asked their father, "Where is Mother?" "How should I know?" her spouse answered. Finally, it occurred to the children to go to the haystack themselves, and from there, with the help of the neighbors, they brought the injured woman home.

Even before this incident, Andrei Andreevich had decided to sew himself a gown. He called a tailor and gave him a piece of homespun cloth of about 27 yards. The tailor took his measure and asked, jokingly, "So, Andrei Andreevich, should I leave you some cloth from the gown for a little cap?" (a gown required 12 to 14 yards) and received the answer, "You know, that's up to you." Andrei Andreevich needed to go out somewhere, so the tailor began sewing the gown in his absence. I don't know what gave him the idea to play a joke on Andrei Andreevich, but he used the entire 27 yards for the coat and indeed barely left anything for a little cap. The gown turned out to be huge, and would have been too big even for Goliath. The tailor made sure to clear out and get home. After returning home and inspecting the gown, Andrei Andreevich at first felt the need to punish his family, that is, his wife and two sons. He dressed them all in the gown, or more accurately, he wrapped them in it and tied it in such a way that they could not break loose, and then began beating them indiscriminately with a set of thick reins. But, to make sure that the blows did not fall on just one of them, he turned his captives around, now this way, now that way. After enjoying himself to his heart's content, he let them go, all beaten up, for the cloth had not been able to protect them from the blows.

But the principal culprit, the tailor, remained unpunished, and—knowing Andrei Andreevich's character—he did not come for his money. When Andrei Andreevich met him at the market, he had a friendly conversation with him and added, "Why don't you come to

my house to get your money? We could also have a beer together."
The tailor was suspicious for a long time, but finally, taken in by
Andrei Andreevich's friendliness, he succumbed to temptation and
went to his house. The master of the house indeed ordered that a
flagon of beer be brought to him. "Here, drink," he told his guest,
who did indeed drink. Then the master poured another ladle and
said, "Drink!" "Have a drink yourself," the tailor replied. "Don't you
worry about me," the master said as he started to become agitated,
"Drink, I say." He drank, but then a third ladle appeared. Again, the
tailor started to say something. "Oh, you swindler," Andrei Andreevich
screamed, "I've been after you for a long time. Remember the gown? I
haven't paid you yet for sewing it." At that he jumped up and went to
the storeroom for the tool for the upcoming execution.* The tailor
took advantage of the time this took, cleared out of the cabin as fast as
his legs would carry him, and ran into the courtyard. But the gate was
already locked and Andrei Andreevich was at his heels, with a picket
in his hands, and started entertaining his dear guest with it.

The guest somehow was able to find a gap in the fence and escaped into the street. Andrei Andreevich quickly unlocked the gate
and ran after his guest with the picket. Even though it was a market
day, nobody could bring himself to stop the pursuer. However, the
victim of the pursuit somehow managed to get out of the village and
ran to safety across the field and toward the woods; as he was much
younger than Andrei Andreevich, he kept increasing the distance
that separated them. The pursuer realized that he would never catch
up with the man he was chasing, and decided to go back. Meanwhile,
drawn by curiosity, a large crowd had come out to the field to observe
the fight. Andrei Andreevich saw the huge crowd, decided to vent his
frustration on them, and charged at them with the picket. The crowd
took fright and ran for safety. The pursuer made use of his picket,
there was a racket and screaming, and turmoil even broke out at the
market. People shouted, "Run, run! Andrei Andreevich is beating
everyone!" The confusion was terrible. Just about the entire market
was thrown into chaos; some ran into courtyards; others hid behind
carts. Finally, seeing the general commotion and the fear he inspired
in everyone, Andrei Andreevich calmed down and headed home.

This hero did not like to indulge those who served with him—
other sacristans, deacons, and even priests. There is no need to mention the witticisms and curses with which he adorned his speeches

---

* *Ekzekutsiia*, i.e., the carrying-out of a sentence of corporal punishment.

even when he was cheerful, but when he felt insulted he would also make use of his fists. Everyone was afraid of him. Strangely, this man, who terrified all his fellow villagers and parishioners, died from superstitious cowardice. One night, he had a "vision," as they say, that the priest was standing under his window and calling him to church to celebrate matins. Andrei Andreevich went but did not find the priest there because the priest had never left his house. A while later, Andrei Andreevich came running home, crawled onto his stove, and started groaning. He had seen some sort of apparition by the church that had so frightened him that he took ill as soon as he got home and died soon after.

[Four other clerics from the area were sentenced to exile in Siberia for various crimes, including one who stole from his own church.] I won't start listing others, but even from the instances I have presented, the reader will have an idea of the morality of the clergy at the end of the eighteenth and the beginning of the nineteenth century! After this, is it any surprise that their kinsmen—whose failure to enter the clergy was not, of course, a consequence of their virtue—could openly become thieves and robbers?

Whatever the origin of Tuma's robber bands, their members were quite numerous and brazen at the time when my grandfather became priest in Tuma.

[The robbers would come to Grandfather's house at night to demand food, and when the clergy went out in the summer to divide up the meadows before mowing the hay, the robbers would offer "advice" on how to do so and expect free food and vodka as "payment." The robbers would prey on travelers but coexisted fairly peacefully with the local population.]

Don't think, dear reader, that my home village of Tuma was the only place where robbers were so uninhibited. No, during the splendid reign of the great and most wise Catherine, robberies occurred virtually everywhere in the state. In fact, hundreds of millions of rubles were being spent in Petersburg on people who enjoyed her favor—the Orlovs, Potemkins, Zavadovskiis, Zoriches, Zubovs, and so on*—and over a million free peasants were being given away as serfs while the great lords of the time were drowning in luxury. So, why blame the lit-

---

* References to Catherine's lovers Grigorii Orlov, Grigorii Potemkin, Petr Zavadovskii, Semen Zorich, and Platon Zubov.

tle people who, deprived of the ability to earn an honest living, would lie in wait for tardy travelers at night by some bridge or creek and rob them of five or ten rubles, a sack of flour, a plain coat, and so on, or who would crawl into a granary, outdoor cellar, or attic and take whatever fell into their hands? After all, these smalltime thieves and robbers made their home in some cave, basement, and so on and would answer with their back and their nostrils when they were caught and end their life somewhere like Nerchinsk.*

Let me say a few words about robberies that took place where I lived or nearby. When Grandfather was still a sacristan in the village of Sheianki, the clergy, especially my grandfather, did not get along with the robber band that made its home in the neighboring woods; therefore, when they went out to work in the fields, especially alone or in small numbers, they would carry a loaded gun that hung from the laborer by a strap. In this manner, during Empress Catherine's reign, peaceful clergymen just over two hundred versts from Moscow had to till the soil just like the line Cossacks who, under the emperors Alexander I and Nicholas, worked their fields in the knowledge that some Circassian or Chechen might shoot them from behind a bush.† [. . .]

Once, Grandfather was supposed go from Sheianki to the town of Melenki, whose district bordered on that of Kasimov. In the hamlet where he needed to spend the night, he saw a long column of carts entering a courtyard. Grandfather was afraid that this place would be crowded and wanted to go to the neighboring house, whose owner had invited him in. Then a peasant who was part of the column said to Grandfather, "Why not join us?" "It'll be crowded," Grandfather replied. "Well, crowded isn't so bad," the peasant went on, "at least your head'll stay whole. But over there you'd better watch out when you're alone, 'cause *a mouse might eat your head off.*" My grandfather took the hint and joined the column. From my childhood, I remember many stories about how keepers of coaching inns would arrange convenient ways of sending many travelers who stayed with them to meet their Maker. For that purpose a beam or tie beam, as it was called, would be fastened to the ceiling. Though it looked as though it were needed to support the ceiling, actually it was arranged in such

---

* Typical punishment for convicted criminals included flogging with the knout (which could be lethal), having one's nostrils slit, and hard labor in the silver mines of Nerchinsk, on the Chinese border, about four thousand miles east of Moscow.

† Alexander I reigned 1801–1825, and Nicholas I 1825–1855. The "line" (i.e., military) Cossacks were settled near the Caucasus mountains as part of Russia's decades-long war against the guerrillas who fought for the independence of the Circassians, Chechens, and other mountain peoples.

a way that it could be dropped to the ground on special chains or ropes. The travelers would be fed a hearty meal and given vodka laced with drugs to put them to sleep, and then they were laid on the floor on the straw in such a way that the tie beam, when it was dropped, would crush them all, preferably falling on their heads or chests. Once the travelers were asleep, the innkeeper and his family or some fellows whom he kept in reserve in his basement would noiselessly lower the tie beam and press it down on those who were sleeping, with some holding it tight while others used various instruments to finish off those who were still alive. This tale is perhaps only a legend, but it does convey the opinion of contemporaries about how safe travel was in the reign of Empress Catherine in Riazan and Vladimir provinces, even for people in large groups.

As recently as 1867, at the time I started writing this *Memoir,* the noble landowner Korenev, an acquaintance of mine, told me about an ancestor of one of the landowners he knew. The venerable ancestor had lived in Pronsk District and, as befitted a magnate, engaged in robbery on a huge scale. He had assembled lackeys, peasants, and other free people into a huge gang, set up depots and caves to store stolen goods, and was friendly with the police and even with governors. Once, a huge column of vehicles traveled past him from Penza Province to Moscow, transporting some kind of food products on sledges whose design was not at all similar to what was usual in Riazan and which were very beautiful. The landowner and his gang caught up with the column on the road and seized all the horses, sledges, and people, with only a few of the latter somehow managing to escape. The people were quickly done away with to prevent them from talking, and the horses and goods were sold. Usually, the landowner-cum-ataman* would burn the sledges, but in this case he had fallen for their beauty and hoped to receive a pretty sum for them, so he ordered that they be hidden. Meanwhile, though they knew who had robbed them, the surviving travelers did not go to court, for it was known that the landowner would find ways to have them sent to prison themselves. However, they did return home and tell everything.

A few of them found the courage to go back to Pronsk District and secretly inquire about what had happened to their lost column. They found out that the people had been killed and the horses sold, but

---

* An ataman was a leader of Cossacks, unruly settlers on Russia's southern frontier who frequently resisted state authority. "Cossack" was a byword for unbridled freedom, machismo, and hostility to Russia's intensely authoritarian sociopolitical order—including, ironically, the landowning nobility.

that all the sledges and part of the goods were still intact and being stored in a cave. With the cunning and persistence that are peculiar to the oppressed Russian people, they decided to track the robber. The following winter, he began sending the Penzan sledges, a few at a time, to the trading village of Perevisk to be sold; the sledges were elegant, beautiful, even quite original, and people eagerly bought them. The Penzans also recognized them, and watched for one that had a particular mark. Finally, this sledge, too, was brought out. The Penzans recognized it, gathered together a large crowd of people, called for the elected local policeman (*sotskii*) and the other village authorities, and recounted in front of everyone who they were and how they had been robbed the previous winter. Then, pointing to one of the sledges, they added that they had awaited its sale in particular to establish the robbers' guilt. They said that there was, on one side beneath the third strut in the sledge's left runner, a hollow space where they had hidden fifty one-ruble coins, so they asked that the sledge be examined at once. The populace had long been suffering from the robbers and insistently demanded that the sledge be examined, so the third strut was removed and the fifty ruble-coins were found. The sellers of the sledge testified that they were selling it on the order of their lord, the well-known ataman. That made it impossible for the land and provincial authorities to continue covering up for the criminal, so a formal search of his house, caves, etc., was carried out, huge depots of stolen goods were discovered, and finally a court exiled the landlord-cum-ataman to hard labor in Siberia. [. . .]

In light of all this it makes sense that, as Grandfather used to tell me, people who traveled from the Meshchora to Moscow under Catherine II made sure to receive communion, just as though they were about to die.

With the end of Catherine II's reign, the golden age for robbers came to an end as well.* In no history of Russia have I encountered this idea, and I will not even dispute that it may not have been applicable to all localities. But the Meshchora—my home region—and all who needed to travel through it should recall with gratitude the reign of Emperor Paul. My grandfather also liked to talk about that reign.

---

* Catherine's reign was called a "golden age" for the nobility, partly because of the untrammeled power they held over their serfs and their dominant position in the state, and partly because of the change in this position during the reign of Catherine's son Paul (1796–1801), who treated them with disdain. Among nobles, intellectuals, and—to some degree—subsequent historians, Paul gained a reputation for being irrational, paranoid, and despotic, and his secret police was widely feared among the nobility. He was overthrown and assassinated in 1801 and succeeded by his son, Alexander I.

The clergy had liked it very much because of one particular circumstance that I will discuss later.* However, the reign itself was remembered by the people as terrifying and burdensome. Even in the villages, people were afraid of informers. According to Grandfather, one of the noble landowners from Kasimov once talked fairly freely about the emperor to his closest friends; some time later, at night, the police took him away, turned him over to an army officer sent from Petersburg, and after that the unfortunate man disappeared to who knows where. The fear of denunciations forced even my grandfather to be cautious, although he was a man who, according to the Russian saying, "did not like to whisper into his fist." My late father would describe how Grandfather, when he was about to tell some story concerning the emperor to his friend, neighbor, and fellow priest Varsonofii, would pause and say, "Hold on, Varsonofii, let's take a look out the window to check whether anyone is eavesdropping from outside," and, after looking out, he would tell his story, but quietly, even though my grandfather usually liked to talk exceedingly loud. However, both my grandfather and my father were in complete agreement that, under Paul, the activities and exploits of the robbers ceased, for the police received the strictest orders to pursue the robbers, and carried out these orders with unaccustomed zeal.

Both before and to some extent after this time, on the other hand, denouncing a robber, capturing him, and even cooperating in his capture was exceedingly dangerous. Most members of the police received handsome gifts from thieves and robbers and liked to give them protection. They therefore secretly gave them the opportunity to escape even from prison, or did not properly pursue them and meanwhile actually informed them about those who had denounced them. Once they were free, of course, the robbers and thieves knew how to take revenge on their enemies. Independently of that, during the reign of Empress Catherine II, the capture of a robber often had ruinous consequences, especially for the wealthy residents of a district.

[Translator's Note: Prior to the judicial reform of 1864, law enforcement and the courts were notoriously cumbersome, arbitrary, and corrupt. Most judges and senior police officers either were bureaucrats (or army officers) socialized in a service culture that encouraged unquestioning obedience to superiors and a harsh command tone toward subordinates, or they were nobles used to lording it despotically over peas-

---

* See p. 108

ants who they assumed were deceitful and lazy. They were not trained judicial or police professionals with internalized notions of legality and due process. The law itself changed constantly and was not codified until 1832, making it nearly impossible to know for certain what was actually legal, so officials tended instead to rely on personal intuition or common sense. As was the case throughout the imperial administration, the regime sought to limit arbitrariness and incompetence by requiring voluminous paperwork, but that only made the judicial process extremely time-consuming and allowed the underpaid clerks who drafted and processed the documents to manipulate cases and extort bribes. Low-ranking policemen were likewise untrained, poorly paid, and had no internalized professional ethic. The population generally distrusted and feared the police and courts, avoided them when possible, and had little recourse against abuse except to hire amateur "attorneys" whose key qualification was a personal familiarity with the staff of the local courts, or else simply to bribe the relevant officials.]

You, dear reader, have surely heard that, in times past, "snitches" were led about the streets of Petersburg, that is, various criminals who ostensibly were supposed to point out to our beneficent government the houses in which they had been harbored or the people who had been their associates or accomplices. When they saw from afar that such snitches were approaching, the residents of the Heaven-blessed City of Peter would seek their own salvation* from the peril menacing them by running into neighboring streets, hiding in nearby houses— in a word, they would make every effort to avoid meeting with the procession, because the snitch who was being led around would, for no apparent reason, point out people who had never seen him before as being his friends. In this regard, the provinces did not lag behind the capital. Our kind authorities—in the person of the land captains, solicitors, or assessors of the land court†—would set out on a stroll around the district with a captured robber. Of course, the robber would not point out his actual benefactors, because he hoped that they would be useful to him again in the future; instead, he would take revenge on his enemies by claiming that they had concealed him.

---

* This is an untranslatable play on words: the phrase "the Heaven-blessed City of Peter" (*bogospasaemyi Petrograd,* literally "the divinely saved City of Peter") suggests that God has granted salvation to the people of St. Petersburg, while "snitch" (*iazyk,* literally "tongue") also means pagan, i.e., a threat to a Christian's salvation.

† The land captain *(ispravnik),* a nobleman elected every three years by the other nobles of the district, headed the land court and was responsible for law enforcement in rural areas.

If the snitch who was being led around did not himself have people whom he particularly disliked, then once more the authorities (of that time) would take upon themselves the labor of suggesting to him the names of persons who should be accused of harboring criminals. For that, of course, well-to-do residents were selected whom the authorities wanted to "teach a lesson." In either case, to make his slander appear credible, the robber usually said either that he did not know his friend's home but knew his name, or that he knew neither the home nor the name but remembered the face.

In any case, the person accused by the robber would be arrested. He would swear "by Christ and by God" that he had absolutely "no idea about anything," which in fact was true. Well, thereupon our most kind and solicitous authorities would say to the accused, "You see, sir, we too know that you're innocent, but what can you do about this swindler? You see, he won't budge from his claim. Stuff his throat with something—just give him a few rubles." It made no difference whether or not the authorities mentioned their own throats, for they would in any case get stuffed with tens and hundreds of rubles, depending on the fortune of the accused. [The police would then make a display of urging the robber to admit his mistake, whereupon the robber would feign contrition for having accused an innocent person.] Our kind authorities would release the falsely accused person, properly reprimand the accuser, and either take him to another hamlet, where the same comedy would be enacted again, or return to town if the excursion had already provided them with a sufficient amount of money. The robber likewise often was not left without a reward, for they would give him the opportunity to escape from prison and resume his exploits in the same places as before. After this, the inhabitants would make sure to be properly solicitous toward such fellows. These nice fellows would live happily ever after, impose tribute on the inhabitants, and share their loot with our kind authorities.

Under Emperor Paul, however, things were different. The police would request help from the inhabitants in capturing robbers and were extremely grateful for any cooperation in this area. At that time, my grandfather acquired great renown in the area for his zeal in helping to unmask and capture the robbers who plied their trade around Tuma, and exposed himself to danger more than once. One time, a bullet that was fired from the woods whistled right past his ear. Not to mention the threats. God knows what all they tried to frighten him with. Until her dying day, my late grandmother would recall those times with horror. "You couldn't sleep at night," she would say, "we didn't go anywhere without a gun and a hatchet." But Grandfather was indefatigable. Many of his honest fellow villagers were inspired by his energy; he took command of them after a fashion and, without the police, captured many robbers himself. The inhabitants, at least most of them, were zealous in helping him, and to tell the truth, they did not treat their captives very humanely. Of course, they did not kill them outright, but [no incident] ever went without a beating, and they tried particularly to deprive the [robbers] of the ability to stand and walk fast on their feet.

My father told me about an incident that was interesting in this regard. The threshing of grain from the drying barns in Tuma would start early in the morning, long before dawn. One day, when most of Tuma's adult residents were at work on their threshing floors, some robber decided to take advantage of the opportunity and break into someone's house for loot, but he was soon noticed. The alarm was raised and people cried, "Stop the thief!" From all the threshing floors, mostly with their flails* in hand, the men came running after the thief who tried to hide in the neighboring woods but was finally caught. The first one who caught up with him swung the flail at the [robber] with all his might, and soon other, similar blows followed. The captive fell to the ground. A great many of the villagers who came running wanted, in their expression, to "lend a hand," or rather a flail, and the result rather resembled a threshing. My father was too young to join the pursuers, so he stayed on the threshing floor by the drying barn, and with the others he heard the sound of the flails raining down blows on the captive. The latter, of course, was beaten half to death.

Finally, thanks to the efforts of the local police authorities, with the assistance of the villagers and especially my grandfather, overt robbery in and around Tuma ceased, that is, there was no more knocking on the windows and shouting, "Hey, young priest, give us bread." Likewise, when the clergy divided up their meadows, they no longer encountered self-appointed surveyors who, after the division was completed, demanded to be entertained, and so on. However, petty fraud, quite often large-scale theft as well, sometimes also robberies and even murders, occurred later on, too, not only in Tuma but also in other places.

[In Tuma, the Saturday markets particularly attracted thieves.] Pious novices at this trade preferred to begin on March 25, Annunciation Day. According to folk superstition, someone who successfully stole

---

* A flail is a rod several feet long that is connected at its end with a shorter rod that can swing freely. It is used for threshing grain.

something on that day between matins and mass would be able to steal all year without having to fear being caught. Once, I think in 1818, I was witness when a peasant whom my father knew was brought to him after being caught stealing. After listening to the report of those who had caught the thief, my father said to him, "What is this, you too have become a thief? And worse yet, on what day? On Annunciation Day, such an important holiday, and already before mass!" "Oh, Father," the simplehearted peasant replied, "what better time to start than on this day? But I failed, so God doesn't wish for me to steal." Mostly, however, the thieves and sometimes also robbers were homeless or dissolute townspeople, occasionally convicts who had managed to escape, and above all fugitive soldiers.

The villagers knew all these thieves and robbers and would have helped catch them, or even caught them themselves, if only the land police had wanted it or at least had not interfered. But that, unfortunately, was not always the case, for the assessors of the land court, later the district police officers (*stanovye*), and sometimes even the land captains gave their protection to the thieves and robbers.

[Rostislavov gives two examples of locally well-known robbers whom local police officers protected despite receiving orders to arrest them. Another peasant was also well known as a thief, and one day, thirsty but short of money, he even persuaded fellow villagers in the tavern to buy him drinks by volunteering a promise to stop thieving. He broke the promise, but his grown sons felt so humiliated in front of the community by their father's conduct that they threatened to gouge out his eyes to make him stop. The threat worked, and the old man stopped stealing. Rostislavov then describes a number of villages that were notorious for harboring robbers.]

When a theft had already taken place, the victims would attempt to strike a bargain with the thieves and ransom their things from them. This was done especially when horses were involved. [. . .] My father found himself in such a situation. When he was already living in Dmitrovskii Pogost,[22]* a horse was stolen from him. It was soon discovered that the peasants of the hamlet of Kasseino had done it. Father did not go to them himself, but instead sent his brother Vasilii Martynovich, the deacon of the village of Prudki, as his envoy to the

---

* He moved to Dmitrovskii Pogost some time between 1834 (when the census listed him as living in Tuma) and 1840. By the 1850s, that community had 8 households and 62 inhabitants.

Spring flooding along a river in Vladimir Province, 1914.
(Source: Russian State Ethnographic Museum, 3307-11/2)

The village of Shemiakino (near Shost'e, twenty miles south of Kasimov), 1910. Note the characteristically wide, unpaved village street and the small religious shrine at the center. (Source: Russian State Ethnographic Museum, 2177-4)

A peasant courtyard, with farm implements and a thatched roof. Village of Uviaz,
near Shemiakino, 1910. (Source: Russian State Ethnographic Museum, 2177-15)

The stove in a peasant cabin. Note the various cooking and household implements, as well as the felt boots on the shelf at the right and the benches and shelves on which people sat and slept. Uviaz, 1910. (Source: Russian State Ethnographic Museum, 2177-13/b)

Traditional wooden church near Lake Onega, Northern Russia, before 1917.
(Source: Russian State Ethnographic Museum, 2521-4/2)

The seventeenth-century residence of the archbishop of Riazan,
in the Riazan Kremlin, as it appears today.

The seventeenth-century Cathedral of the Assumption in the
Riazan Kremlin, as it appears today.

The Alianchikov mansion in Kasimov (presently the Kasimov Regional Museum),
as it appears today. The main entrance faces Cathedral Square. The Kasimov Church School,
since destroyed by fire, was located just past the last building on the left edge of the picture.
The street in the foreground goes down a steep incline to the banks of the Oka.

The eighteenth-century mosque in Kasimov, as it appears today, with the fifteenth-century minaret on the right. Salekh's house is located just past the left edge of this picture.

Gavriil Vasil'evich Riumin's mansion, as it appears today, on Astrakhan Street in Riazan (presently the Riazan Provincial Museum of Fine Arts).

negotiations. He came to the hamlet and addressed the peasants with his most humble petition. The peasants gathered in council in the street and, after a lengthy argument, resolved not to give up the horse even for ransom. My father had brought this disfavor upon himself by the fact that, not long before, when he had participated in the investigation of a theft of which one of the inhabitants of the hamlet of Kasseino was found guilty, he had greatly aided in establishing the guilt of the thief, who was then exiled to Siberia. The people's parliament *(veche)* of Kasseino announced its resolution to my uncle in these words: "You go tell the archpriest of Dmitrovskii Pogost that we won't give him back the horse—we'll send it to Tambov Province instead. Why did he have to help get our boy Van'ka exiled to Siberia? Now he'll know not to pick a fight with us."

I will not conceal that, sometimes, the police also skillfully pursued thieves, especially if an honest and energetic land captain was elected. Just such a land captain was the landowner of the hamlet of Uzhishchevo in Kasimov District, Karl Vasil'evich Kronstein, from whom, as I mentioned earlier, we bought our female servants. To you, my future readers, the character of this lord will most likely appear enigmatic. He was a very honest and unselfish man; after ten years of being elected by the nobles to the lucrative posts of land captain and district judge, he died and left his family in utter poverty. However, in governing the Russian common people, he followed the ideas of the famous Arakcheev in being sincerely convinced that only the cane, the lash, the rod, and slaps in the face could maintain order among the peasants, and on that basis he was extremely cruel in his punishments. [23]* [. . .]

---

* Born around 1780 as the son of a noble lieutenant named Heinrich von Kronstein from St. Petersburg Province, Karl von Kronstein virtually grew up in the artillery, where he served first as a cadet (from 1792 on) and then as an officer until his retirement in 1804 at the rank of lieutenant. One of the most influential figures in the Russian military and government during those years was Count Aleksei A. Arakcheev, an artillery officer notorious for his brutality in enforcing obedience to his orders. The surviving archival records tell us that, in 1807, Kronstein was "under investigation" for having "punished" one of his wife's serfs—such investigations were very rare, so Kronstein's brutality must have been quite exceptional—but the Senate eventually dismissed the charges, a decision confirmed by the tsar in 1814. By 1823, we find him living in Kasimov District with his wife Praskov'ia Aleksandrova—a local landowner who was listed as having 268 male serfs in 1816 and 167 in 1823—and their three young daughters. Kronstein himself owned only one male serf, whom he had bought, in the district. Elected by his fellow nobles to the office of land captain for Kasimov District in January 1824, he was still alive in 1854 when he was being investigated because of doubts about his family's noble credentials. He was one of many ethnic Germans in Russia's officer corps and bureaucracy. Russians generally admired their work ethic, respect for rules, and high level of education and professionalism, but also stereotyped them as arrogant toward Russians, lacking in humor or emotional warmth, and merciless in the enforcement of regulations—in a word, the embodiment of the authoritarian, bureaucratic, modernizing spirit of the imperial regime.

I was personally witness to an execution [i.e., infliction of corporal punishment] that the land captain carried out in Tuma one summer holiday between matins and mass. A rumor had spread among the peasants that they were supposed to be resettled on state lands, which would of course free them from the power of their landlords. The main culprits in spreading this rumor were peasants of the landlord Troumpel's hamlet of Shchurovo, one and a half versts from Tuma. From his head to his toes, Kronstein was a dyed-in-the-wool serf owner, and he thought it necessary to crush any thought of freedom in the peasants. In this case there was the additional circumstance that Troumpel's peasants had been placed under Kronstein's direct supervision by their landlord. The land captain established himself in Tuma in the house of the economic peasant* Leont'ev, who lived across the street from us. Here were gathered both the guilty and the righteous peasants, who formed a wide circle. The land captain stood in the middle and summoned the three guilty ones, and his coachman at once brought several pairs of bundles of birch rods, with fairly thick switches, which in such cases are called canes. He then launched into a speech about how foolish it was to revolt against the landlords, spread absurd rumors, and so on. The speech was directed to both the guilty and the righteous, all of whom were standing with their hats off. [After that, the three guilty peasants were each given between one hundred and two hundred powerful blows.]

This lover of the lash and the rod was an excellent land captain when he was dealing with criminals, especially horse thieves and robbers, though here too he could not give up his Arakcheevan habits. At that time, any thief was exiled to Siberia if the object he had stolen was worth over one hundred paper rubles. On that basis, as soon as he had captured a horse thief, Kronstein would order the official estimators (tsenovshchiki) to assess it at a price higher than one hundred rubles.† Peasants would mostly carry out his order unquestioningly, but if, among the estimators, there happened to be merchants, townsmen, or even peasants who were reluctant to assess some nag at a hundred rubles, the land captain would tell them, "It's true that the horse isn't worth a hundred rubles, but then again, without it a peasant is destitute—he has no way to plow, move his sheaves, go out for firewood, etc. Just add up the loss he must have sustained through

---

* Economic peasants were peasants who had belonged to the Orthodox clergy until 1762, when they were secularized and placed under state authority.

† Rostislavov elsewhere describes an incident in which a peasant bought back his stolen horse from the thief for twenty rubles, which puts these sums into perspective.

the theft of his horse—and besides, are we supposed to wait for the thief to steal an expensive horse? No, let's get rid of him now." And indeed, they almost always did get rid of them, so rumor had it that, during the first three-year term to which Kronstein had been elected as land captain for Kasimov District, about thirty thieves were exiled. In catching robbers he proceeded even more harshly.

[In one case, a hamlet offered refuge to a robber whom Kronstein was unable to capture. Kronstein finally lost patience, rounded up the entire population of the hamlet, and ordered that every man and woman be flogged. Chastened by this experience, the inhabitants turned in the robber. In another case, Kronstein also used a combination of cajolery and pressure to obtain the population's help. In this case, the peasant bailiff whose aid Kronstein needed was afraid that the robber, if captured, would escape from prison and take revenge on him. Kronstein suggested that the bailiff and his posse break the robber's legs in order to make escape impossible. Harming captured criminals was illegal, so judicial officers routinely extorted bribes from civilians who brought in injured criminals. In this case, however, Kronstein promised the bailiff that he would be safe from such blackmail, and kept his promise.]

However, the villagers themselves did not wait for orders from the land captain or trust in the justice of the judicial and land authorities, but enforced their own Russian lynch law and personally carried out the sentences. These were usually death sentences, and the condemned escaped only very occasionally. The thief Grishka from Tuma did, it is true, end his life at home after receiving communion, but not quite in the usual manner. The peasants captured him, or rather, they caught up with him in the woods in possession of stolen goods and decided to settle accounts with him once and for all. They set about beating him to death, and when they saw that he was no longer breathing, they decided he was dead and left him to be eaten by the wolves. However, after lying there for a while, Grishka regained consciousness and managed to crawl all the way to the road. He was brought home, where he wasted away for several months and died a so-called Christian death. Remarkably, he did not say who had tried to beat him to death in the woods, or for what.

With others, things were done differently. The Meshchora is a marshy country, and there are marshes with a watery mud that is several *sazhens* deep. If a robber or thief had been finished off, they would usually tie a rock to his neck and dump him in the marsh. Sometimes even a live one, a rock around his neck, was thrown exactly the same way into the mud of the marshes, where, of course, he disappeared forever. The reason why marshes were preferred to rivers and lakes in this case was that in the latter people went fishing, and with a dragnet or seine they might dredge up a drowned man with a rock around his neck. In that case there would be investigations, and people would have to pay not only with money but even with their backs. On the other hand, no one fishes for anything in a marsh, and besides, the mud there soon covers objects that sink to the bottom. Why look for anything more convenient and safer than that place?

[In areas where there were no marshes or deep rivers, the following method was used. In the forest, a tall, thick tree was selected. On one side its roots were cut, and then the tree was pulled in the opposite direction (where the roots remained intact), so that a gap opened up on the side where the roots had been severed. The robber—usually dead, but not always—was stuffed into this gap, after which the rope was released and the tree returned to its natural upright position.]

This form of burial was called "hiding under a post." Remarkably, the entire area sometimes knew about such a killing, but they would remain silent, that is, they did not bring it to the attention of the authorities. In the house of the priest of Birenevo, Kuz'ma (the father of the priest of Narma, my sister's husband, Vasilii Kuz'mich Lebedev), there once sat a large crowd of people waiting for mass on a holiday. The conversation turned to a certain townsman, a well-known thief, of whom nothing had been heard in a long time. People asked what had become of him, whereupon one of those taking part in the conversation said, "Why this desire to talk about a thief? You probably want him to come back and start stealing again?" "Well, no, he's not coming back," another peasant retorted with a stutter. "What makes you think he's not coming back?" "How could he come back? He's already been lying *under a post*" for so-and-so long. Everyone began laughing, though half of them had already known before.

Of course, the lynch law that I have described was unavoidable as a result of extreme necessity and the indulgence that the authorities displayed toward inveterate thieves and robbers who were able to obtain and keep their favor, but it also manifested and actually aggravated the coarseness of people's morals. Unfortunately, lynch law was sometimes applied to people who were guilty of absolutely nothing. To illustrate the point, I will describe one such incident. In this case, of course, there were no thieves, theft, or robbery involved, but instead an entire hamlet acted worse than a gang of robbers.

[In 1840, the father's workwoman, Anna, told the following grisly story that occurred in her native hamlet of Ershovo (near Dmitrovskii Pogost). When she was a child, there was an old man who had no children or grandchildren and therefore lived alternately with different distant relatives. For that reason, he was accidentally overlooked during a census* and left off the tax rolls. This was a serious offense for which the village would be made to pay a heavy fine, and the community elder would face harsh punishment. So, the villagers gathered in the courtyard of one of the houses and announced that they had decided to kill him to avoid trouble with the authorities.]

Anna, who had watched this scene from the street with the other children by peering under the fence, said that the old man had pleaded desperately with his executioners not to touch him, that he would die soon in any case. But they ignored his plea, made a noose in the middle of a long rope, placed it around the old man's neck, and then all without exception, women and men, took hold of the ends of the rope, pulled, and the entire community strangled the old man. I suppose they must have given a handsome bribe to the priest, for he buried him without legal proceedings or investigation. Anna added that, at the time she was telling the story, many of the women and men were still alive who had taken part in this horrible crime. By now, as I write, it is likely that none of them remain on this earth. This event occurred during the reign of Emperor Alexander I.

---

* Either in 1811–1812 or 1815–1816.

CHAPTER EIGHT

Our Home Life in Tuma

• In Tuma my father could not, in every respect at least, live as he had in Palishchi. Tuma was something of a center, a little capital for the Kasimov section of the Meshchora. There was a bazaar there every Saturday. There was not only a tavern, but also a liquor depot *(vinnyi podval)*, as well as the so-called agent *(poverennyi)*, that is, the liquor-farmer's representative who managed several nearby taverns.[24]* The officers of the land police, and even the land captain himself, sometimes came there. The presence of the main road from Kasimov to Moscow led many merchants and nobles to stay over, and the landowners from the vicinity would come simply to dispel their boredom. My father was made district superintendent as well as senior priest; as a result, both parishioners and clerics began coming to see him, not only from Tuma but from many other villages as well. Furthermore, one of the priests in Tuma, Ivan Petrovich, lived "like a gentleman," that is, he had a samovar and lived in a clean, heatable annex where none of his farm animals ever entered. Lastly, the landowner Petr Vasil'evich Ivanov, an old acquaintance of my father's and my godfather, lived two and a half versts away.

[During the first winter in Tuma, the entire family—fifteen people—lived in Grandfather's cabin. However, the keeper of the coaching inn vacated Grandfather's other cabin during the warm months, and that spring Father bought a four-room wooden building

---

* The imperial government sold to concessionaires (called liquor-farmers *[otkupshchiki]*) the right to sell liquor to the public at a price set by the government; the liquor was stockpiled in depots and then sold in taverns. Liquor-farming was abolished in 1819 because the "farmers" were finding illegal ways to keep too much of the proceeds from the sales. However, the direct takeover of the lucrative trade by the state produced such extensive corruption among the officials in charge that liquor-farming was restored in 1827. The fiscal importance of the trade is apparent from the fact that state revenues from alcohol sales (117–134 million rubles annually in the 1820s, out of total ordinary revenues of roughly 400 million) usually exceeded those from direct taxation, and Finance Minister Egor F. Kankrin actually expressed the hope in 1826 "that the moderate [!] use of spirits among the simple people should increase" in order to boost government revenues.

(known in the family as "the mansion" [*khoromy*]) in another village, dismantled it, and reassembled it in Tuma. A few years later, Grandfather's first cabin was replaced with a two-story structure.]

Our family's life in Tuma was not lordly and differed little from life in Palishchi. First of all, I should say that all of us continued almost always to have lunch and dinner together with our servants, even when together we consisted of eighteen or nineteen people; usually, only little children up to six or seven years, and Grandmother after she lost her eyesight, ate lunch and dinner separately from the others. [This rule was broken only when there were guests, whom Mother and Father would receive alone in a special room.] When we had dinner together, plates, forks, and knives were out of the question. We had round, wooden spoons, the kitchen knife was used to cut bread, and beef would be cut into chunks on a wooden platter with that same knife, though it was most often held in place with a fork. Then, our cabbage soup, cold liquids, porridge, and other foods that had to be eaten with a spoon were poured into a single common wooden bowl. All used their hands to take cut-up chunks of aspic and roast beef, mutton, suckling pig, etc., from the common platter. On the other hand, when a separate meal was prepared for guests, they would place before each guest a flat wooden plate on which he could put his spoon, and for roast meats each would use, not (as we used to say) his five fingers, but a fork. For guests who were really honored, for example landowners, or archimandrites* who were passing through, deep tin plates were set out and hot foods were poured into them for each person individually.

The food that we all ate when there were no guests was very simple. I will begin with fast days.

[The first course consisted of rusks (dried and rebaked slices of bread) that had been softened in water, with kvass (a beerlike drink made from barley, malt, and rye) poured over them and onions and cucumbers added. In the winter, kvass with white cabbage and cucumbers was substituted. That was followed by cabbage soup mixed with wheat flour or whitened by the juice from hempseeds, and with mushrooms when available. Finally, to end the meal, there would be buckwheat porridge with hempseed or linseed oil or with the same juice that whitened the cabbage soup. Other foods included potatoes (which were beginning to come into use) and beets—both of which

---

* High-ranking clergymen, usually the heads of large monasteries.

were sometimes mixed with kvass—mushrooms, berries, peas, oat flour soaked in water, and fish (which was rarely available).]

On holidays, especially when we had guests, pies were baked with wheat flour and filled with cabbage or with bilberries and raspberries; the berries were mixed with honey, which is why the pies themselves were called sweet. Usually, however, we never had more than three courses at dinner on ordinary days.

Before describing the foods that our family ate on meat days, I think I need to explain that, until long after we moved to Tuma, it was difficult in summer and even in autumn to obtain fresh beef from any trader; instead, it was brought frozen to the bazaar in the winter. It was only just before I finished the seminary that it became possible, on Saturdays during the meat season,* to stock up on fresh meat for the entire week, so long as one could store it in snow to keep it from spoiling. Because of that, in almost all houses, even the affluent ones, fresh meat meant veal, mutton, suckling pig, duck, goose, and other small domestic animals. Then, toward the end of autumn, when frost had already set in, every affluent householder would slaughter one or several cows and swine and stock up on salted beef and ham. In the summer, they were the main items for those who had the means to afford meat on meat days.

[On ordinary meat days, the family would eat kvass or cabbage soup with rusks, sour cream, and pieces of meat or eggs.] With both cabbage soup and kvass, all would begin by taking only the liquid with their spoons, but then, when less then half the food was left in the bowl, the eldest would say "help yourselves," which signaled permission to take one chunk of beef at a time—but no more—with one's spoon. After the magical "help yourselves," the children, and sometimes also the adults, would dip their spoons into the soup or kvass a little more often in order to fish out more chunks. But generally it was rare for each to get more than four or five pieces. The cabbage soup was followed with either fried potatoes or sour milk, rarely both together, but almost without fail the final item was porridge, less often wheat than buckwheat. The porridge was mixed with either butter or fresh milk, the latter being just about the tastiest and most popular dish. On meat holidays, our simple list of foods was supplemented or replaced by other foods. [These included various roast

---

* The "meat season" *(miasoedy)* is the time when eating meat is permitted, especially between Christmas and Shrovetide *(maslenitsa,* equivalent to the week of Mardi Gras, the week before the beginning of Lent). In 1820, for instance, Shrovetide was February 2–8, followed by Lent from February 9 to March 21 (Palm Sunday), Holy Week from March 22 to 28 (Easter Sunday), and Easter Week, March 29–April 4.

meats and fowl; a soup made from chicken and the innards of a chicken or another bird; and various noodle, milk, and egg dishes.]

At the table, in the presence of our elders, we would sit very quietly. Carrying on a conversation was reserved to them alone, but sometimes just about everyone would take part, though the rules of propriety had to be observed. No one worried about formalities regarding how long to sit at the table—when someone no longer wanted to eat, he got up from the table, so that sometimes fewer than half remained by the end of lunch or dinner. I must add that my father, as district superintendent and priest in a wealthy village, kept a better table than many others in the clergy. In those times, it often happened that I would have lunch and dinner with relatives and not see a single piece of meat. All their food on meat days consisted only of sour milk, milk with porridge, cabbage soup with sour cream, and so on.

In the summertime, when it was warm, the kitchen served as lodging or bedroom only for a few of us. [The rest slept in the various other, often unheated, rooms. However, from September on, most of the family began sleeping in the kitchen, and on the eve of holidays they were joined by many villagers who were afraid of missing matins the next day.] In the chilly and cold seasons, the kitchen served not only as the common meeting place for almost all of us, but it was also, so to speak, the classroom for those who were learning to read and, in some cases, to write. Grandfather and Grandmother were almost always there. My sisters would spin here and sometimes sew, embroider, and so on. In the evenings it was almost always lit with torches, while upstairs and in "the mansion" only candles were used. Regarding domestic animals, the same customs were observed that I have already described. [In addition, the house was located on a low-lying site and was very damp.] You can easily imagine that the air in the kitchen was not exactly very good, though of course we didn't notice that. Twice, while I was a seminarian, a fever broke out among us, and then almost everyone except Father, Grandfather, and Grandmother was forced to make its acquaintance. Later on, a heatable cabin was built for the livestock, but even then it still happened that some newborn from the animal kingdom was temporarily housed in our kitchen. From my account of how we lived, you can imagine the living conditions of priests in poor parishes, and of sacristans and deacons in general. When I was preparing to enter the seminary, almost all priests and maybe a few deacons had separate heatable cabins in addition to their kitchens, but most sacristans still lived the old-fashioned way.

CHAPTER NINE

Hospitality

• My father was a great believer in hospitality. In Palishchi it had been difficult for him to exhibit this quality, but in Tuma, where so many people came to him with or without urgent reasons, his hospitality was fully on display, and truth be told, it did not come cheaply. In the countryside, the time I am describing was a time of struggle or, perhaps, of amicable compromise, between the old ways and the newly introduced method of entertaining one's guests. Tea was just beginning to come into use at the time. My father had already bought a samovar when he was still in Palishchi; in the entire parish, only the noble lady from Ovintsi and the landlord of Golovari had preceded him in this. I won't even talk about us children, who at first looked with a certain shyness upon that hot and noisy contraption, but grown people as well, even deacons and sacristans, were amazed and could not understand how it could so quickly heat water and bring it to a very intense boil. "Well, my goodness, isn't that something," they would say as they stood around the samovar.

But drinking tea back then was not exactly easy. I don't remember what price we paid for the tea, but I know for certain that when we lived in Palishchi my father paid no less than two paper rubles a pound for sugar in Riazan and Kasimov. No wonder that few chose to adopt such an expensive way of entertaining, one that only filled the stomach with hot water and caused one to sweat but gave no "Dutch courage" to the head. The costliness of drinking tea was further aggravated by the fact that, at first, people would put enough sugar into the tea cup to make the liquid that was poured into it sweet enough. Soon, however, there arose the art of drinking tea while holding a lump of sugar in one's mouth, but even so, not many among the clergy drank it, and even fewer drank it every day.

However, Father's samovar came into extensive use after the move to Tuma. There, the priest Ivan Petrovich had long been a tea drinker, and the liquor-farmers' agents considered it a must for themselves and their guests to drink tea. Another priest, my uncle Nikifor Mironovich, soon also bought a samovar. But the remaining clerical and lay folk were reluctant to get acquainted with the new drink. Almost right down to 1829, when I was to leave Tuma forever, just about the only native, permanent residents who had samovars were the priests, the sacristan Luka Semenov, the townsman Sazanov and the peasant Leont'i Maksimov, and around the parish, only the two bailiffs Ivan Astaf'ev (of Shul'gino) and Dement'i Efimov (of Kiriaevo). If someone wanted to serve a cup of tea to an honored guest, he would either borrow a samovar from someone in the village or use a copper teapot which he would heat on a trivet in the hearth of the stove. In the hamlets, they would sometimes resort to earthen-ware and cast-iron pots. [One peasant woman actually made tea with an earthen pot and wooden ladle usually reserved for cabbage soup.] There were times when some peasant woman, on her own or even af-ter consulting with her husband, would put the tea leaves directly into the earthen or cast-iron pot while the water was being brought to a boil, but when she saw that this produced a sort of flavorless liquid, she would think it necessary to add buckwheat, onions, or some other flavoring. I was never personally present at a tea drinking of that sort, but I heard of many such cases during my childhood.

Entertaining the old-fashioned way principally involved our own Orthodox vodka, or *sivukha*.* Depending on the person being enter-tained, the time of day, and other considerations, various things might be served as appetizers. Sometimes only a slice of bread with salt was put on the table,† or sometimes they would set out a plate with chunks of beef, a bowl of cucumbers, or something else. They would empty wineglass after wineglass, or tumbler after tumbler, and not so much eat as drink. By the 1820s, many—not only clergy, but peasants too—had started buying grape wines for special occasions, Russian ones that were known as "white" even though the color was reddish. If wine was required but these ["white" wines] were unavail-able, then particularly pious hosts (or people entertaining pious guests) would use the so-called ecclesiastical red wine.

My father combined the new and the old methods of entertaining. For landowners, government officials, priests, respected bailiffs,

---

* *Sivukha* ("gray stuff") is a cloudy, unrefined vodka, in contrast to the costlier, clear, higher-grade variety.

† Bread and salt was the traditional symbol of hospitality.

merchants, and so on, the samovar was normally brought out and then tea was served. Before tea, there absolutely had to be vodka, either "plain" or as an infusion, especially the then famous *erofeich*, that is, liquor infused with the herb called St. John's wort. After a few cups of tea, punch was served. Rum was still little known in the villages and hamlets of the time, so the famous vodka from Kizliar* was used instead. If none was available, people would sometimes pour plain vodka, *sivukha*, into the bowl, but that never happened with Father. [In the family's home, tea was served only when there were guests, or else on special occasions.] For a long time, Grandfather didn't like tea. "Why would you want to fill your belly with hot water? Better to drink a glass," he would say. But later, he too came to like tea, so that we would sometimes even hear him say to my father, "How about it, Vaniusha, isn't it time for a little tea? We've been working pretty hard." Entertaining "the old-fashioned way" did not cause my father any great expense. As was customary at the time, the liquor-farmers gave him, as district superintendent, a quantity of vodka that was quite adequate for home consumption. Father liked to make various sorts of infusions (with rowanberries, raspberries, cherries, currants, *uglianka*,† and so on), and bottles were sometimes stored for several years.

So far, I have spoken about entertaining chance guests who came for a few hours. However, the rural clergy, like the other villagers, have special occasions when their hospitality has to be exhibited in all its splendor: the patronal festivals for the clergy, and, for the peasants, sometimes the patronal festivals but especially Easter. I will describe the celebrations of the clergy, not only how they were in my youth but also earlier. Let me begin with the old times.

Even now, but far more so in the past, relatives and acquaintances would come in very large numbers to visit the ordained clergy and sacristans on patronal festivals. There would be not ten but twenty and even thirty guests, so that the horses and the carts or sleighs would take up a significant part of even a large courtyard, while a small one would be filled entirely. Because of that, people would say that the priest had "a whole courtyard full" or "an entire wagon train" of guests. The same thing went on during weddings at the homes where they were celebrated. Nor did the entire wagon train, complete with horses, stay for just a day, and it was all at the host's expense. In the summer agricultural season, at least, pressing field

---

* A grape liquor from Kizliar in Dagestan, near the western shore of the Caspian Sea.

† From *ugol'* (coal). Perhaps this drink was filtered with coal or had a dark color.

work would force the guests to clear out quickly to get home. But in the fall, after the work was finished, and in winter, particularly on the holidays of the Protection of the Virgin, the Mother of God of Kazan, the Presentation of the Blessed Virgin, and St. Nicholas the Miracle-Worker,* they would not just stay for three or four days, but a whole week, sometimes actually against the host's wishes. Once, visiting Father when I was already a professor at the academy, I heard about how people at a neighboring priest's house had recently celebrated his son's wedding. The guests had drunk and overstayed their welcome for almost a whole week. [. . .]

Let me begin with the way guests on patronal festivals and other festive occasions were entertained in the old days, that is, when my father was a boy. By his account—which Grandfather would confirm by smiling and commenting that "you're right, you're right, it's true, you couldn't do it any other way, that's how it was done" and so on—guests were entertained in the following manner. An hour or two before the guests were supposed to get up, the host would approach them with a *shtof* † of vodka, nudge each one in turn to wake him up, and humbly request that he have a little wineglass or tumbler. Once he was awake or even only half awake, the guest would prop himself up on one arm, and, in this half-lying position, use the other arm to have a drink, then wipe his lips on his sleeve, lie down again, and fall asleep right away. Afterwards they would nudge and awaken another, then a third, and so on.

It was a truly remarkable scene. Since it was impossible to find enough bedsteads and feather beds for all the guests, a few bundles of straw or hay would be brought in for them and spread out in a thick layer on the floor. Sometimes it was covered with something, but otherwise the dear male guests were laid out directly on this improvised bed, while the women mostly slept in the kitchen area, on the benches, or in the annex if it was warm out. Imagine a room that is dimly lit by either a torch or the remnants of a tallow candle, or sometimes a small, waxen church candle. The light is held either by the host's unkempt and sleep-deprived wife, or by some workwoman in a homespun skirt or a workman. The latter two usually watch with a sarcastic smile. The guests are snorting and snoring, as people liked to say back then, "like the great Kremlin bell tower." The host, the

---

* October 1 and 22, November 21, and December 6, respectively.

† Equivalent to 1.23 liters. The term refers both to the unit of measurement itself and to a container holding that amount.

shtof in his hand, is on his knees, shaking the guests one after another to wake them up. One by one they half get up, drink, and then return to their "bell tower."

After completing this first prelude to the holiday, the host would lie down somewhere to make up for his lost sleep, but the hostess almost always had to get started with her cooking, unless she had a special, experienced woman as cook. At last, the guests begin to awaken, stretch, cough a little, say a word or two, and so on, but they don't yet think of getting up. If the host doesn't have the sense on his own to get up at this time, one of the more senior or importunate guests will call out, "Hey, host, where are you? Get up, time to get to work." Either responding to this call or on his own, the host comes back with the shtof and a tumbler or wineglass, and again, on his knees, serves his guests one after the other. The sound of the voices grows stronger, and the guests who were still asleep either wake up on their own or are awakened by their neighbors. The host sits down on the floor or straw, everyone joins in the conversation, and before they even see a need to get up from bed, the vodka in the shtof dwindles further and sometimes a new container is even brought in. Finally, either on their own or because the hostess reports that breakfast will soon be ready, the guests get up, put on their shoes and clothes, start washing up, clear their throats and expectorate and groan, but without fail each prays to God and even bows to the ground a number of times. Then they have to straighten out their long, disheveled hair; they call their wives to plait it into braids, or sometimes they braid it for each other.*
[Breakfast is accompanied by continued liquor consumption and noisy conversation among the men and women, after which some of the guests lie down again while the others either stay at the house or visit neighbors, all the while continuing to eat and drink.]

Although lunch was not particularly refined in the present-day sense, it was extremely filling and included a large variety of dishes. [. . .] Never in Grandfather's time, and not always later on, would the host and hostess take part in lunch. They would only "make the rounds," that is, go from one guest to the next and serve them either individually or all at once. Of course, the host was mainly in charge of drinks, and the hostess of the food. They would try everything, from nagging pleas to displays of deference, flattery, and complaining. "Why won't you eat anything? You don't love us, right? I'm a bad cook, right? Be so kind, and eat." And so the guests, whose stomachs

---

* Orthodox clergymen traditionally wear their hair long.

were already stuffed with all kinds of things, would seek to humor their hosts by bravely taking on the food and drink. Lunch would end and people would leave the table if they were still able to get up, pray to God if they could still raise their arms, and start thanking the host and hostess, who in turn would apologize and say, "But you didn't eat anything, we weren't able to please you, please excuse us, we're glad to share what little we have, we entertained you as best we could." [Most of the guests would take a one- or two-hour nap after lunch.]

A little more sober and rested, they would then leave for other houses to continue celebrating the holiday. On different days, they would make the rounds not only of the clerics, but also laypeople, especially people who were well-to-do and hospitable. Once more, the refreshments would appear—all manner of food would be set out on the table and liquor would be served, but they also did not leave out beer, or rather the village home-brew. In those times, it was usually brewed in cauldrons somewhere outside the back gate, fermented and malted in vats, and stored in kegs and jugs. This home-brew was not especially tasty, but it was thick, bitter, and strong, and those were the qualities required. Prosperous, hospitable householders would make a "March beer." They would brew it in March, fill it into sturdy kegs, place these in ice cellars, and cover them with snow in such a way that they remained covered until June and even later. That sort of home-brew was called March beer. In the absence of ice cellars or during other seasons, the kegs would be lowered into wells and kept there in the water for a few months. In that case, the home-brew could not be called March beer because they brewed it whenever they could, but it too was quite strong.

On holidays, home-brew was consumed mostly after lunch, when it was brought in copper containers called flagons and drunk from large glasses and mugs. Sometimes, clever guests managed to go to more than one place after lunch. Of course, if they went nowhere at all they would get more rest, but once they got up they would again be served one thing or another, especially home-brew. The result was that, by dinnertime, almost all were not only tipsy but actually drunk, and some couldn't even eat dinner but instead "collapsed" somewhere to go to sleep. Of course, dinner was not as copious as lunch, but there still was plenty to eat, and sometimes hostesses felt they had to heat up the stove again to make dinner. As for liquor, it goes without saying that it was served and poured just as generously as it had been at lunch, so that, by the end of dinner, the guests went away completely soused. The hosts would hasten to carry the table out of the cabin or move it aside, bundles of straw and hay were brought in and spread thickly across the floor, and soon all started snoring and snorting; they even forgot, or rather were unable, to pray to God. The next day, the very same rituals and drinking bouts would start all over again, and as I said earlier, this could sometimes go on for an entire week.

With such prolonged, continual and intense drunkenness, things could not always go peacefully. Down to this day, and even more so in the past, the clergy love to boast of their learning and erudition, talk about their affairs large and small, and argue and even sound off noisily, especially when they have "noise in their head." Add to this the fact that, living as they do in the same village, they rarely get along with each other. Likewise, the relations between ordained clergy and sacristans of neighboring villages are not free from conflict, rivalry, and especially envy, and even relatives find many grounds to quarrel. That explains why holiday feasts could not pass without quarrels. There often was wrangling, and sometimes they would even go after each other's "worthies" ("aksiosy"),* that is, grab each other by the hair or regale each other with fists and kicks.

At weddings, they would permit themselves to do all sorts of stupid and downright vile things. I won't even speak of the fact that, the day after a wedding, they would lead the newlyweds to the bathhouse while drumming on iron pots and stove doors, or that the bride's shirt would be examined for proof of her virginity and maidenly innocence—even back then, you no longer found that nonsense and nastiness everywhere.[25]† But for some reason, virtually down to the present there still survives the custom, on that same day, of smashing all the earthen crockery, that is, pots, jugs, mugs, and sometimes even glassware. Before morning on that day, prudent housewives would do their best to hide any crockery that they needed for cooking, and for the lovers of smashed crockery they would leave only things that no longer had any use and which they sometimes got from their neighbors. But without those precautions, everything would get smashed, so the floor of the vestibule and sometimes also the cabin became covered with a fairly

---

* "Aksios," the Greek word for "worthy," is used in the Orthodox Church to indicate that a man is worthy of being consecrated as priest.

† A German observer was appalled to find similar customs among the upper class in Moscow in 1805: "With the wedding guests still assembled, the marriage is consummated to the final degree and the evidence is then presented to the entire company, whereupon the newlyweds receive their congratulations. You can imagine that this cannot pass without the coarsest jokes, and so, in the end, the young bride is truly rid of any vestige of virginal innocence."

thick layer of broken crockery. [Such destructiveness was less common on occasions other than weddings.] Some people would break things simply out of habit or mischievousness. Among our relatives, this was particularly the case of my mother's brother, Stepan Nikitich Arbekov, priest in the village of Podlipki.[26]* He was an intelligent and intellectually curious man, and modest to the point of sometimes being shy, but only as long as he was sober. As soon as he would start boozing, it was as though the demon of mischief and destructiveness had taken hold of him, and with amazing composure he would smash anything that fell into his hands and then die laughing with pleasure. Don't think that the drinking bouts and foolishness I have described are things only of my grandfather's time. No, they continued afterwards, and some still go on today.

[Certain rituals were involved in drinking among the clergy. Hosts felt a moral obligation to use every form of psychological pressure to get their guests drunk. Guests, in turn, were expected to feign reluctance but ultimately give in. The first glass would be downed in honor of the oneness of God, the second for the dual nature of Christ, the third for the Trinity, the fourth for the four corners of the cabin, and so on, including the seven universal councils, the nine ranks of angels, and the twelve apostles. A new series of drinks would begin when the guest was about to leave—two drinks were a minimum because the guest needed to walk on two legs. Persuading guests to keep drinking was thus an art form. When Rostislavov returned to Tuma from the academy in St. Petersburg and told his friends and relatives that he would not drink alcohol at all, they were dumbfounded and incredulous, and the men and women of his acquaintance made every effort and exerted every pressure imaginable to get him to drink anyway.]

I will now go on to the way holidays were celebrated in our home. My mother was never drunk. I don't remember her ever drinking vodka, and even grape wines she would drink only in the most moderate amounts, to show her respect for the host, and usually she did not even drink those. My father would drink both vodka and punch, but with restraint. Sometimes he would go for several months and

---

* As of the 1834 census, Stefan Nikitin, 40, priest of Podlipki, was married to Elizaveta Vasil'eva, 38, and had a 19-year-old son who was attending the Riazan seminary as well as 3 younger children. Podlipki was a small settlement, with 8 households, 45 residents, and 1 church.

even years without drinking any alcohol. I remember exceedingly few cases when he got drunk, and those occurred because he had gradually given in to zealous hosts. Furthermore, he frequently received the visits of landowners and officials who had refined manners, and by associating with them he adopted many genteel habits. Finally, he himself quite disliked the nonsense that the clergy permitted themselves at their parties and drinking bouts. Because of that, there was no outrageous behavior when holidays were celebrated at our home, or even at our relatives' when Father was there, or at least it did not happen often. Sometimes my late grandfather would permit himself old-fashioned jokes, but he would fall silent when he met with disapproval, and later he gave them up entirely. Then there was the priest from Parakhino, our distant relative Ivan Antonovich, who liked to have a good time, but he was a good-natured and simple old man and, even when drunk, was merely funny. Only Uncle Stepan Nikitich would become intolerable when he was lit up, but they would use force if necessary to get him to calm down.

Although outrageous behavior was not welcome in our home, they still felt that they had to entertain guests as well as possible. On patronal and other holidays, after the guests had risen, washed up, and prayed to God, before tea, they would be served a glass of vodka; then they would have tea, and each would be served some punch. This was followed by a very copious breakfast, after which vodka was served, but not in large amounts. Between breakfast and lunch, if the guests did not go to visit one of the neighbors, time was spent in conversation. My uncle Vasilii Martynovich in particular was a master at arousing general mirth.[27]* Grandfather himself would die laughing when he heard him, and would sometimes say, "My goodness, how do you do it, where do you find the words, you joker?" Father knew many funny stories and was well-read and a master at telling tales, but his conversations were absorbing rather than amusing. Lunch would be copious, of course, for my mother was inventive in preparing a broad variety of dishes. Father would serve vodka, white wine, and infusions, but the latter only on special occasions. Naturally, many would leave the table tipsy, but I say again that nonsense or outrageous behavior were exceedingly rare, and when these occurred, something was done about it right away. After lunch, almost all would lie down to sleep; only the women would find a quiet place some-

---

* Born around 1800, he had left the seminary in 1820 to become deacon in Prudki. By the 1834 census, he was a widower, apparently childless, and still holding the same position.

where in the annex, sit together, and exchange their news with each other. After their naps, in the evening, people would have tea. Punch would be served two or even three times, but always in small teacups, so a pair of such servings could hardly compare with one glass. When they were finished drinking tea, they would go to other houses if they had been invited. Toward dinnertime, they would all come back. Dinner was copious, of course, and vodka and white wine were not forgotten. After dinner, they would sometimes carry on long conversations or play cards, but never for money—my father could not stand that. If there were many guests, they would go to sleep on the floor of the "mansion" or in the upstairs cabin,* but straw or hay were rarely brought in because Father had a supply of several feather beds and so-called traveling rugs (large, white strips of felt).

I was at home and attended the wedding feast when Natal'ia, the oldest of my sisters, was given in marriage to Ivan Filippovich Voskresenskii, a teacher at the district church school in Sapozhok. The wedding took place on the Sunday immediately before Shrovetide, so the wedding celebration coincided with the Russian carnival. [. . .] Almost all the guests celebrated the wedding for just about the entire week. Even though the two wildest Russian celebrations were here combined, and spirits of course were high, no outrageous scenes were permitted. The day after the wedding, not only was my sister's shirt not shown around and there was no smashing of pots or jugs, but Father did not even have the bathhouse heated—that deviation from the supposedly sacred customs of the shameless old times made him seem like a kind of heretic or schismatic. For an entire week, the feasting was as merry as could be.

During the day, in addition to tea, breakfast, and lunch, the main pastime was driving sleighs. There were about fifteen horses in our courtyard, ours and the guests'. They were harnessed by threes or in pairs, and to each shaft-bow was attached at least one little bell if not two. In this way, four to five troikas or six to seven pairs would go out at one time, joined by some villagers from Tuma on their horses. They would sometimes ride on the village street, but there they had little space, so mostly they would drive across the fields and through the neighboring hamlets. They did not usually go slowly, but instead, where the road permitted it or the snow was not too deep, they would start chasing each other. Here, their Russian audacity showed itself in full force: they gave their horses the reins, let them run

---

* See pp. 82–83

freely, and drove them on with shouts and whips, but the horses themselves were also fired up and did not want to concede victory to each other. The men would stand on their feet and wave their hats; the women and girls were frightened at first but would then sit back and relax. All were tearing along, flying, utterly heedless of the risk of being hurled out of the sleigh. Of course, people were chosen as drivers who were healthy, strong and sober. They were in any case in control of the horses and only gave them the freedom to run as fast as they could, but when the horses needed to be stopped, they would turn off to the side where the snow was deep and naturally would soon come to a halt. Going through hamlets, they usually would not drive very fast but instead sing songs, and many people would come out into the street. Once they had reached the fields, they would race again or at least resume a fast trot. There I experienced for myself that fast driving, especially with a troika, has a kind of bewitching effect on a Russian, and nothing seems to matter anymore, life itself is worth but a kopeck, just so long as you can keep racing so fast it makes your head spin.

In the evenings we had fun in a different way, playing cards and various other Russian village games, but our favorite pastime was singing wedding and other songs. My sisters had beautiful voices, and they would invite their girlfriends and be joined by other men and women. And when the whole harmonious, lively chorus would take up some catchy song, "your feet would start tapping," as they say, but there was no dancing, for my father neither liked nor allowed it.

CHAPTER TEN

Household Work

• When we moved to Tuma, my father became the senior priest and district superintendent there, and he was already around thirty years old, yet neither he nor my mother at once became the full masters in the house they owned. Among the clergy at that time, or at least among many of its members, the same custom prevailed that survives to the present in peasant families. Here, the old man and old woman—the father or grandfather, and the mother or grandmother—rule until the day they die, unless they voluntarily step down, even if their children are the actual householders, hold honored positions [as elected community leaders] such as foreman *(starshina)* or elder *(starosta)*, support the family entirely by their own labor, and so on. I knew Ivan Maksimovich, the bailiff of the hamlet of Korobovskaia in the parish of Dmitrovskii Pogost, a sprightly, intelligent man who was the despot of his estate. Yet this very despot occupied only second place at home, where his father, a man over seventy, would not let him take charge of anything. "In the estate office or the communal assembly, you're the bailiff," the old man would say, "but here I'm the head of the family, and you'll do as I tell you." Something of that sort also went on in our family: in managing the household, Father and Mother had elders over them, whom they had to obey

Village households divide their work into two parts, called the women's household and the men's household. Women's work includes taking care of those domestic animals whose meat or other products are used for food (cows, sheep, swine, chickens, geese, and so on) as well as preparing and storing cheese, butter and milk, and—the most important thing—managing the kitchen. In this department, so to speak, the mistress of the house is the commander. Men's work includes looking after the horses and all the field work; here the master is the one giving the orders.

In our home in Tuma, the mistress at first was my great-grandmother, Grandfather's mother Avdot'ia Mikhailovna, who already had over seventy years "on her shoulders." Even so, she was a tireless worker who would get up earlier than almost anyone else, make sure the cows were milked and sometimes milk them herself, in the summer she would often drive our livestock out to graze with the other livestock of the village, and she would decide what food should be prepared that day. She would not leave the stove once it was lit; some foods she would prepare by herself, others she would assign to someone else, and both Grandmother and Mother were admitted only as helpers and advisers. During lunch and dinner, she almost never sat down at the table, instead pouring cabbage soup into the pot, cutting up the beef, preparing the porridge, and so on, and sometimes she would even serve up the food. Don't think that anyone forced her to do this—no, my late great-grandmother was not one who could take orders from someone else. She was a woman of extremely tough, unbending character who kept all her direct descendants under her thumb; even Grandfather was a little scared of her and did what she said. On the other hand, both Mother and Grandmother would have been happy if the old woman had transferred control over the household to them, because she did not much like to take advice from anyone, paid no heed to any needs that were new to her, and kept everything in her hands the old-fashioned way. She was in charge because she was accustomed to it and considered it both her duty and her right. I am amazed even now when I think of how she would walk across the muddy courtyard, barefoot and slightly stooped, and shout at the workwomen or the workman. Here, she would drive the sheep into the shed. There, she would milk the cow or check whether it was being done right. Almost every evening, she would count the sheep, lambs, chickens, and so on. She would strain the milk and crawl into the outdoor cellar to set up the milk jugs or have someone else do it in front of her, and so on. She was always busy, allowing herself to rest only after lunch and at night, and she almost always slept on the stove without ever spreading anything under herself.

She even, as the Russian saying has it, "died in midstride." [Following a popular custom,] she would, as a very old woman, go to confession and receive communion every six weeks and, so to speak, permanently prepare to die. On the eve, or actually the very day of her death, she was active as was her habit; she had merely been saying for two or three days that she was growing tired quickly, but still she was running the entire household. After dinner, she stayed with Mother, the bought girls, and my oldest sister in the cabin, where they were spinning. Great-grandmother climbed onto the stove and apparently went to sleep. Suddenly, she began to snort strangely, which the girls found funny, so they started laughing. But Mother made them stop and, when the same snorting recurred several times, she decided to examine the old woman with a light. When she looked at her and saw with horror that a deathly pallor was spreading across her face, she began rubbing the dying woman's temples and gave orders for Grandfather and Father, who were sleeping in the annex, to be awakened at once. They came running, and when they lifted her from the stove she was still alive but unconscious. Following custom, they laid her down in the icon corner and placed a burning wax candle in her hands; she was still breathing, but after a few minutes she died. I was sleeping in the annex that night when I awoke and saw Father looking very grave. "You've slept long enough," he told me, "our grandmother has died." I was puzzled by these words, and could not figure out which of our grandmothers—his or mine—had passed away, since I had seen both of them in good health just the evening before. How could one of them have died? When I reached the cabin, I saw the deceased who had already been properly arranged. The Psalter was being read over her, and a few strangers were already standing about who had come to gaze upon the deceased and mourn her death. They made me kiss her. For the first time in my life, I kissed a dead person, and touching the cold lips seemed somehow strange and terrifying to me. I was sorry that she had died. Although she had been querulous, for some reason she had loved me and often indulged me, giving me some milk to drink separately from the others, or a bone with some meat still on it, or discreetly slipping some goodies into my hand. Altogether, her funeral was an important event for me. For the first time, I saw a death in my own home, and, both at home and in church, I watched with curiosity the various rites and traditions with which it is our custom to see off the deceased on their final voyage.

[After Great-grandmother's death, and with Grandmother Fekla Akimovna being sickly and losing her eyesight, Mother became the head of the women's part of the household. This meant that she alone had to spin, weave, and sew the clothing for the entire household. She also directed the home schooling of their six children, though Rostislavov, by the time he was seven or eight, was expected to help his younger siblings learn to read and to babysit the youngest.]

My sisters, however, spent little time on scholarship and reading, and that mostly between the ages of five and seven. At that time they were learning to read, that is, they would read through and learn the alphabet, the Book of Hours and the Psalter. Later, they would also learn to write, little by little, to while away the time, on holidays, sometimes by teaching themselves. For that reason you could not expect them to be like the girls of the urban clergy and show much intellectual curiosity when they were young. Only my oldest sister liked reading books in the civil print even before she got married. Once they were married, however, hardly any of my sisters were averse to listening to a book or reading it themselves, and not only saints' lives. Talking with their brothers, getting to know noble landowners, the ideas that were spreading about the vital importance of education, their own sons who returned from school and talked about what they had learned, and so on—all of that awakened their curiosity. My sister Mar'ia was even quite familiar with European geography and all of them knew Biblical history quite well, a knowledge that my sister Aleksandra very ably passed on to her own children.

At the age of seven and sometimes even six, my sisters were put to work on women's tasks or handicrafts, especially spinning, and that is where I will begin. For the purposes of the household tasks of my sisters, and indeed almost all village women and girls, the year was divided into two parts: the "working season," when the field work and other agricultural activities took place, and the "nonworking season," when there was little or no such work to be done. When the nonworking season began, in September or October, they would usually sit down on their *donets* by their distaff to spin.* Initially, as it always is with children, my sisters themselves wanted to start spinning, especially once they grew tired of learning to read. At first they were taught little by little how to spin, but by age seven or eight each of them had become a pretty good spinner. It may be that they sometimes became tired of spending entire days sitting on the donets, but by then getting away was difficult. Each one usually received lessons and was held accountable if she was careless. But by age ten or eleven they were already becoming very competitive in their work—each wanted to spin as much and as well as possible, and they were prepared to sit up all night. When that occurred, Mother sometimes had to force them to go to bed to protect their health.

I have to admit that I also enjoyed being there when they were at work. At the time when I was finishing my seminary education, it

---

* A *donets* is a wooden board, several feet in length and a few inches wide, that lies flat on the ground. One end curves upward and supports the distaff, a wooden staff whose cleft end holds the flax from which the thread is drawn.

would happen that my four sisters, Mother, the two bought girls, the old woman Praskov'ia, and sometimes even Grandmother before she lost her eyesight, would all be sitting at their distaffs. It was fun to watch the seven or eight spinners, spread across all the benches, pinching the flax on the distaffs with their left hand and drawing it out into a thread, while their right hand turned the spindle around which the finished spun thread was wound. They usually did not sit in silence, but instead talked, joked, and above all sang songs. The latter especially happened in the evenings. I already mentioned that my sisters had very good voices. Both bought girls, especially Tat'iana, sang masterfully, and even Mother, when she was younger, did not refuse to add her excellent voice to the general chorus. And so, it would happen that six or more of them would start singing soulful Russian songs, with harmony, dignity, and emotion, and you would listen spellbound. No wonder that almost all of us would gather by torchlight in the cabin in the evenings to listen to them— that is how I first discovered my love for Russian songs, which has not left me even in my old age. Sometimes they grew tired of songs, or they were not permitted to sing them, for example during fasts. Then someone would tell Russian tales, of which my mother knew many. Grandfather also sometimes told about life in the olden days. However, I was not always an idle spectator and listener. My sisters liked it very much when I wound the thread they had spun into skeins; for the Christmas season, when I came home from the seminary, they would ready their cops, that is, the thread that had been wound around the spindle during spinning, and I rarely refused to wind the thread into a skein.

Spinning ended at the beginning of spring, around or after Easter, and they would prepare their looms to weave linen. From Easter until St. Peter's Day* and sometimes almost until September there was weaving in our house, on not just one, but even two or three looms. [. . .]

Even those persons of the female sex who were not sitting at the loom did not remain idle. Some unwound the skeins onto "drums" (cylinders made from tree bark), some wound the thread from these drums onto a thin rod, that is, wound them onto spools that were used for the filling in weaving linen fabric. But most were occupied with sewing linens *(bel'e)* and also with plaiting lace and making designs with all sorts of needlework. Another handicraft that was considered indispensable for unmarried girls was knitting stockings with five needles and with one [needle]. I, too, knew how to knit with

* June 29.

five needles and sometimes knitted mittens for my hands when I was at the church school.

Nor were my sisters excused from washing linens and even floors. In the annex, the floor was usually washed on Saturdays, though not every week, but in the kitchen it was done only before Easter, the Christmas holidays, the patronal festivals and any particularly festive occasion. Hunched over and barefoot, with rags and brooms in their hands, my sisters and the bought girls would wash the floors. As for the linens, almost the entire female part of the family was involved in washing them at home and especially by the little river. As long as she was in good health, even Mother would go with them the two versts from the village to the river Narma, past the hamlet of Kabanovo, where she would wash clothes by hand and pound them with a wash-board* just like the others. Truth be told, none of us lived like lords.

The dress of the female half of our family was not poor, but neither was it very rich. [Grandmother would wear traditional village clothes, particularly the *kokoshnik* (a tiaralike female headdress) and *suknia* (a colorful, sleeveless dress that was made of coarse cloth and buttoned in the front), but never cotton print dresses. Mother, on the other hand, apparently never wore the kokoshniki that were part of her trousseau, and in Palishchi and initially in Tuma she wore a suknia only for everyday use around the house but printed cotton dresses for special occasions. Later on, she abandoned these old-fashioned clothes completely and wore only cotton, woollen, and even silk dresses. On her head she never wore a cap or hat, but always a kerchief. The sisters dressed in the same way as their mother.]

I might as well also tell you what sort of dandy I was. I must say that I never was, nor did I even know how to be, a dandy. My parents were burdened with a huge family—they had to prepare trousseaus for five daughters and provide for the school and seminary education of four sons—so expecting them to dress us "like lords" would have been absurd.

[Except for special occasions, Rostislavov wore typical village garb—long, tuniclike shirts *(rubakhi)* and long johns, both made from homespun linen, as well as traditional peasant coats. He was already a seminary student when he received his first nankeen cotton pantaloons (more elegant, close-fitting trousers) and his first frock coat made from store-bought, factory-made cloth.]

---

* The wash was wrapped around a cylindrical roller *(skalka)* and then cleaned by pressing the roller against a flat, corrugated washboard *(valek)*.

CHAPTER ELEVEN

Agricultural Work

• As I explained in the preceding chapter, my mother became the head of the female part of the household long before Grandmother died. That was not the case with Father. Of course, the house where we lived was his inalienable property, and of course, he was the actual (temporary) owner of the piece of church land that was his share as priest, while Grandfather was only a retired priest who had transferred the house to the full possession of his successor and had no rights even, so to speak, to a single plot of land. Regardless, the actual master and virtually autocratic ruler of the house in agricultural matters was Grandfather. That is easy to explain. Grandfather's character was hard, one might say unbending, and he was neither fond nor even really capable of deviating from his convictions and habits. For over thirty years, in Sheianki and Tuma, he had been the absolute master of his house; only in the women's department of the household had there been any limitation to his power. To have placed him in a different, dependent position in this respect, or even to have freed him from all work obligations out of respect for his age, strikes me even now as unthinkable, for life would have become an ordeal for him.

And in fact, truth be told, it was difficult to find anyone who was (by village standards) a better, more energetic, more experienced householder. His experience gave him an outstanding knowledge of when and how particular kinds of work needed to be done, and in this regard he was the oracle of the entire village. "Isn't it time to start plowing or planting?" a young member of some family would ask. "What are you worrying about that for?" his old father would respond, "Father Martyn hasn't started yet." But when Father Martyn started to plant or plow, it was like an order to the entire village to start the same work.

This opinion about Grandfather among his fellow villagers was bolstered by the fact that experience often enabled him to divine whether the weather would be bad or good the next day. His best barometer was his lower back, which he had overstrained through excessively hard work when he was young. When it hurt, that told him that bad weather was coming. There was also the setting and rising of the sun, the greater or lesser redness of the clouds at the morning and evening twilight, the varying positions of the moon, and many other, so to speak, meteorological signs that sometimes gave him the opportunity to pass for a prophet, although it cannot be denied that he sometimes also made mistakes. For some reason he particularly liked to try to discern the onset of bad or good weather by watching certain birds, such as magpies, crows, and swallows. If a magpie flew to the threshing floor and started chirping in a particular way, Grandfather would be delighted: "There, thank God, tomorrow will be a fine day." But the cawing of crows and the swift flight of swallows close to the ground meant bad weather. And so, the magpie was Grandfather's favorite, while he could not stand crows and swallows.

Furthermore, not only did he know how to do this or that kind of work, but he was an expert, a real artist so to speak, at each one, and proud of it. Not many could stack grain more skillfully than he, mow a meadow more cleanly, scatter rye, oats, and so on more evenly when planting the fields, dry out a drying barn better and more safely,* and so on. He was tirelessly active and utterly incapable of remaining idle. When there was a job to be done, he would choose the hardest part or try to serve as a model for everyone else. At mowing time, he would take the lead and, depending on the circumstances, he would not miss an opportunity to mock or reprimand others who failed to keep up with him. [Similarly, he made great exertions when the grain was threshed, and often did not trust others to do the arduous, complicated, and unpleasant work of moving the grain into the stiflingly hot drying barn, despite the entreaties of the others and his own excruciating back pain.]

When there was no work to be done in the fields, especially in the winter, he would be in the cabin, making and fixing rakes, repairing flails, twisting rope, or examining and repairing the horse's harness. When those jobs were not needed, he would walk or drive into the forest, where he might have his eye on an oakling that was good for a *padubka*—that was the term for the short part of the flail—or on a birch tree that was suitable for making shafts or torches; both trees would need to be felled. In our courtyard, he would examine and repair the sleigh and the cart. Even on holidays, he would set off across

---

* Inside the drying barn, the sheaves of grain were dried during the night over a fire that burned in a pit dug beneath the building.

the field to check whether the cattle had damaged the crops, inspect the shoots of the vegetables, see whether the rye and oats were almost ripe, whether it was time to start mowing hay, and so on. When it was harvest time, he would walk across the grain fields, here pick up and put back a sheaf that had fallen from a small shock,[28*] there rearrange a small shock that was crooked or collapsed. In the field he would keep an exact count of everything. He knew how many haycocks were in every meadow, how many small shocks of grain in the grain field, even the total number of sheaves of oats or rye that had been harvested. With him, nothing went to waste; even if no more than two or three dozen pounds of unripe grass could be mowed on some meadow, he would still mow it, stack it up around him, and move it somewhere else where there was more hay.

It should be easy now to see whether my grandfather could have taken on a subordinate role in the very household that he had ruled for several decades. Could he have remained idle and sat around, in his expression, "with his arms folded"? And if he took on a job, whom would he have found worthy enough to accept being subordinate and dependent on him? No, he needed to either be the unrestricted commander, the autocratic ruler, or do nothing at all. Since the latter was unthinkable for him, the only option was to take command of everything. That outcome was favored by the fact that Father was distracted by his duties as district superintendent and the need to be prepared at any time to receive officials and nobles, so he could not constantly be in charge of, and supervise, the work in the fields.

Grandfather, who retained control over our agricultural work and set an example of energy and skill in every activity, would become indignant if he noticed lack of effort, sloppiness, or inconsistency in people's work, and, in keeping with his character, he was not one (as the saying goes) to "whisper into his fist," but instead would make clear his annoyance to absolutely anyone without beating around the bush. Anyone who was at all able had to go out to work. Being absent or even just coming late prompted a stern reprimand, especially when for some reason the job needed to be finished in a hurry. In those cases, Father would also catch it. If he failed to show up for some reason, Grandfather would not hold back: "Why isn't he coming? Go tell him to hurry up," he would say as he sent somebody, "there's no time to lose."

---

* After grain was harvested but before it was removed from the field, it was gathered in small shocks *(krestets)* of 13 sheaves *(snop)*, bundled and placed on end; 4 small shocks would be combined to form 1 large shock *(kopna)*.

In extreme situations, even guests might catch it. I have particularly strong memories of one such episode. The grass on the threshing floor had been mowed before St. Elijah's Day,* but the constant bad weather had prevented us from stacking it into haycocks. However, on St. Elijah's Day and the day after, the weather turned beautiful. On the holiday itself, Grandfather left everyone alone, but the next morning he began insisting that the hay be gathered up. We had plenty of guests, but, truth be told, the closest relatives were Grandfather's sons or sons-in-law. They began arguing with the old man to allow another day for partying, but he would not listen and went to break up and dry the grass with the help of the workman and the other farm hands. Meanwhile, the townsman Sazanov, a relative of ours, had invited Father and his guests over, and I too went along. It was already after lunch. We were sitting around and talking when Grandfather suddenly came in wearing the same clothes that he wore when working on the threshing floor, that is, only a shirt and long johns, and barefoot. "You've been sitting around here long enough," he said categorically. "It's getting cloudy out, and if we don't rake up the hay before it starts raining, it'll all spoil." We began arguing and making excuses, especially as his concern about rain was not really justified. But Grandfather absolutely wanted to gather up all the hay, which he could not do with only the farm hands and my sisters. He again firmly demanded that we all go. "And you have no business sitting around here, either," he added, speaking to the guests, his sons, sons-in-law, daughters, and so on. "Let's all go. We can celebrate later." There was nothing we could do. We all got up, said goodbye to the host who had just begun serving tea, went back home, took off our holiday clothes, and went for our rakes. All the hay was gathered in haycocks, and it was only in the evening at home that we finally sat down for tea.

[. . .] Only in one situation would Grandfather lose his poise as commander: he was terribly afraid of thunder. He shared and proclaimed the traditional belief that thunder was caused by the Prophet Elijah riding in the clouds in his flaming chariot and pursuing the Evil One with his red-hot arrows. When Father was still in the seminary, in the philosophical or theological class,† Grandfather was taking him to Riazan and they had stopped for lunch in the hamlet of Kel'tsy. Afterwards, Grandfather went ahead on foot and told Father to grease the cart, hitch up the horses, and catch up with him. While Father tarried,

---

* Elijah's Day is July 20.

† The last 4 years of the 6-year seminary education. This episode must have occurred between 1805 and 1809.

storm clouds began to gather. Since he knew how frightened his father was of thunder, he left the village and hastened to catch up with him as quickly as possible. From afar, he saw that Grandfather was walking with haste. Father drove up to him and asked:

"Father, sir, why are you in such a hurry?"

"What? You mean you don't see the clouds and hear the roar of the Prophet Elijah?"

Being a seminarian, my father knew a thing or two about what actually caused thunder and lightning, and he also seems to have wanted to have some fun. "Oh, come on, Father, there's no Prophet Elijah in there. And even if there were, why be afraid of him? As far as I'm concerned, let him make noise, what do I care? Here, have a seat."

Grandfather had in fact been about to climb onto the cart, but when he heard these words, which he considered blasphemous, he ran away from the cart and, despite all my father's entreaties, the old man would not sit with him until the clouds had gone away. Later, whenever we would start talking about that incident, Grandfather would say with a smile, "I thought, for sure, that the Prophet Elijah was going to kill you, Vaniusha." This fear of thunder stayed with Grandfather until the end of his life.

[Boys aged six or seven would help carry sheaves of grain from one section of the barn to another. Ten- and eleven-year-olds, for whom Grandfather made special child-size rakes, helped gather the grain in the fields after it had been mowed. Children also took part in threshing. In all these activities, the children initially took part out of curiosity, but soon their participation would come to be expected. All available workers were mobilized to help mow the grass in the meadows. It was then gathered into haycocks, which in turn were consolidated into tall haystacks—those jobs involved very hard labor and spending all day in the meadows, in the heat, with little opportunity for food, drink, or rest. Another labor-intensive job that required every available worker was threshing, which began when the rye was brought in from the fields and was usually finished by mid to late September. Threshers were awakened around two or three in the morning and went to the barn. They would form teams, each of which took on a quantity of sheaves that were arrayed on the floor. To thresh one row of sheaves of rye, each person had to strike three hundred to four hundred very powerful blows with the flail. After this exhausting work, the grain had to be collected, separated from the straw and chaff, and transported to the granary. Reaping rye and oats was done with a sickle and was considered women's work that the men regarded as beneath their dignity.]

Since my sisters belonged to the female half of mankind, they, like the others, would work at reaping both rye and oats. Fortunately for them, we were able to assemble so-called teams of helpers *(pomochi)*. To explain that expression, I should point out that the parishioners assisted the clergy, especially the priest, when there was work to be done. Under Emperor Paul, this assistance was turned into a labor obligation, and many clergymen all but ruined forever their good relations with their parishioners by summoning the men or women just as a noble landlord might, and feeding them badly; indeed, some gave them neither bread nor kvass, and the workers were expected to bring everything along themselves. For that reason, when this labor obligation was abolished after Alexander I ascended the throne, the parishioners in many places began to refuse to provide any sort of labor assistance. But Grandfather and many other priests in the Meshchora succeeded in preserving the old tradition by being friendly to their workers and providing refreshments, so that after Emperor Paul's death the peasant men and women continued to come to help them with work in the fields and elsewhere.

[Such community help was used for a variety of tasks, but especially for reaping. In those cases, Father would tour the parish households at sunrise, before the peasants left for the fields, and recruit up to forty or sixty women. The women usually welcomed the opportunity to work for the priest, since the work was not exhausting, the atmosphere among the reapers was merry, and the priest's family provided plenty of food, some vodka with breakfast and lunch, and enough vodka with dinner that the women were usually tipsy. That would be followed by outdoor singing and dancing. Finally, the group would slowly wander back to the village, often joined by the young men and pausing for further singing and dancing. Another job in which the villagers, both women and men, helped the priest was transporting manure and spreading it in the fields. The job of breaking up the dungheaps (which were left to build up for a year) and loading the manure onto carts was particularly difficult, filthy, and unappealing. Other aspects of farm work included plowing, sowing, and harrowing, weeding the flax fields, watching the geese and swine, and so on. The children were also sent into the woods for mushrooms, which grew within one to three versts of home, or berries, for which they would sometimes walk five to ten versts each way.]

Once I was fourteen or fifteen, I was no longer sent out to gather berries, but my sisters, who counted on my male strength, would always urge me to go with them and protect them from the village boys and girls who, in words if not actions, liked to pick on the priest's daughters. [. . .]

A worker like me, especially when I was over sixteen, had to hurry home [from the seminary in Riazan] as soon as vacation began. After my first year in rhetoric,* I stopped on the way home at the house of Stepan Nikitich, my uncle in Podlipki, and stayed with him until St. Elijah's Day, that is, only three or four days. But when I arrived home on the actual holiday, I received a very unfriendly welcome from Father and Grandfather. "What took you so long? You mean you don't know how much work we have around this time?" and so on. I never made that mistake again. At vacation time, my parents and Grandfather awaited me as a reliable worker. My sisters were also happy about my coming because I was quite a humorist, and my jokes would make them laugh even when the work was hard. Father and Mother liked my effort and skill at farm work, and they loved and praised me for that, and Grandfather was delighted about me, except, of course, when I annoyed him by arguing or clowning around. Toward the end of my vacation, in the second half of August, he would try just about every day to thresh as much as two drying barns would hold. "We have to thresh all we can while he's still here," he would say, pointing at me, "because when he leaves, it'll be like losing my right hand." Often, for that reason, I would leave for Riazan only by September 5 or 6. "Nobody studies there anyway during that time, you're just hanging around town," Grandfather would say, "so you might as well stay here with us and thresh."

One time, the old man even said that he wished to see me get settled in a job as soon as possible. In Tuma, the deacon Ivan Pimenov had died. Grandfather now suggested to Father and Mother that I be appointed to that position, which meant leaving the seminary.

"What kind of idea is that, Father," my parents responded, "you know he's a good student and would be breaking off his studies for no reason. Why take away his happiness?" "Come on now!" Grandfather objected. "What, is being deacon in Tuma such a bad position? Better than many priests'. And you'd both be living together, in one household, you'd have two shares of farmland, the priest's and the deacon's, and I'd be in charge of everything. The grain we'd have! Come, Vaniusha and daughter-in-law, do what I tell you—I mean it,

---

* The first 2 years in the seminary.

life will be glorious." But they would not obey the old man, and later, to his great regret, they sent me to the academy.

You would usually be so busy with various chores that you hardly noticed how all six vacation weeks went by. Truth be told, you would often be tired when you came back from the field or the threshing floor; sometimes you would be so exhausted you could barely drag yourself home, had a quick supper, and went straight to bed. During my last years at the seminary, I developed lower-back pains, not from hemorrhoids—I was not yet acquainted with those—but from the way that, all fired up and overestimating your strength, you would lift excessive weights or overstrain yourself threshing, stacking hay with a pitchfork, and so on. By the end of the vacation, your face would be tanned and take on a harsh sort of color, and your hands would bear the traces of many calluses. And yet, almost no time of my life was better for my health. Of course, you would get tired, but then, lunch and dinner were magnificent. How sweet it was, going to sleep and sleeping all night without waking or even turning over from one side to the other! They would have trouble awakening you, and you would be incredulous that the entire night had gone by and it was already time to get up again; it would feel as though you had just gone to bed, and still, you would get up with your strength refreshed, your head clear, and a healthy appetite. When you got back in Riazan, your schoolmates would be amazed at how fresh and full your face looked. "Wow, you sure must have eaten well and relaxed at home," some joker would say. "Your mother must have fed you nothing but pancakes *(bliny)* and flat cakes *(lepeshki)*."

And the joy I felt in my soul! Father might say, "Thanks, Mitia, for all the work you've done. We couldn't have done it without you." Not to mention Mother—it was a rare day when she did not thank me for my labor, with her eyes if not with words. Even my stern grandfather, demanding as anyone could be and forever dissatisfied, might say, "Hey, Mitia, you're a great guy! Stay with us for a while longer—without you, it's as if I'd lost my own hand." Also, what pleasure you feel upon finishing some difficult job that requires prolonged effort, when, for example, you see that all the sheaves have been carried to the threshing floor and stacked in *odon'ia.*[*] How good it felt, after threshing the grain from the drying barn, to walk into the granary carrying a sack with three or four measures of rye or oats, and to see that the grain bin that had been empty two weeks earlier was now full, and soon we

---

[*] A stack of 25 to 40 large shocks (between 1,000 and 2,000 sheaves) of grain.

would need to use a different granary! With a touch of pride, I would feel that I, too, had made my contribution, and that, as the Russian saying has it, "I had earned my keep," that I did not eat my bread for free during my vacation. Oh yes, those were truly glorious times! Never was I as cheerful, content, and healthy as then. Who knows—maybe Grandfather spoke the truth when, in suggesting that I be made deacon in Tuma, he said that we would live wonderfully?

When Father heard that I had been chosen for the academy, he personally came for me to Riazan. When he and I arrived back at home, it was already night, but Grandfather, although he had been sleeping, got up and joined us. After blessing and kissing me, he asked Father in an odd tone of voice:

"Well, is that it, thank God?"

With a peculiar smile whose meaning I initially did not understand, Father said, "That's it, Father, thank God."

"Well," Grandfather added as he crossed himself, "thank God, for I already thought the boy was about to leave us for St. Pete."

Then my father said, jokingly, "You go ahead and ask him, Father."

"What," the old man objected a little nervously, "you mean it's all over?"

"It's over, sir," Father answered.

"Then why did you go—didn't I tell you not to let him?"

The issue was that the difference between the ecclesiastical and the medical academy was not very clear to the old man; what mattered most was that both were in Petersburg and whoever went there ceased to live in the village. He was sorry to lose in me the splendid worker that he thought I was. "Well, isn't that a pity! Not only next year, but already this year he won't be working during his vacation." Actually, both my father and mother would have preferred to see me in the Moscow academy rather than the one in St. Petersburg, since Sergiev Posad was not far from Tuma* and I could come home during vacations; in addition, someone from the family could probably have dropped in at the academy. Petersburg, on the other hand, was then God knows how far—almost beyond thrice-nine lands, in the thirtieth kingdom.[29]†

---

* The Moscow Ecclesiastical Academy was located at the Trinity St. Sergius Monastery in Sergiev Posad, 120 miles northwest of Tuma. St. Petersburg, by contrast, is over 500 miles away.

† An expression that means "unimaginably far away." The number "thrice-nine" is derived from an archaic, pre-decimal number system that counted by nines.

CHAPTER TWELVE

Community Life in Tuma

• When we moved from Palishchi to Tuma [in 1817], the latter counted only a little over fifty households, but the inhabitants belonged to a variety of estates. First place, of course, belonged to the clergy—three priests, two deacons and six sacristans. Then, fifteen households each belonged to peasants who were serfs of the nobility and to economic peasants (who later were renamed "state peasants"). Also, a few townspeople and discharged soldiers had their own households, and one of the townspeople, Sazanov, periodically registered in a merchant guild.* All these homeowners could call themselves native residents. Among the clergy, there does not seem to have been even one who did not have a father or father-in-law, and in some cases a grandfather and great-grandfather and so on, who was native to the place and, as the clergy put it, had served at the Lord's altar in Tuma. Of the townspeople, every last one was descended—either personally or through fathers and grandfathers—from the clergy of Tuma, so that it was a rare townspeople's family that was not related, and fairly closely, to some member of the clergy. Our relatives included the Sazanovs, the Sirotinins, and also Dmitrii Ivanovich, whose last name escapes me. The serfs and economic peasants may also at one time have been related to the clergy, but the memory of that time had already been lost. As for the soldiers' children, they belonged to those unfortunates who, while in active service, are in our Christ-loving army, are sung by poets, and bend their backs to the cane and the birch, but who are consigned to a life of utter destitution upon leaving the service.[30]† Our soldiers

---

* Presumably, he was an ambitious and reasonably prosperous man who hoped to escape the lowly condition of townsman but whose fortunes allowed him only in some years to pay the taxes required for claiming merchant status. Elsewhere, in a passage not included in this translation, Rostislavov mentions that Sazanov earned his money by working as a liquor-farmer's sworn official in Tuma (ch. 11, p. 74 of the Russian original).

† Men who were drafted into the army ceased to be serfs, state peasants, etc., and instead became life-long members of the military estate, as did their wives (*soldatki*) and children (*soldatskie deti*). When a

were men from Tuma who, with the help of their relatives, had managed at least to build themselves little cabins with small properties.

In addition to the native local population, there were also, so to speak, outsiders, transients, temporary residents of Tuma who came and went. The most important among these were the agents (*poverennye*) and sworn officials (*tseloval'niki*) of the liquor trade. As long as there were liquor-farmers, the agents were mostly townsmen and merchants from Kasimov. I remember one of them, Iakov Petrovich Kurbatov. He had done well by this trade, for he had a two-story stone house in Kasimov, and he himself weighed no less than 360 pounds, so his legs had a bit of trouble carrying such a massive body. During the brief interval when, under Emperor Alexander I, the liquor-farm system was replaced with direct state management, there would always be two agents from the government living in Tuma. As was proper, they were state officials, "Their Well-Borns,"* and following time-honored custom they robbed the treasury both for their own profit and for that of their superiors. I still remember two of them, Aleksandr Petrovich Storozhevskii and Ivan Stepanovich (whose last name I don't recall). When they arrived in Tuma, they were, as the saying goes, poor as church mice, and received nothing like the salaries of the excise officials of my time. However, after a year they already looked like lords, especially Aleksandr Petrovich. They soon married the daughters of noble landowners, received their dowries, and added their own "well-earned little capital." By now they have probably already ended "their earthly path," as the preachers of the church say, "and are resting from their righteous labors." Aleksandr Petrovich was even close to setting up a menagerie in Tuma—he had a fox, a wolf cub on a chain, and a bear cub that long wandered free in the street and would play together with us.

[The clerics in Tuma, aside from Father, were all drunkards. Some of the peasants and townspeople, on the other hand, were energetic, enterprising, and able at least intermittently to achieve a modest prosperity, particularly two townsmen who worked as sworn officials for liquor-farmers.]

The individuals I have described were known for their worldly and, so to speak, natural qualities. However, a large village of the Orthodox

---

man was conscripted, his wife and children (if he had any) therefore ceased to be members of the village community and were no longer entitled to a share of village land, plunging many into utter destitution.

* "Your Well-Born" was an honorific title for any noble as well as for officials and officers of a certain rank.

Russian tsardom also could not do without supernatural powers, without people who had close ties to the denizens of Hell, in a word, sorcerers. First place went to the townsman Gavrilo Khormashov, a good-natured, affable, and affectionate old man. It seems that nobody ever saw any harm coming from him, and yet almost all were convinced that he was a fearsome sorcerer who could put a hex on your grain harvest, turn people into animals, give people hernias, cause women to be possessed by demons, and so on. The reason for all these tales was probably just that he had thick, beetling eyebrows, from underneath which gazed, indeed almost gleamed, a pair of bright and expressive eyes. "Just look, honey," some gossip would say to her neighbor, "how Khormashov's eyes gleam like burning coals, as though the Devil were stoking the fire in them." And we would run away from this fearsome man. After his death, the majority of the villagers were saying—not in jest—that an aspen stake should be driven up his bottom—that was considered the surest protection against a sorcerer's rising from the grave after his death and coming back to haunt the living.[31]* When the priests did not want to accept this suggestion, they too came under suspicion, for either being too lenient toward Gavrilo or taking a bribe from his son.

Another sorcerer was the economic peasant Gavrilo Sidorov, who lived across from us. This little old man liked to drink, but if anything he was even nicer than the other Gavrilo (Khormashov), and still he was said to be a sorcerer. However, no actions were attributed to him that brought harm to others. Instead, it was only believed that hardly a night went by without the Dragon Gorynych[32]† flying to him, bringing a large quantity of milk, and pouring it into jugs that were supposed to be left in a corner of the cabin near the door. If, by mistake, the jugs were not left out, and the dragon were to arrive and not find the containers in the proper place so he could pour in the milk he had brought, he would give Gavrilo a thrashing. In addition to milk, the dragon also brought other things, even cash. If the neighbors' cows gave little milk in the morning, it meant that Gavrilo's dragon had milked them dry and taken the milk to his friend.

---

* A contemporaneous survey of Russian folk beliefs reported similar practices: "Usually, to make the sorcerer lie quietly in his grave and not haunt the living, an aspen stake is driven between the shoulders of the corpse, and that, according to popular opinion, puts an end to visitations from the [dead] sorcerer."

† The Dragon Gorynych is a stock figure of medieval Russian folklore whom the *bogatyr'* (chivalric hero) Dobrynia eventually slays in heroic combat to rescue a princess whom the dragon had abducted. The dragon is also a symbol of paganism and the devil.

Under no circumstances would any of the neighbors ever borrow milk from Gavrilo's house: "*You* take it," they would say, "it might be devil's milk." In the mornings, the gossips would whisper to one another, "Have you heard that the dragon just came to visit Gavrilo? Mar'ia saw for herself how the cursed one burst all into sparks over his house, and yesterday Agrafena visited them and saw for herself the six big, empty jugs that were set out by the corner near the door, all ready for the milk." "That's awful," the gossips would chime in, "how long is that old devil still going to be alive?"

Whenever the old man was not well, and especially if he started complaining about lower-back pains, the rumor would spread in the village that he had caught it the night before from the dragon for having forgotten to set out the jugs. "Look at that—yesterday he was doing great, but now he can't even climb off his stove; he sure caught it."

All the same, even after Gavrilo's death the dragon continued to visit his son-in-law Sergei and his daughter Agrafena. "Where do they get their money from?" the philosophers of Tuma would reason. "You know they don't do anything, they don't practice any trade, and still they have plenty of everything. Who else could be bringing it to them, if not Gavrilo's dragon?" The mystery was solved when it turned out that the worthy Sergei, who was probably not receiving the necessary aid from the dragon, was himself a thief.

Finally, in addition to the two sorcerers, there was also a sorceress, Dar'ia, wife of the economic peasant Anton Sintsov. She had her own specialty. According to her neighbors—whom most of the villagers of course believed—at night, if a storm was coming and the thunder was already rumbling in the distance, Dar'ia would throw her gate wide open, pace back and forth under the awning of the gate, and say "heeeere, chick, chick, chick," the sound you make to attract chickens. Here is what that *really* meant. As I already said, my grandfather "believed and professed" that, during a storm, the Prophet Elijah would mount his flaming chariot and hunt devils with his red-hot arrows. The devils would flee from their fearsome enemy and look for cozy little places to hide, but probably, because they were frightened, they would panic and run without thinking and not be able to find safe refuges on their own. At those critical moments, the sorcerers who were devoted to them would throw open their gates and, with their "heeeere, chick, chick, chick," invite the poor fellows to come in and hide from their pursuer. Of course, an entire legion of them would swoop down. This sort of harboring of fugitives was what Dar'ia did. Woe to her if she overslept after a stormy night and was late in taking her cows out to the village pasture. "Well, look at that," one gossip would say to another, "looks like Dar'ia hasn't brought out her cattle yet!" "She's still resting, honey," a friend would reply, "you know, it was thundering all last night and she had to receive her guests, so now she's still sleeping." And they would all start to laugh.

I should point out that there were not only sinister people in Tuma, but also sinister places nearby. The most important was one verst away, near the hamlet of Kabanovo, by a stream that was often dry and that flowed out of the so-called Nightingale Marsh. There was a bridge across the stream, and that was where the devils were especially prone to hiding. Once, my sisters and the bought servants returned home at night, in extreme terror, from the little river Narma where they had done the laundry. All of them were frightened and told how they had almost been seized by devils in the Nightingale Marsh. Such tales were repeated very often when it was not wintertime. [In fact, the space under that particular bridge served as a refuge for stray sheep and swine. The animals would become startled when a cart passed over the bridge, and the resulting noise and commotion in turn frightened the unsuspecting people in the cart, who were quick to suspect that they had encountered devils.]

So it was among these people, and devils, that we lived. Father and Mother would exchange hospitality with the clergy, but not with all equally. We were closest to Uncle Nikifor and the sacristan Ivan Nazarov, and the latter was also a relative. Of the peasants and townspeople, my parents would visit the Sazanovs, the Sirotinins, and Leont'i Maksimov. My father was on especially close terms with almost all the liquor agents, because he found their lifestyle—which was at least somewhat genteel, and sometimes very much so—far more attractive than the coarse way of life of his fellow villagers. Once I was sufficiently grown up, I would go out on visits with Father and Mother, but I didn't like being with the liquor agents and almost never went to visit them; somehow, I felt freer among clergy, townspeople, and peasants than with Their Well-Borns. As a child, however, until I was fourteen or fifteen, and also afterwards, I needed companions my age with whom I could run around, play, and have fun.

The clergy in the village had quite a few sons who were almost exactly my age: Uncle Nikifor's son Vania, Father Ivan's Andriusha, the deacon Ivan Grigor'evich's Akim, and the sacristan Mikhailo's Vasilii, whose hair was a strikingly red, flaming color. However, my cousin [Vania] was a terrible troublemaker, was naughty, had a sweet tooth, and would sometimes even steal money from his father to buy himself a spice cake or *kalach*.* I did not wish to be particularly friendly with him, nor did my parents encourage me to do so. Andriusha was a wonderful boy, but his father did not allow him to come outside often and almost always kept him in the annex. He and I became good friends in school. Besides, Vania and Andriusha did not live long. Akim was a little too dim for the education system of the time, so his father sent him to Riazan to work as an assistant in the shop of a merchant, and he later became a merchant himself. Vasilii the Red lived at the other end of the village and rarely came over to our end.

As a result, I had to become friends with the children of the townspeople, the soldiers, and the peasants. My closest friends were the soldier Simakov's son Elisei ("Liska"), the townsman Davyd Stepanovich's son Gerasim, the peasant Leont'i Maksimov's son Ermolai, Ivan Baliazin (also a peasant's son), and others. Of this group, Elisei and Ermolai later served in the Imperial Guards, the one in the Lithuanian Regiment and the other in the Horse Guards. They would come to see me when I was already a professor, especially Ermolai, who often drank tea and even had lunch with me. Father and Mother were not entirely happy with my friends. "Why don't you stay home, like Andriusha? Now there's a good boy! He doesn't act like you do." Or else, "Why do you keep spending your time with peasant kids? You should go see Andriusha and spend time with him." However, what my ardent, active nature needed was not to sit indoors but to chase around after others. It may be, of course, that I did not learn much from my plebeian friends. On the other hand, through them and through their stories about their families, I gained an excellent understanding of how our common people live, and came to love them, from the time I was a child. And that was truly of great value to me and prevented me from developing any social snobbery.

My sisters likewise had girlfriends, though it was not easy to find any among the clergy, since my uncle was just about the only one with daughters my sisters' age. Therefore, they too had to find friends for themselves among the daughters of peasants and townspeople.

On weekdays, after finishing the Book of Hours, the Psalter, and my other studies, and also after work, I might be able to find an hour here or there, in the evening or at lunch time, to run around with my friends. My sisters, however, were rarely able to leave the house and go outside on those days; at most, they might sit by the gate and work on their embroidery or some other task. On holidays and Sundays,

---

* A white, wheatmeal loaf.

on the other hand, we did not have to stay at home. Tuma was a fun-loving village whose older inhabitants liked to drink while the younger ones liked to sing and horse around. The principal gathering place for young men and women was almost right across from our house. Of course, we could have seen and heard it all from our house, but—please!—there was absolutely no way for us sit still.

Holiday fun varied depending on the season. During the entire Easter week,* people would do nothing but ring the bell in the church tower, roll eggs around like balls, hide little stacks of eggs, and so on, but no one dared, as they say, to "open his mouth to sing." And if some liberal had dared such a thing, he or she would have been regarded as almost godless, or at least an unbeliever. But the customs bequeathed by our great-great-grandparents did permit the singing of songs by the Sunday of St. Thomas. Their début was marked by so-called choral songs. Let me describe a few of them.

Typically, the older unmarried girls and young women would stand in a circle, each would join hands with her two neighbors, and they would begin to sing songs and perform a round dance. Soon a pantomime would begin, something rather like a ballet or operetta, with a chorus but no music. Some nimble young peasant wife or grown, unmarried girl would step into the middle of the circle; they were to play the role of groom or bride. If the former was required, they would take a hat or cap from one of the men sitting or standing nearby, and the young wife who had stepped into the middle of the circle would put it on. The song conveyed the groom's wish to propose to some girl, and so, with all of them singing in chorus, the young wife would approach one of the unmarried girls, throw off "his" hat, bow, and ask her to come and join him. Of course, rejections would ensue, and sometimes the hat would have to be thrown off in front of two, three, and even more girls. At the end, when at last there was a couple in the circle, they would hold hands and walk around while the chorus sang about asking permission for them to go out with each other—or even marry—from the father, mother, brother, brother-in-law, and so on. In that case, the circle would get in motion, approach the seated men and women, and open up, and the couple would come out and prostrate themselves before some older man while the chorus sang, "Give me leave, my dear," or "Bless me, my dear." Of course, after hesitating for a moment, the old man would give them leave and his blessing. The participants in the

---

* The week from Easter Sunday to the Sunday of St. Thomas.

round dance would step away and reform, change their refrain, and, in the same way as before, go over to some older woman and start asking her to give them leave and bless them. Then came the turn of the brother, the brother-in-law, and so on, for which young people were chosen. When I was a grown-up seminarian, I found myself playing the role of such brothers and brothers-in-law and especially giving up my visor cap to cover the female groom's head. Sometimes, the bride would start walking alone in the circle and choosing herself a groom. To that end they would go up to the young fellows, and if one of them did not consent, he was pushed forcibly into the circle, and then the same ceremonies that I have already described, or ones similar to them, would begin again.

These round-dance songs were sung every holiday and Sunday, and more than once. However, the young people of Tuma also had a dramatic round-dance song with a warlike theme. They would sing it only two or three times a year; it was called "To Kazan Town," for through this song, in folk-rhythm verses and to the sound of round-dance singing, they would retell Ivan the Terrible's campaign to capture Kazan.* The unmarried girls and young wives would form a huge circle, and both sing and maneuver. This is not the place to describe these maneuvers, the gist of which was that, at one point of the circle, a passage was formed over which two tall young women held their hands, and the entire round-dance party was supposed to file through these Caudine Forks† without breaking the circle. In this way, singing and maneuvering, or actually doing both at the same time, the round-dance party slowly advanced. Then the young men, who had lined up in several rows, would start moving, armed sometimes with pickets, poles, sticks, or whatever happened to be handy. At times, they also joined the chorus, stopping, advancing, and so on. In addition, a whole swarm, one might say, of little boys and girls would run ahead of the round-dance party, or else they would spin around near it, run between the rows of the men, or imitate them by arranging themselves into warlike formations of their own. Finally, the adults and even the old men and women would rise from their seats, saying, "Why shouldn't we go to Kazan Town? You know, we used to go, too, when we were young," and try to keep up with the

---

* Ivan IV ("the Terrible") led the Russian campaign to capture the Tatar city and khanate of Kazan, located on the Volga, in 1552.

† Mountain passes in Central Italy, where the Romans were defeated in a 321 B.C. battle in the Second Samnite War. The victorious Samnites humiliated the defeated Romans by making them march through a specially constructed arch. I thank Mikhail Dolbilov for this information.

others. Even the clergy would often walk with the honored elders. And so, the entire, continually growing crowd of a hundred to a hundred fifty people would advance from one end of the village to the other and finally reach the outskirts. There they would sing some victory hymn, and go home victorious. People would usually march to Kazan Town toward evening; the last entertainment of the day, it went on for an hour or more, and so it was almost always already night when the participants returned home. [Parents would normally call the young people home for dinner, but they were usually indulgent and made a special exception for this particularly beloved occasion.]

However, any round-dance songs and hymns "To Kazan Town" could be sung only until Trinity Day.* After that, even on the Day of the Holy Spirit, singing one of our songs even at home was considered a sin, a kind of heresy. I don't know what ancient council of old peasant wives issued that law, but it was scrupulously observed. I encountered deviations from it only occasionally, at wedding feasts of the clergy, where people became so tipsy that they forgot these canonical rules right along with the other ones.

Trinity Day, when round-dance singing ended, was also special for another event that recurred each year. It was prepared three days in advance, on the so-called *semik*.† On that day, a Thursday, the unmarried young women would ask each of their mothers and grandmothers to give them a few eggs, and they would go alone—without young men or even little boys—somewhere into the woods and hide the eggs in various places. On Trinity Day, almost every mother would prepare food for her daughters, such as omelets, pancakes, pies, butter, and so on. The girls would gather in a dense crowd to which the young men were now admitted as well. With loud and merry song, the entire crowd would head into the woods and the girls would find the hidden eggs, after which all would set about weaving garlands out of birch twigs and flowers. After a snack, or better, after consuming all the victuals that had been brought along—all present were invited to take part—they would return, singing and with garlands on their heads, to the village, to be welcomed by the old men and women. After that, they would sing round-dance songs without interruption until deep into the night, and almost always end by marching "To Kazan Town."

---

* Trinity Day (Pentecost) is the seventh Sunday following Easter Sunday. The next day is the Day of the Holy Spirit. In 1820, for example, with Easter Sunday falling on March 28, Trinity Day was May 16. The week that begins with Trinity Day is one of the few weeks in the Orthodox year when there are no fast days.

† The feast of the seventh Thursday after Easter.

Even when there were no round-dance songs, however, the merry folk of Tuma knew how to have fun. Of course, few were rich among the villagers, but neither were many poor—whether through labor and trade or trickery and theft, all were able to earn some money, all had enough for bread and groats *(kasha),** and therefore they were full and always merry. Even after Trinity Day, songs would still fill the street on every holiday, not round-dance songs but purely traditional Russian ones, whose tunes were either gentle and melancholy or rollicking and full of zest. Some of the voices were beautiful, especially among the women and unmarried girls. They were too civilized, in a way, to carry on in crude peasant fashion when they sang; they did not sing merely to drown each other out but developed a real sense of music that compelled them, if not to worry about harmony, then at least to notice and avoid dissonance. Not only the older locals, but also the transient liquor agents and their city-bred wives and others enjoyed listening to the songs and would give gifts of nuts and other delicacies to the women and girls who sang. Only the fall of night, and the voice of mothers calling them to dinner, would disperse the singers, male and female.

There were also various other holiday entertainments besides singing. Little boys would play checkers, also called *babki,* at which I never had much luck and which I therefore stopped playing at an early age. Furthermore, young and old played *gradki.†* Not only sacristans, but sometimes even the priests, would take part in this game. The losers were supposed to carry around the winners—that was how those played who had no money to spare. More affluent and staid folk would play for beer, which the losers would buy after each game and which they and the winners would share. Shared games for the youth of both sexes were swings and catch. Swings, up to twenty or thirty feet tall, were actually set up for Easter, but then stayed not only until Trinity Day but right until the fall, so long as some kind person replaced a torn rope with a new one. Even the solid citizens of the village were not above enjoying the swings. There were usually two ways to swing, alone or "in a bunch." The former involved fastening the rope to a small board on which someone would then take a seat. Then, using a special rope that was fastened at the middle to the rope of the swing, two attendants would swing the person, sometimes

---

* Groats are hulled grains that are broken into large fragments and cooked (e.g., oatmeal).

† A game that involves constructing a figure from pieces of wood and trying to knock it down with a stick.

making him go up very high. In the other case, the bottom of the rope was fastened to a board, at each end of which stood one person who both pushed the swing and swung himself, and another two to four people would sit on the board. If the people standing at the ends were strong, the boards would go up very high, reach an almost vertical position, then come back down very fast and rise just as high in the opposite direction. [. . .]

In Tuma there was also, one might say, a wet sort of amusement. It was sometimes played out on the Monday of Easter Week.* The unwritten code of canonical village rules required soaking every man who had not been to matins that day, especially if he belonged to the clerical estate. [In one such instance, one cold morning, he and his grandfather took refuge in the basement after they had overslept and his father had jokingly threatened to have them soaked.] But there was also another day when, according to the same unwritten code, all were supposed to get soaked, that is, have water poured over them from head to toe: that was August 1, known in the countryside as "Wet Savior Day." The soaking would begin immediately after lunch among the boys, who, by and by, were joined by more and more adult folk, and at last it turned into a general water fight. If someone gave himself up without resisting, he might have no more than a bucket poured over him. But, if someone had resisted for a long time and it had been hard to get him, well then, excuse me, they would pour ten or more buckets over him and sometimes stick him in a trough and fill it up with water. When we first started living there, not even the priests were exempted from this, though they were allowed to buy their way out with a shtof or two of beer. Later on, they and a few honored old men and women were no longer touched, but all the others were still soaked with water.

---

* I.e., the day after Easter Sunday.

CHAPTER THIRTEEN

How the Clergy
Would Tour the Parish

• In India, where the division of the people into castes has such deep roots, it is natural for every father to train his children from a young age for the trade which fate had earlier selected for him as well. As soon as they are able to make use of their arms, the tailor's son takes up the needle, and the blacksmith's son the hammer, and by increasingly honing their skills they fully master the arts of sewing clothes or forging iron. With us also, one often observes this sort of thing. The peasant usually trains his son to perform the same work by which he himself earns his bread and the means to pay his landlord and his taxes, while the merchant takes his son into the shop and shows him, verbally and by his actions, how to cheat gullible shoppers. What distinguishes us from India is that, since the abolition of serfdom, every father can prepare his son for any occupation, and the law presently does not forbid any adult to change his trade.

At least in very recent times, like the inhabitants of India and of our hamlets and towns, our clergy also liked to train their sons from an early age in what might be called their father's trade, to prepare them to become priests or deacons and sacristans when they grew up. "And how could you blame the clergy for that?" is what many ordained clergy and sacristans who are my contemporaries would say. "Is it such a bad thing to train your children from a young age, so that, in time, they will be worthy servants of the altar, worthy of proclaiming the Word of God, administering Christ's sacraments, and guiding people toward salvation in the life to come and toward fulfilling their Christian duties in this one?" For my part, I would not blame the clergy for doing this, if only the children's preparation for the pastoral calling were carried out in a sensible way and in a true Christian spirit, but that unfortunately was not the case.

Our Orthodoxy, like any positive religion, consists of three components, the dogmatic, the moral, and the ritual. Primacy must be accorded to the moral component, for what could be the use of deeply studying dogma and zealously fulfilling every conceivable ritual if man nevertheless remains immoral and comes to resemble those tombs which, in Christ's words, are beautiful on the outside but within are filled with the remains of a rotting corpse?* Dogma should serve merely as a support for the requirements of morality, in case man does not find that support in his conscience or in his heart. And ritual is meaningful and should be considered indispensable only if it enhances, inspires, and sustains a religious state of mind. Therefore, if our clergy wish to see their children as their successors, they should concern themselves principally with developing in them a sense of Christian morality, and only afterwards, or perhaps in so doing, familiarize them with religious dogmas that are accessible to a child's mind and give them the opportunity to be present when the liturgy is performed. However, under no circumstances should they regard religion as a trade, or their children as future guild members of this trade to whom this or that state of mind can be imparted mechanically. Later on, when I introduce my readers to the ecclesiastical educational institutions and the morality of the clergy, I will talk about moral education and the approach to introducing dogma, but for now I will talk about the ritual side. I feel all the more entitled to do this because, in essential ways, the clergy of my time focused their attention on the ritual side and trained their children for the practice of rituals.

Following traditions established in times long past, the clergy of my time—with a very few exceptions that started to appear later, in the second half of Nicholas's reign—devoted especially great care to training their children for the clerical calling, and for that they selected the weakest and, one might say, ugliest side of their way of life. It is well known that, in addition to the so-called church rites that are considered indispensable rather than optional—such as baptism, marriage, and burial—the clergy have the custom, on the holidays of Christ and other holidays, to visit all the households in the parish, one after another, without being invited and even against the parishioners' wishes. [. . .]

The clergy seek to give their walks about the parish at Christmas a special religious flavor by calling the practice "exalting Christ." A few enthusiastic homebred archaeologists regard this "exalting" as an imi-

---

* Matthew 23:27—"Woe unto you, scribes and Pharisees, hypocrites! for ye are like unto whited sepulchres, which indeed appear beautiful outward, but are within full of dead men's bones, and of all uncleanness."

tation of the glorification with which, so the Gospels tell us, the angels welcomed the Newborn in Bethlehem. No one knows how many minutes or hours the angelic glorification lasted, but the clergy, particularly in the villages, convey their exaltation of Christ with very few canticles, mostly just two: "Christ is Born! Glorify Him!" and "Thy Nativity, O Christ Our God." That is how the exalting of Christ usually began and how, even now in many places, the children of the clergy begin their training for the calling to which their parentage and their fathers' merits before God supposedly destine them. They would begin these studies very early, sometimes at just about the same age when they were first made to sit down with the alphabet. The future priest or sacristan would begin his service career under the leadership of his father, his older brother, or some other grown-up seminarian; sometimes, though, a group of three or more young boys would be gathered and allowed to go out alone to exalt Christ with their innocent lips, and they would be likened to the children of whom Jesus Christ said, "Forbid them not: for of such is the kingdom of God."* I should add that the fathers would let their children go by themselves only within the village, and then only if it was not very large, but they would always accompany them when they toured other hamlets.

My own exploits in this field began very early (when I was six, to be precise), when we still lived in Palishchi, and I started right away with the hamlets of the entire parish because our village consisted almost entirely of members of the clergy. Of course, I was still a small child at my début in ecclesiastical practice, but others were introduced to it even earlier. After my father had already been transferred to Tuma but had not yet moved there from Palishchi, he took me there with him at Christmastide and, together with him, Grandfather, and so on, I toured the entire parish and exalted Christ. From then on, every single year until I entered the academy, I had no way of escaping this obligation. As a result, I wandered fourteen times amongst the households of the entire parish and had the opportunity to observe all the peculiarities of these wanderings. Also, I am adding to my own observations what I have heard from others, and I will present all this material to my readers, in whose time, God willing, exalting Christ either will have been abolished entirely or will have lost the primitive, un-Christian, largely commercial or beggarly character that distinguished it particularly in my childhood.

---

* Luke 18:16—"But Jesus called them unto him, and said, Suffer little children to come unto me, and forbid them not: for of such is the kingdom of God."

It has long been common for the clergy in the towns to tour the homes of their parishioners at Christmastide, and now, so I hear, in some places the entire parish clergy walk together, the priest with the stole around his neck and the cross in his hand, and in chorus they sing and exalt not only Christ but also the householder, whom they wish "Many Years" in words and in song at the end of their canticles. In earlier times, however, and even now in most villages, exalting Christ was done quite differently. Even in a one-staff village,* where the entire clergy might consist of three people, the priest would go by himself, the deacon likewise, and the sacristans would usually go as one party.

The reason is easy to explain. The clergy have an unusually large number of children,[33]† and frequently each member of a parish's clergy has two or even four sons to take around the parish in accordance with established tradition. In a case like that, the campaign can involve a party of ten to fifteen people. That is quite a large number and may not even fit comfortably into the cabin of some peasants. Besides, every peasant finds it most important to give full satisfaction to the priest, who seems a particularly indispensable figure, while the deacon and sacristan have to content themselves with just anything. If the entire parish clergy were to walk together, the priest would lose out while the others would be the winners, for the peasant would either give the whole group a lump sum of money and they would have to divide it up according to the law, or else, if he starts giving to each separately and the priest were to ask for a supplement for himself, he might reply, "Look, Father, I don't have much left—if I give it all to you, there'll be nothing left for them." It would then be awkward for the priest to say, "Pay me first and let them go empty-handed." On the other hand, a priest who is persistent and comes alone is more likely to receive whatever he decides to ask for, as there are no rivals. When the deacon and the sacristan arrive, the peasant tells them, "Come on, it's not my fault, I already gave everything to the priest," or "I have to save it for the priest." The children would represent an additional problem. The priest would start asking on behalf of his children before it was the deacon's or the sacristans' turn, and the deacon would also try to go before the sacristans. People would start arguing and pleading, the priest—who already has his

---

* A clerical "staff" (*shtat*) consisted of one priest and the lower-ranking clergy who assisted him. Depending on the number of households it served, a village church might have one, two or (like Palishchi and Tuma) three staffs.

† The clergy had the highest rate of natural demographic increase of any estate in Russian society.

share—would start feeling bored, and possibly guilty, about sitting around, and the peasant would say, "Where am I supposed to find more money when I've already given it all to Father?" Is that what goes on when the priest goes alone with his children? No—he is completely free then, with nothing to inhibit him.

If the village had several staffs, exalting Christ almost always took place in all sections of the village. In that case, the parties were arranged differently. The priests would join together, the deacons would form a separate group, and the sacristans would split up into several parties. Walking together was very advantageous for the priests. Every priest would try, in his section of the village, to help his beloved brothers in Christ by urging his parishioners to be as generous as possible to them, since they were after all the same as he, their priest, and might substitute for him if the need arose. It is striking, however, that it was exceedingly rare in three-staff villages for all three priests to go exalting Christ together, since they almost never got along with each other. Only their material interests sometimes made them set aside their mutual hostility. In many three-staff villages of the Meshchora, not long before my retirement and also afterwards, all the priests would join together at Christmastide for a particular purpose. They found it a hassle to tour the entire parish but did not want to give up potential gains by limiting their walks just to their own section, and making up the loss by suddenly raising the fees on their own parishioners' households was also difficult because the peasants were unlikely to give in right away. So, all three priests would go together but start asking the householders to "give" to them as a group rather than to each individually. Since the leading figure was always the priest in whose section they were, the "gifts" were satisfactory. They would repeat this maneuver for two or three years, and then each priest would start touring only his section and ask for the same compensation for his labors that had previously been paid to all three. Of course, the peasant would object, but it would be pointed out to him that none of the other priests were going to come this time, that this one was collecting for all of them, and that, had the others come in person, the householder would be paying the same amount as last year and as he was being asked to pay now. The peasant would have his doubts, scratch himself, and argue, but usually give in, and thus the new tax, so to speak, went into effect.

With the parish clergy breaking up into separate parties as I have described, there could be no question of giving the exalting of Christ a fully religious character. The priests themselves never took the stole or cross with them, while the deacon and sacristans were forbidden to do so. The peasants, for their part, mostly received the exalters without the ceremonies that are required when church rites are performed. It is well known that, in those circumstances, the peasant will always initially ask the priest not to begin the rite until he has had time to light the wax candle before the icon. During Christmastide, however, this custom was observed only in a few homes, even when the priests were exalting Christ.

[Rostislavov then gives a very long, detailed description of these tours of the parish. The operation involved between six and seven hundred households, scattered over almost thirty hamlets, and needed to be completed by New Year's Eve; time was therefore of the essence, especially since the priests needed to be in church on Christmas Day and on Sundays, and on Saturdays many peasants left their homes for the weekly market in Tuma. Wandering in the predawn cold and dark, slipping on the ice, being harassed by dogs whose owners refused to restrain them, facing irritated householders, listlessly singing a few hymns at maximum speed and haggling afterwards over every kopeck, sometimes using brute force to extort payment from recalcitrant peasants—the entire experience was degrading and humiliating.]

One might think that not much was appealing about exalting Christ, and yet I met many who enjoyed it. I am not referring to the members of the village clergy, for established custom made it impossible for them not to go, they had no other way of supporting themselves and their families, and lastly, prolonged practice had inured them to it. However, I met lovers of exalting among more or less grown-up seminarians as well. Some of them would look forward impatiently to Christmastide, not only to see their family, but also to walk about the parish exalting Christ and then, after their return, describe with enthusiasm or at least cynical equanimity how they had talked some peasant out of the odd two- or five-kopeck coin and with what arguments they had succeeded in softening his hard heart.

Acquiring that mindset takes time. A boy sees his father return from a hamlet after exalting Christ, sit with his wife as they count the money he has brought home, and then jokingly describe the scenes that took place while he was out exalting Christ. The child starts wishing that he, too, could see all that and get at least a little money. Then they actually take him along into the parish. His mother dresses him in his best shirt and they sit him down in the sleigh, wrap him up in a sheepskin coat, and then reach a hamlet and go from house to house. Growing up in the home of a clergyman, the boy is unlikely to have been told the truth about what it means to go around the parish begging for money—on the contrary, they teach him to regard it as a sacred custom. And so, going from house to house and stretching out his little hand for a kopeck or even a half-kopeck, the child (at least in most cases) has no idea of the humiliation to which he is subjecting himself. What he likes and what interests him is the money, not the means by which he has obtained it. Subsequently, even if he realizes sooner or later the utterly humiliating nature of the exalters' role, it would still be quite difficult to renounce it, for not all mothers and fathers are like Father Ivan Fedorovich Glebov and allow their son to throw four quarter-kopecks into the snow and then completely give up walking about the parish. No, he has to go, whether he wants to or not, and if he disobeys, they resort to strong means of encouragement. [Flogging was common when sons resisted instructions to exalt Christ.]

Furthermore, money has a magical power over children, perhaps more even than over adults, because they have it so rarely and in such small amounts. In order to take advantage of this passion when they were exalting Christ, many fathers in the clergy would allow their children to collect the one- and two-kopeck coins and later let them keep some or all of them. Even if they did take them all back, they would still promise to use the sum they had acquired to buy their son something new. Well, how could anyone *not* walk about the parish under these circumstances? And so, little by little, a person is drawn into the rut. Sometimes he may even realize how humiliating the role is that he has to perform. But the example set by his elders, the desire to emulate his father, and the wish to please his parents will make him ignore that feeling. Eventually, given the absence of alternatives, the demands of his own self-esteem will lend even the most humiliating role a pleasing appearance. Thus, even if a person does not become a lover of exalting Christ, at least he comes to regard it simply as business.

Turning now to myself, I will speak honestly about the impression that exalting Christ made on me. I seem to have liked it at first, and, as the saying goes, I was developing a taste for it. After I had managed to exalt Christ once in Palishchi and once in Tuma, I wished to take part in walks about the parish on other occasions as well when neither Father nor Mother did anything to compel or invite me to do so. For example, at Easter, the Tuma parish clergy limited themselves to collecting money as a group and did not take along their children;

the same must be said of funeral banquets. Even so, both before entering the church school [in 1819] and for a few years afterward, I would go on my own, without permission from my parents, together with others in the parish. My grandmother Fekla Akimovna had a great deal to do with that. After a lifetime spent among the village clergy, she would never have dreamed that there was anything wrong with not only the sons, but even the wives of the clergy walking about the parish. She was actually amazed that my mother would almost never spend time in the parish. She, on the other hand, continued to go to funeral banquets and Easter even after Grandfather had retired, and—for company and perhaps out of a desire to train me for the clerical calling—she would take me with her and even defend me if people made remarks about my hanging around the parish.

I was fortunate in that I never did acquire a passion for exalting Christ and for the clergy's various walks about the parish, or more accurately, for begging and cadging. It may have helped that I was not allowed to keep the money I got by exalting *(vyslavlivaemye mnoiu den'gi)*,* but always had to turn it over to Father and Mother. In addition, they never tried to encourage me by saying, "Go ahead and exalt; with the money you get by exalting, we'll sew you a frock coat, a vest," and so on. Thus, the love of money did not develop in me and consequently did not hide from me how base it was to go exalting Christ and roam the parish like a tramp. Meanwhile, other circumstances began to arise that inspired me with revulsion for both. Most of all, I began finding it burdensome to have to exalt Christ around the village. I always rode to the hamlets with my father, grandfather, and uncle, and there, the humiliation was disguised by the respect for the priests that was at least feigned by many of the inhabitants. There, I did not have to ask personally for a little extra, or appear all alone before the bearded householders and look each one in the eye; I was shielded, so to speak, by my father's cassock. But in the village, for some reason, all three priests would walk together and take none of the children, so at first I had to go with my uncle Vasilii Martynovich, and later all by myself, and that on the first day of the [Christmas] holiday. At that time of year it was rare to meet a householder who did not have guests who were feasting. You would walk into a cabin and find yourself facing a whole company that was merry and sometimes drunk. Naturally, even a bold child feels shy in a situation like that. My voice was bad, and my singing was not powerful, not harmonious, and

---

* *Vyslavit'* means "to obtain by exalting," implying that the activity has a purely monetary object.

even downright unpleasant. Not only did it fail to draw the attention of the revelers, they could not even hear it. Because of that, I often had to stand and wait for the master of the house to take leave of his guests, for him even to notice me, and even that did not always happen because not everyone would soon turn and look around. Of course, he would give me something, but often it was with a look of annoyance at having his conversation interrupted by some little boy, even if it was the priest's son. Also, it sometimes happened that Father would (though with restraint) vent his irritation at what he called the need "to wander or drag himself around the parish, to go collecting two-kopeck pieces," and so on.

Furthermore, one Easter I was in the hamlet of Snokhino, and while the collective public prayer was being conducted in the field, I was standing on the road next to my cart, which was filled with loaves of bread, unleavened bread, small round loaves, and so on. The landowner of the hamlet, my godfather, walked by with his oldest son.* When he saw me, not only did he not greet me or kiss me to wish me a happy Easter, but instead he said with the most malicious and sarcastic smile, "Well, gotten spare change yet from anyone?" (That is what people usually say to beggars.) Then he and his son burst out laughing and walked on. I was already twelve or thirteen years old and could really feel the sting of their gibe. After that, I stopped wandering the parish as an enthusiastic volunteer. I could not refuse to go exalt Christ, but the more I grew up, the more unbearable and even repulsive I found it.

Here I was, a good seminarian who enjoyed my classmates' respect and the favor of at least some of my teachers, beginning to develop pride and self-awareness and to discover at least a few liberal ideas— and then I was supposed to go from house to house, stand before some bearded householder, stretch out my hand to him as though begging for alms, and receive maybe a two- or one-kopeck piece in paper-ruble currency.† I would have been willing not go home at all for Christmastide and instead live somehow in Riazan, but I could not do that, and that only further deepened my revulsion against exalting Christ. At the time I was still very religious, even somewhat fanatical, but the idea had already taken root in me not to enter the priesthood. I did not know yet how I would live and support myself, but I absolutely detested the idea of becoming a priest.

---

* The landowner was Petr Vasil'evich Ivanov (the brother of Aleksei Ivanov, from whom Rostislavov's father borrowed copies of Voltaire's works—see p. 24–25, 82).

† I.e., kopecks that were worth 1/100 of a paper ruble.

CHAPTER FOURTEEN

The Kasimov Church School

[Boys from the clergy who had no formal schooling were often drafted into the army. At the beginning of 1819, to preserve their son from this fate, Rostislavov's parents broke off his home education in Old Church Slavonic, Russian grammar, arithmetic, and Latin and Greek, and enrolled their ten-year-old son in the parish church school in Kasimov, thirty-eight miles from Tuma.* The boy had heard awful tales about school life and was very reluctant to go. Once he arrived in Kasimov, he lived in squalid, overcrowded quarters that he shared with several other boys.]

[Translator's Note: Conditions at the lower church schools (the parish and district schools to be completed before studying at a seminary) were notoriously bad. Imperial regulations mandated that teachers engage their students intellectually; that corporal punishment be avoided; that needy boys be provided with decent room, board, and clothing; that all students receive moral supervision from the school inspector; and that hopeless underachievers be expelled. None of this actually occurred. Extreme lack of funds forced many schools to operate with student-teacher ratios in excess of 100 to 1, though Kasimov had 136 students for four teachers.[34†] The low-paying teaching positions were filled by mediocre, unmotivated seminary graduates, and schools had decrepit, desperately overcrowded facilities and few or no textbooks or other supplies. All this made a mockery of progressive pedagogical ideas. Students mostly lived as lodgers in lower-class homes, making moral supervision impossible. Further, the tight budgets provided stipends for only a minority of those who needed them. Faced with these daunting conditions, and largely free from interfer-

---

* This, as he explains elsewhere, is where he was given the last name Rostislavov, which his father chose for unknown reasons and later adopted for himself and his other sons as well.

† Seventy-two in the parish school and 64 in the district school, as of 1822.

Kasimov

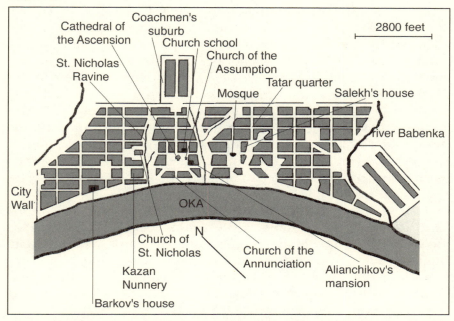

(Sources: Mikhailovskii, Il'enko, *Riazan', Kasimov,* 206. N.F. Gulianitskii, ed., *Moskva i slozhivshiesia russkie goroda XVIII-pervoi poloviny XIX vekov* [Moscow: Stroiizdat, 1998], 305.)

ence by higher authorities, the schools ignored both the letter and the spirit of the regulations. The overburdened teachers demanded unstinting deference, relied on rote memorization and corporal punishment, delegated much of their authority to student assistants, and made decisions arbitrarily. Alongside this brutal authoritarianism and demand for the purely external appearance of discipline, the traditional Russian communal spirit also survived—while the very worst students were held back, they were rarely expelled, and the available stipends were divided among the largest possible number of students.[35]* The result was that the boys lived and studied in unimaginable squalor and deprivation, removed from adult guidance, and exposed to constant abuse and depravity, but the schools somehow functioned and most students who wished were able to continue their educations there.][36]

---

* Of the 72 students in Kasimov's parish school, for instance, 67 were promoted at the end of the academic year 1821–1822, 3 were held back, and 2 were expelled.

• Before describing my studies at this school, I think I should start by talking a little about the school building. It stood at the corner of a broad square, and its fairly wide courtyard was almost entirely enclosed by the large main building and two wings, a stable, a coach house, a bathhouse, ice houses, and so on. At the time, rumor was that it had earlier belonged to the deceased priest of the Church of the Assumption, and that, through some fraud, our headmaster had taken it away from the dead man's wife.[37]* She lived next door to the school in a little house whose courtyard was connected with us by a wicket gate, which showed that both houses had once belonged to the same owner. The rumor was borne out by our headmaster's indulgence toward his neighbor, the priest's wife. As we shall see, he was a proud and touchy man who was widely respected and, as the Russian saying has it, "let no one step on his toes." But when the old priest's wife would meet him or see him on the porch of his little house in the school courtyard, she would start shouting that he was a brigand, a robber, and a swindler, and remind him that he had stolen her house. Sometimes our whole school heard this, yet the "venerable" reverend archpriest would "humbly" endure all these insults.[38]†

The main building held the headmaster's residence. Each of the wings consisted, to put it simply, of two cabins, separated by large vestibules with one or two store rooms. One wing held the upper and lower divisions,‡ the other, the [two-year] parish school and the kitchen. Our classrooms were not especially elegant in their décor. In each room, right by the door, stood a brick Dutch stove that had never even been whitewashed. On the wall opposite the door was a mediocre, tarnished icon, and beneath it a few nails held the class

---

* The house, built on church land, had belonged to a priest who left a widow but no heirs who were members of the clerical estate. As a consequence, the widow was ordered in August 1811 to sell the house and vacate the property within six months so it could be returned to clerical use. Her appeal to the archbishop to reverse the eviction order was turned down, and the property was used for the newly established church school. The original school building, along with much of the town, burned in 1828 and was replaced with the neoclassical structure that is still there today.

† The headmaster, Polikarp Polikarpovich Kistrovskii—or, as Rostislavov spells it, Kistrusskii—was born around 1770, educated at the Riazan seminary, and owed his surname to having been ordained as priest in the nearby village of Kistrus' in 1795. After a few years spent as district superintendent and missionary to Old Believers, he was made cathedral priest in Kasimov in 1799 and head of the Kasimov Ecclesiastical Board in 1801. His career presumably also benefitted from the fact that he joined the local Committee for Smallpox Inoculation and the Russian Bible Society, two ventures that enjoyed strong governmental support. He died during the cholera epidemic of 1831.

‡ The two divisions of the four-year ecclesiastical district school, which boys entered after finishing the parish school.

roster and a list of holidays when there was not supposed to be school. All the walls were lined with benches, like the ones one sees in village cabins, so even the teachers sat on a bench, not a chair. Of course, there was a table by the teacher's seat. There were tables for the students on both sides along the length of the cabin, but these were unlike those commonly found in educational institutions, for they were made from three thick boards that were fastened together and supported by four thick legs; all of this was of the simplest, crudest workmanship. Some students sat on the bench by the wall, and the others on a bench across the table from them, with their backs to the middle of the class and the teacher. However, sometimes there was no bench, and some had to stand. There also might be insufficient table space for half or more of the students; when that happened, they would sit on the benches, but if they needed to write, they would get on their knees, face the bench, and put their paper on it.[39]*

Our classrooms were filthy in the extreme. I cannot remember the floors ever being washed. Meanwhile, we would all track dust, snow, or mud into the classroom, all of which of course stayed on the floor to be trampled by our feet and slowly accumulate, until it formed a layer that covered the floor and from which hardened knobs of mud rose up here and there. When the weather was damp, a fairly thick mud would form and the floor would become slippery, so that, when our play became too wild, we would fall right into the classroom mud which was impossible to wash or even scrape off the floor. We would walk on the benches and tables with feet that were covered with mud from the street and the classroom. As a result, when you sat down on a bench or propped your arms on the table, you risked dirtying your coat. Of course the walls and ceiling were not as filthy as the floor, but you could not call them clean. A great deal of dust gathered on them, but in our case there was another element as well. When the classrooms were cold and we warmed them with our breath, the vapors would slowly condense and form droplets on the walls and ceiling. Some of these droplets would fall onto us from the ceiling, but the rest stayed there and mixed with the dust into a kind of putty that

---

* This sorry picture is borne out by a November 1822 memorandum from the school's inspector, Ioakim Krasnov, to Kistrovskii, the headmaster: "As you know, all classrooms in the school entrusted to you have a significant shortage of desks and benches, owing to which many students are forced to stand the entire four hours and have no means for writing their assignments because they have no desks. Please have the kindness to take steps to remedy this defect, not to mention the other ways in which the school is decrepit and of which you are well aware."

dried and coated the ceiling. The same happened along the walls, except that the droplets did not fall onto us but instead mingled and ran down the walls, covering them with intricate hieroglyphics. [. . .]

[One] classroom housed both the first and second years of the parish school, even though the two were supposed to be separate and each have their own teacher. In our school, that was not the only irregularity with regard to the teachers. According to the regulations, there were supposed to be six of them: two in the upper and two in the lower division of the district school, and two for the parish school's classes. Instead, there were only three, with the headmaster as the fourth, but he was expected only to teach geography. Such economy in teachers did not mean economy with money, however, since the three and the headmaster shared the salary of six teachers.[40]*

After describing the classrooms, I will now describe the people whom they temporarily housed. I will begin with the officeholders, who were divided into two categories, junior and senior. The former included the auditors (*avditory*), the censors (*tsenzora*) or elders (*starshie*), and the orderlies (*dneval'nye*), all of them students; the latter were the headmaster and the teachers.

When I entered the parish school, there were only two auditors for both classes, Solov'ev and Veselkin. Their job was to check how the boys had done their lessons (the technical term for this was "to examine"). Whether the lesson was done well or poorly was written down in the *notata*, a booklet of several pages. On the first page, in large, beautiful letters, stood the words *Notata for the students of such and such division or year, for such and such month or term; auditors: so-and-so and so-and-so.* On the following pages were the students' first and last names. Opposite each one, spread over two pages, were little boxes in which the auditor noted how well or poorly the students had known their lessons. In the parish school we knew absolutely no Latin, and only toward the end of the second year did they teach us to read Latin letters and the rudiments of grammar, yet long-standing custom required that grades be noted with the beginning letters of Latin words, which we pronounced our own way. These abbreviations and words were the following: *sc* for *sciens* (knows), *ns* for *nesciens* (knows nothing), *nt* for *non totum* (knows part of the lesson), *nr* for *non recitabat* (refused or had no time to recite), *er* for *errans* (does not know it

---

* According to regulations issued in 1820, institutions such as this were supposed to employ 6 teachers with annual salaries ranging from 180 to 350 rubles, for a total of 2,030 rubles. In fact however, an 1822 document indicates that Kasimov's 4 staff members were each paid from 437.20 to 638.70 rubles, for a total of 2,130.06, so Rostislavov's calculation appears to be roughly accurate.

well). In addition, there were the marks *ag* for *aegrotus* (sick) and *ab* for *absens* (did not come to class, out of laziness or some unknown reason). However, we pronounced these words as *ssiens, nessiens, nontot, nonprestsens, yerans, yeger.* Only *absens* was pronounced correctly.*

The auditors were only boys, like all the other schoolchildren, and had no pedagogical tact. To them, knowing a lesson meant reciting it verbatim, with no omissions or additions. One who recited in this way was *ssiens.* But should a boy leave out or add anything, or replace a word with another that meant exactly the same thing, e.g., if he said "consequently" instead of "thus" [. . .], that was enough for *yerans.* An auditor could write you up for not knowing your lessons even if you actually knew them, because the teachers usually felt obliged to trust them and back up their authority. If a student had been given *nontot, yerans,* or *nessiens,* but recited the lesson properly in front of the teacher, the auditor would defend himself by saying that "he only learned that later, but when I examined him, he didn't know it." That defense was accepted without appeal, the grade in the *notata* remained unchanged, and if a similar incident occurred three times in one week, the student would be declared lazy and would not only be made to sit on his knees but was even caned. On the other hand, if the teacher personally examined the students and found a *ssiens* who did not know his lesson, then the auditor was also in trouble. The student might sometimes be forgiven or punished lightly, though usually they had him caned, but the auditor was almost always caned thoroughly, albeit by students other than those whom he examined. To ensure that no bias was shown, the teacher closely monitored the caning and, at the slightest sign of indulgence, screamed at the student administering it; some teachers would even take the rod themselves and thrash him.

The auditors understood both their rights and the dangers facing them, and were not only nitpicking in the extreme but also expected to be rewarded by their subordinates for their labors. If you had brought in a slice of bread or a bun, or if you had purchased a white wheatmeal loaf, a buckwheat bread, or something else of that sort, you

---

* *Nonprestsens* probably stands for *non praesens* (not present) rather than *non recitabat.* The point is that the words were pronounced as though they were Russian, ignoring Latin pronunciation rules. This seems to be part of a pattern—also evident in such words as "censor," "auditor," and (later) "executioner"—in which Latin words, imported from Western Europe and connected with the vocabulary of the government as well as the church, were associated with corrupt, authoritarian power and were sometimes mangled by church-school students who did not grasp their meaning. The terms "the authorities," "subordinates," "commander," "crime," and so on likewise evoke a governmental rather than an ecclesiastical or educational institution.

always had to share with the auditor. He would come and ask for it himself, but it was better to go to him and offer it without his asking. Otherwise you might be told, "Look out, brother, and don't pretend you don't know me. I'll get you for that." If you did not bring what you had eaten into the classroom, your lack of consideration toward the authorities would be pointed out to you: "Brother, you haven't given me anything in a while, but I'll get you. You'll get to know me."

Or else, without saying a word, he might start writing *yerans* or *nontot*, even though the boy knew his lesson, and then, as I said, the consequences were unpleasant. The auditors also had special means to avenge any lack of consideration toward themselves. It was customary to examine students only before "the bell rang." But now, the auditor would say to the particular boy, "Wait, I'll examine you now." Yet, time was passing, and already the handbell rang, so he would write down *nonprestsens*. In other cases, if a boy was lost in thought or playing or cramming his lesson, the auditor would run up to him from behind, grab his shoulders, and say, "Come on, hurry up and recite, recite, the bell's about to ring." When the startled boy failed to remember the first words of his lesson right away and paused for a minute, the auditor would tell the bystanders, "Look at this, brothers, he doesn't know anything," and write *nessiens*.

For all these reasons, we would come to class as early as possible, an hour or even an hour and a half ahead of time, to make sure we were examined, and we were terribly afraid of the auditor and did everything possible to mollify him. He, on the other hand, realized how powerful he was and could tyrannize over us.

Another authority position in every class of the church schools was that of censor or elder. The top student was chosen for this post, although sometimes they picked a particularly strong, strapping young fellow instead. He was a kind of tutor or inspector's assistant. Until the bell rang, the students usually wandered around the classroom or ran on the desks rather than sit in their places; they also got examined by the auditor, played, made noise, and so on. Even then, however, a nitpicking and cautious elder had the right to pacify his overly rowdy classmates. But once the bell had signalled the officially approved beginning of class, the full scope of the censor's power became apparent. After hearing it, he would shout arrogantly and loudly, "Hey, you, to your seats! Why aren't you sitting down? I'll note that in the record!"

The record was the name for a little scrap of paper on which were written the first and last names of students who were guilty of some offense, e.g., making noise, fighting, running out of the classroom, disobeying the elder, and so on. [. . .] When the students heard the fearsome "I'll note that in the record," they tried to gain their seats as quickly as possible. Meanwhile, the elder mostly stood in his place or paced around the room, looking around at everybody, shouting at this one, threatening that one, and sometimes pulling someone's hair or otherwise meting out manual punishment. Once all was quiet, the elder still occasionally looked at his subordinates; our strict discipline made it a crime not only to whisper to one's neighbor, but even to communicate with someone by making faces or gestures or even to turn in one's seat. "Hey, you, what are you doing there—turning around, whispering! There, I'll put you in the record."

After the bell rang, none of the students dared to leave the room without permission from the censor, who made sure that anyone who asked to be excused did so at the proper time. Supervision by the elder continued even when the teacher was there; if he noticed anyone being careless or acting improperly, he reported it to the teacher at once. Our commander was first Solov'ev, and later Dobromyslov; they happened to combine the two qualities needed in an elder, that is, they exceeded us both in academic achievement and in age and strength.

The auditors and censors were appointed for an indefinite term and were removed from their positions when something showed them not to be capable. In addition to these two aristocratic positions, there was a third, plebeian one, which was held by all students in turn except for the senior officeholders—the position of "orderly." He was required to lock the classroom and keep the key when the students were not in class. Because of that, he had to come to school before everyone else in the morning and after lunch, so the students would not have to stand in the vestibule or the courtyard. Any deviation from this law, especially if it was very significant, entailed not only annoyance among one's classmates but also punishment by the teacher. Furthermore, in the evening or in the morning, in any case before the teacher arrived, the orderly was required to prepare a sufficient quantity of rods. In a very small number of schools that were, so to speak, "well regulated," the rods were stored by the school staff, most often in the kitchen; they stayed with the staff, were brought to class as needed, and were then returned to the staff, to whose discretion it was left to decide whether they were reusable. With us, the orderly was in charge of everything, and if he failed to prepare the rods in the hope that the teacher would not cane anyone, or if the rods were too few or were unsuited for their special purpose, then the orderly was almost always punished very hard.

Our rods were mostly supple willow or birch switches, not too thin but not thick, either. Individual ones were not used for caning, except that now and then a fairly thick willow switch might be used to cane little boys, but usually they tied several together in a bundle, never fewer than three. Smart teachers had the bundles tied together only at the top, the end that they held in their hand. This was done for a particular purpose. When they needed to cane someone, they would "spread out" the rods, that is, they separated the switches at the lower end (which was meant to strike the body) so that each was as far as possible from the others and might, so to speak, act independently and not interfere with the blow of its neighbor. They needed to be bound tightly enough that, no matter how powerful the blow, no switch came loose from the bundle; otherwise, the orderly might get into trouble for carelessness. [. . .]

[The orderly] was also required to sweep the classroom when it was convenient, but, of course, before the teacher arrived. The authorities provided no brush, broom, or bundle of twigs for this. [. . .] In the absence of a bundle of twigs, the student's sash or the skirt of his coat took its place. Some even took off their sheepskin coat, gown, or short caftan and swept the classroom with that. [. . .] Lastly, the orderlies were required not only to heat the stove during the winter, but also to chop firewood for that purpose. Here, too, the authorities provided neither axe nor poker, so we brought them along from our lodgings. Burdened with so many duties, the orderly had to receive at least some sort of reward. Almost everywhere, his reward consisted of not needing to recite his lessons before the auditor, being listed in the *notata* only as the orderly, and, in many places, standing or sitting near the door or the place where the rods were kept and executions* were performed, so he could be ready the moment he was called upon. Whenever the orderly fulfilled the duty of executioner, students who expected to be caned that day tried to win him over and begged him to be as gentle as possible with them.

Above the class elders and auditors there was, aside from the teachers, one more important authority figure for the entire school—the elder of the upper division. He was the elder not only for his class, but for the entire school, something like an assistant to the inspector. He had the right to enter every classroom in the teacher's absence and take measures to suppress disorders, that is, he could pull students' hair, slap them in the face or on the back of the

---

* I.e., corporal punishment.

head and so on, or report them to the headmaster and the inspector. He saw to it that we all went to church on Sundays and holidays for matins and mass and behaved reverentially. He was our leader and commander when we went out for "herbs," which I will describe in another chapter, etc.* I repeat, he was something like an assistant to the inspector, although when he became careless, he was caned just like the others, almost even harder.

Our higher authorities, the teachers in our parish school, consisted of a single individual, the cathedral priest Mikhail Iakovlevich Mirtov. He was of extremely small stature, perhaps four feet, ten inches tall.[41][†] Since we did not know the word "midget," we called him [and taunted him as] "pipsqueak" *(kapsiuk)*. He was a classic exemplar of a church-school teacher of that time. He hardly bothered with explaining lessons. His lectures on Russian grammar and the catechism were limited to telling us to memorize from this word to that word, or memorize another two verses, two or three examples, the remaining half-page, and so on. I have absolutely no memory of his ever explaining anything about these subjects. When the subject was arithmetic, he would usually ask, "Does anyone know how to go on from here?" If someone answered "I know," then Mikhail Iakovlevich made him do one or two problems from Kuminskii's arithmetic textbook on the blackboard. However, since the impromptu mathematician risked getting caned if he did poorly on his little assignment, there were not many volunteers for this temporary office. As a result, most of Mikhail Iakovlevich's lectures on arithmetic did not go beyond telling us to memorize the rules, say, of multiplication, and to ask the students of the lower or higher class how to do multiplication. Likewise, when he had us perform grammatical analyses, he examined only one or two notebooks, obviously those of the elder or the auditors, and instructed them to find the mistakes in the others.

---

* Elsewhere, Rostislavov describes how the church-school students were sent to gather medicinal plants for the physician and pharmacist Barkov.

† Born around 1790, Mirtov had been educated at the Riazan seminary at the same time as Rostislavov's father. In 1814, he became a teacher in the Kasimov parish school, whose administration reported in 1822 that his conduct was "praiseworthy" and his work "correct and reliable." Besides being responsible for his many students, whom he was supposed to teach for twenty hours a week, he served as priest of the Cathedral of the Ascension (a stone's throw from the school) until 1825, when he was made priest of the nearby Kazan Nunnery and also joined the Kasimov Ecclesiastical Board. Most likely a poorly educated man, he must have struggled with a staggering workload and perennial financial penury. The 1834 census found him still serving as priest at the nunnery. He was by then 45 years old and had a 37-year-old wife and 6 children (5 daughters, and a son who was attending the Kasimov church school) ranging in age from 1 to 15 years.

However, in the teaching of singing from sheet music and penmanship, Mikhail Iakovlevich did not use the pedagogical techniques just described, perhaps because he knew church singing well and wrote in a very good hand. Each singing lesson he would first perform alone or together with us. He also reviewed every single one of our penmanship notebooks. [. . .]

The correctional measures practiced at the school in Kasimov were identical to the ones that almost all schools, with at most a few exceptions, employed to a greater or lesser degree at that time. It was considered the weakest correctional measure, not even really a punishment, if the teacher pulled your hair or ear with only his thumb and index finger. Mikhail Iakovlevich particularly liked to pull or tear at our hair. He was quite generous with slaps in the face and on the back of the head, and generally blows to the head; we found those more painful than his slaps, which rouged our faces better than any cosmetics could have.* At times there was "pulling" or "shaking," when our esteemed educator grabbed our hair with all the fingers of one or both hands and gave our head a multidirectional motion that could spread to the whole body, so the victim lost his balance and his entire body swung from side to side, touching the floor only with the toes; if this punishment was inflicted with particular zest, one could become dizzy and lose consciousness. Oddly, though, even bouts of pulling that left us with many fewer hairs on our heads did not strike us as very serious matters, and we ranked them below many other punishments because they were soon over and required no preparations.

Real punishment, we felt, included standing motionless or kneeling, at our places as well as "in the middle" (as we called the space not taken up by our desks) or by the stove or the hole in the floor. This method was very widely used with us. It was a rare class period when several students were not standing motionless or kneeling, sometimes one-fifth or more, and in a very few instances, all of us. If you were standing near your seat, you could lean against the table, or stoop and put your hands on the bench. But the middle was different. There, whether you were on your feet or on your knees, you had to stand straight, virtually at attention; if someone who was kneeling started to sit on his heels, and the teacher noticed, instant punishment would follow for the part of the body that had forgotten school discipline and lowered itself onto the heels. Sometimes, the sheer

---

* Non-noble women were fond of coloring their cheeks bright red to make themselves more attractive.

number of people assembled in the middle, usually near the door, made it difficult for anyone who wanted to come in to find a way through those who were standing and kneeling. These included not only offenders sent there by the teacher himself, but anyone returning to school after being absent because of sickness or any other reason, including even going to church on his name day and so on.* They all had to stand and wait until the teacher, either on his own or after the elder's report, thought to ask, "Why are you standing there?" If he was satisfied with your answer, he allowed you to go to your seat. That is why students were sometimes caned "by mistake," as we used to say. Mikhail Iakovlevich was harder on those standing in the middle than on those seated in their places, for he would make the latter stand or kneel for offenses for which he unfailingly caned the former. Fairly often, some carelessness or fault would be noticed in a student who had just recovered from an illness, returned from home, or come back from his name day. The teacher would assume that the culprit was standing in the middle as punishment for something else and at once order him caned. Of course, the order was promptly carried out. Many were so shy and timid that they were afraid, as they say, "even to open their mouth," so they would lie down and suffer patiently, but others—especially the elder and the auditors—were bolder and would report to the teacher, "You know, he's standing there for such and such reason," and then the caning was most often replaced with some other punishment. It was striking that someone recovering from an illness would be rescued at once, but few bothered to help those who had had their name day or were returning from home. Everyone loved it when a name day boy was caned. That was seen as an omen that he would be caned often, very often, throughout the year. "You sure got yours, name day boy! Happy name day!" they would say to the victim once the teacher had left.

My future readers will hardly guess why everyone liked it when those who had just come back from home were caned. Because of their savage mindset, the students particularly enjoyed it when someone came under the rod who had not been caned in a long time and had no welts or other purple or blue marks on that particular part of his body. All who could watch would gloat repulsively as the rod fell on the naked, perfectly clean, white or slightly reddened body and started painting red and blue welts on it, and the executioner would

---

* The name day—the day dedicated to the saint after whom one is named—had a significance similar to birthdays today.

say with delight, "Wow, was it ever fun caning him—there wasn't a speck on him before, but I sure painted him!" They also enjoyed it when the victim was wearing clean linens, since that almost always guaranteed that his body was nice and clean. Given this savage, repulsive mindset, is it any surprise that they enjoyed seeing someone caned who had just returned from home? Naturally, you see, his mother had washed him thoroughly in the bathhouse before sending him on his way, and dressed him in his best shirt and long johns. Surely, you see, they had not caned him at home. So, how could one not be happy to see a little sissy like that brought down at once to the level of the others whose linens had become black and on whom that particular body part was covered with paintings? For the same reason, they loved it when someone was caned who had been to the bathhouse that very day. It is painful even to recall it, but when they would inform the teacher that the victim had just had his name day or returned from his father's home, usually everyone would start laughing, and even the teacher would smile and add, "Oh well, don't worry—you'll get over it, and I'll count it in your favor later on."

Whether from forgetfulness or by design, the teacher would keep some on their knees in the middle not only for a whole class or day, but for a week, even a month. And since they were on their knees not from the moment the teacher came in, but from the very beginning of class, as soon as the bell rang (the elder strictly enforced that), almost everyone was horribly weary by the end of class. Days, weeks, especially months of kneeling would wear through your linens and cause bruises, especially since you sometimes even had to remove the skirts of your coat from under your knees. In that case, I think, it would have been better to be caned than to be kept on your knees. Sometimes you were even caned and then still left to kneel, although other teachers usually told people who were standing or kneeling to sit down after they had been caned. Could this have been a hellish plan to make the victim sit on the very part of his body on which the effects of the caning made it painful to sit down? It may well have been.

We had another punishment, which might be called special because it was applied almost only for faults in penmanship. [. . .] [Our school used] a thick, wide, fairly long ruler. Mikhail Iakovlevich would take one end in his hand, and with the other he would strike our hands with full force on the palm and fingers. [. . .] Since the right hand is used for writing, he probably believed that it should be the one punished for carelessness in that subject, but we were allowed to put our left hand under the ruler as well when he struck more than one blow. More than two blows in a row were actually almost impossible to bear, but sometimes they were dealt out in threes and fours; the many blows to the palm and fingers caused such swelling that it became completely impossible to write. [. . .]

But the punishment we feared most was, of course, the rod, which Mikhail Iakovlevich used very generously. That unhappy procedure usually began when our esteemed educator uttered the words "the rod." Of course, those who faced imminent punishment or expected it during that class period sadly hung their heads and sometimes shed tears of anticipation, but the other students not only remained calm but even seemed happy at the coming spectacle. As soon as the word "rod" was uttered, the silence in the class was broken and gave way to a kind of excitement. Those sitting on the bench facing the middle of the room would turn around, while those sitting along the wall would rise slightly from their seats to try to see the punishment in all its detail. However, they rarely succeeded in this and therefore envied those who sat near the middle, who in turn would actually brag about their privileged position. "We can see perfectly," they would say, "not like you." If the culprit was still at his seat, they made sure nobody blocked his way. If he tarried in going to the execution site, they would tell him, "Move it, move it, why aren't you going?" and nudge him forward.

The execution required at least three people—one to cane the victim, two to hold him—but the number increased if the victim was caned, as we put it, with two rods, and two could not possibly hold him down. In that case, six or seven people might be needed—two to cane him, two to hold his legs, two to hold his arms, and one to rest on his head. As I said, the orderly was supposed to act as executioner, but boys who were weak were not only excused from that duty—they were actually barred from it. But there were many lovers of caning who would take up the rod even when it was not their turn to be the orderly and who actually argued over it with each other and with the orderly. There were also several expert executioners, so to speak, and Mikhail Iakovlevich himself would call on them if he wanted someone caned especially hard. In our parish school, these tough fellows included Evsei Petrov, my cousin Vania, and especially Ivan Smirnov, whom we called "the hangman" and of whom we were extremely afraid. The duty of holding the victim down was not reserved for anyone in particular, but there were all too many volunteers, even rivals, for the job—instead of two, at least ten would offer their services. [. . .]

It is no surprise, given such zeal, that the condemned boy could go barely three or four steps "in the middle" before the requisite number of people surrounded him to carry out the sentence. If he moved too slowly, attempted any resistance, or tried to plead for mercy, they would seize him under the arms, push him from behind, pull him down by the head, leave him prostrate at their feet, and within five or ten seconds he would be sprawled on the floor, with one holder on his head and another on his legs. Then they quickly began to lay bare the body part that, in children, has to answer for all the mischief caused by the head, hands, and legs, even though it had no part in it; jokers—themselves no longer children, of course—called it the "educational body part." The boy sitting on the legs pushed the skirts of the coat and shirt* toward the one sitting on the head and at once removed what Englishwomen call the "inexpressibles,"† while the one sitting on the head turned the coat and shirt up onto the victim's back. He was assisted by the executioner, whom we called the "secutioner" *(sekutor)*.‡ Sometimes the victim expected to be punished and had tied his inexpressibles so tightly that they were difficult or even impossible to remove; then both the two holders and the secutioner would go to work, one taking hold of them from below, one from above, one from the sides, and if that failed, they used a knife. In any event, the educational body part was laid bare, but not it alone. To make sure the rod or any of its parts did not strike the coat or linens, by the secutioner's intention or not, the inexpressibles were pulled down to the knees and the coat and shirt were pushed up almost to the waist, both in front and in back; as a result, the culprit shivered not only from the anticipated punishment, but also because much of his body, from the knees to the navel and sometimes the chest, was touching the cold floor. After that, the holders took steps to prevent the victim from extricating himself. [. . .]

Once the preparations were completed, the beginning of the execution had to await a particular signal, which Mikhail Iakovlevich gave by either nodding his head or saying "go." But even before that, the one who was, as we called it, "spread out on the floor," already had the pleasure of feeling the touch of the rod. While awaiting the order to go to work, the secutioner practiced his aim, so to speak, by resting the rod on the naked part of the victim's body. If he felt malicious toward him, he would run it lightly along his body;

---

* The shirt *(rubakha)* is designed like a tunic and covers the upper part of the legs.

† In English in the text.

‡ *Sekutor* (and the related *sekutsiia,* or "secution") blends the Latin *executor* with the Russian word *sek,* from which *sech', sechenie,* and other words referring to caning or flogging are derived. Dal' identifies this usage as "humorous" (4:692), suggesting that it is a sign of linguistic playfulness rather than ignorance.

we called that "tickling." Of course, such tickling inflicted no pain, but still it caused an involuntary shiver in one's entire body and almost made one's heart stop beating. Usually, this torture soon changed into a physical pain from the rod, but sometimes it went on for a while, even a long time. Sometimes our esteemed educator was busy with something at his table, looking over a letter from someone, fixing his pen, making a list, or interrogating someone, so he did not say "go" or nod his head. Then the victim, fully readied to be caned, the rod already lying on his naked body, just had to lie there and feel that rod tickle him. Sometimes, when the culprit was already completely readied and all that was left was to say "go" or nod his head, Mikhail Iakovlevich would suddenly be called into the vestibule by someone. If Mikhail Iakovlevich could tell, when he opened the door and saw his visitor, that he would need to talk with him for a while, he would turn and say, "Let him go for now." They would half let him go, so to speak. The rod was taken away from his body and the holders got off of his legs and shoulders but sat down on the floor. The culprit also got up but did not dare to put on his long johns or lower his shirt and coat, so he sat down on the floor on his naked body. Sometimes the coat and shirt fell down by themselves. But the holder by the head almost always tried to prevent this either by tucking part of the victim's shirt tails into his cravat or even by holding it up with his hand. If the culprit was someone they disliked, a priest's son or a "little gentleman" (this term will be explained below), then his coat and shirt might be wrapped around his head and often covered it up; that was called wearing a bonnet, a hat, or a nun's headdress.

There were also times when Mikhail Iakovlevich would go out the door without giving the order to "let him go." It was good if he returned quickly, for then the torment did not last too long. But sometimes his conversation lasted several minutes, even over a quarter of an hour. Just lying there, fully readied for the caning, was not very pleasant, but now various additional refinements appeared. If the boy on the floor was a priest's son or a little gentleman, or if the elder, the secutioner, and the holders did not like him, they would start amusing themselves. The secutioner's "tickling" would become more frequent, or else he would raise and lower his rod as though demonstrating a caning, only without inflicting pain. The holders likewise did not feel like being idle, so they would stroke the naked parts of the body with their hands, pinch them ever so slightly, and even—just saying it is repulsive—spit on them and rub in the saliva. That was called "putting on varnish." A more daring holder would gently slap the naked, soft body with his palm or rub it with his hands—that was called "rouging the ass." They also did much else that was stupid, and of course the audience snickered as they watched all these repulsive things. But then the door would open again and Mikhail Iakovlevich would come in. Seeing that the culprit had been on the floor the entire time, he would announce with a smile: "Oh, so you were just lying there all this time and resting? Well, let's get started." If the boy had been sitting on the floor, the holders hurried to lay him down and stretch him out on the floor.

One way or another, sooner or later, the word "go" was uttered or the head nodded, and then the rod quickly started falling onto the body. Even had he wished to spare the victim, it would have been dangerous for the secutioner to do so. It was rare for Mikhail Iakovlevich not to observe the execution with his own eyes, and sometimes he would come up to the boy on the ground or sit down near him on a bench. Besides, he would in any case have known at once if the secutioner was not striking hard, or if the rod or even just one of its tips was hitting the coat or floor, because one of the holders or spectators who could see where the rod was falling, and who wished to ingratiate himself, would at once report it to him. Besides, we could tell just by the sound whether the rod had fallen on clothing or the naked body. If the former happened, there would be fairly loud whispering that "he hit the shirt, he hit the shirt." If he showed any indulgence, the secutioner was almost always subjected to the rod, which Mikhail Iakovlevich would wield himself or entrust to a secutioner of proven ability. Thus—for the sake of self-preservation—there was no way to avoid striking hard, and most considered it their duty to oblige Mikhail Iakovlevich and worked their arms as hard as they could. As a result, it was a rare blow that failed to leave on the body a visible mark, even seen from a distance. Our word for the stripes that the willow switches made was "ribbons," the ones from birch switches were called "red calico designs," and drops of blood that appeared on the body were "red sequins" or "little stars." We had tough fellows, especially Evsei Petrov, who could wield a single strong willow switch in such a way that the "ribbons" were arranged in order and parallel to each other and you could use them to keep count of the blows that had been given, so long as there were only ten or fifteen. If there was an abscess or itch-mite boil on the naked body of the victim, the secutioner would unfailingly aim his strongest blow at its center and try to cut it in half. That was taken as a sign of prowess, but it caused horrible pain that made even a weak boy wrest himself free from his holders unless they had previously tightened their grip.

All too rarely did the victim receive five or six blows—that was hardly considered punishment. "Big deal," they told anyone thus punished, "you barely got to lie down and scream when it was already time to get up again."

Most often, ten to fifteen blows were "dished out." That was already considered punishment, with ribbons and designs in large numbers being painted on the educational part. However, for serious "offenses," as we called them, e.g., [for those occurring] during singing class or if someone's name was "underlined" [for serious or repeated misbehavior] once or twice in the "record," for open insubordination, rudeness toward the elder or an auditor, repeatedly not knowing one's lessons, and so on and so forth, the number of blows could reach between twenty and fifty. Then it became impossible to distinguish individual ribbons and designs, for they all blended together. The use of willow switches would leave black marks, and birch switches made not only little stars, but stripes, "streams of blood" we used to say. But God forbid that one committed a very serious crime, such as beating someone bloody (even if the blood flowed only from the nose and from a single blow, and not even a very strong one), or swearing at or—even worse—hitting the elder or an auditor, or hiding or running away from punishment, so that the mutineer needed to be tracked down or caught, and so on; well, in that case, you could expect no mercy. The number of blows would reach a hundred and more, and the rods needed to be replaced several times with fresh ones. The secutioner could strike no more than thirty or forty blows, then another took his place. The entire educational part and the nearby parts of the waist and legs would turn black or become covered with blood, which also splattered all over the victim's linens, the floor, and even the holders. Such canings were, in a way, milestones in our life at school, and we talked about them and remembered them for a long time afterwards. [. . .]

Mikhail Iakovlevich never announced the number of blows at the start of an execution, except for the very rare cases when he was out of time and charged the elder with carrying it out. He usually observed the work of the rods himself and ended the caning by saying "enough." Then the secutioner, often interrupted in midblow, would turn around and restore the rod to its place; the holders rose and shook the dust of the floor from their coats; and the victim slowly got up or quickly jumped to his feet. If the punishment had not been severe and had not, as we used to say, "scrambled his mind," he would go back to his seat, arranging his clothes and continuing to weep or sometimes sob, and wiping away his tears. Ten or so minutes later he would already be trying to see how, in the very place where he had just been stretched out on the floor, another was being caned.

Often, however, the punishment did scramble the victim's mind, and he would get up in a daze, go to the small, unoccupied sections of the benches by the door and the stove, kneel on the floor, put his arms on the bench and rest his head on them, and sit there for a long time, crying and gathering his strength. In those cases, scenes took place that should have inspired pity and revulsion, but instead always aroused general hilarity. A boy who was dazed from pain would get up from the execution site and forget to pull up his inexpressibles. That by itself was not so bad, but in the summer we did not wear shoes, so the inexpressibles (which were already lowered to his knees) fell off the victim's legs entirely when he took a few steps, or they hampered his legs, or sometimes stayed on only one leg and dragged behind him on the floor. In addition, the skirt of the victim's coat was often wrapped around his shoulders, and in extreme cases, his shirt was tucked into his cravat. [. . .] In those cases, if the dazed victim did not straighten out his coat, then his behind remained naked from the waist to the knees just like during the caning. Add to this that the barefoot boy's inexpressibles had fallen off completely or were down at his toes. With this disgraceful appearance, the poor boy would sit down by the bench near the door, leaving most of his body naked. Sometimes he might stop on his own or hear the shouts of "pull up your pants" or "let down your shirt," but the shirt might be tucked into the cravat and not obey at once, the inexpressibles had sometimes fallen down completely or become tangled, so he would have to bend over to straighten them out, and that still left the shirt needing to be let down. Believe me, such situations almost always sparked general laughter. Rarely did anyone help the unfortunate boy arrange his clothes, and sometimes he remained for a long time by the bench in that repulsive way; only on an order from Mikhail Iakovlevich might someone loosen the coat from his shoulders. One who had been punished too cruelly might not make it to the bench and instead lie down on the floor by the stove, where he might stay for a half hour or an hour to "rest from his steam bath," as we used to say. [. . .]

In order to provide a complete picture of the educational activity of Mikhail Iakovlevich and just about a majority of church-school teachers of the time (with a few variations, of course), I will describe a typical school day. For Mikhail Iakovlevich, there were two types of school days—when he celebrated late mass [as priest of the nearby Cathedral of the Ascension] and when he did not. In the former case he would come early but not stay long, instead leaving for the cathedral to perform the liturgy and ordering us to occupy ourselves with "reading." For this assignment, each of us brought some book with him, usually one printed in ecclesiastical letters, and read it. To make sure that nobody was merely pretending to read his book while mentally "flying above the clouds," we were ordered to read audibly and loudly. The elder, who might stand in one place or pace around the room, vigilantly saw to it that no one stopped or sat without reading. In any case, it was rare for one's neighbor to notice that very thing without reporting to the elder— "Look, so-and-so isn't doing any reading." The culprit was at once entered into the record, where the culprits' names were followed by the words, "These students did not read." Both classes of the parish school had about forty students one year and fifty-five or sixty the next, so you can imagine the noise we made when we were all reading loudly and at the same time. In the summer, when the windows were open, the noise carried far across the entire square and to the neighboring streets.

When Mikhail Iakovlevich was not celebrating mass, he would come later, close to nine o'clock, whereas the bell usually rang at eight.[42]* Naturally, all of us would rise from our seats when he entered. The elder read aloud the prayer "To the Heavenly King," and we bowed our heads and crossed ourselves. Then we bowed to Mikhail Iakovlevich, who almost never responded with any sort of greeting. After laying his cane on the bench and his hat or cap on the table, he would order us to be seated and would go to the elder for the *notata* and the record, in case anyone was guilty of something other than not knowing his lesson. At first he would review the record, and those listed on it would almost always be summoned at

---

* Officially, though, it was reported from Kasimov that "the [parish-school] teacher both arrives and leaves his classroom when the bell rings, at the same time as the district-school teachers." Classes were supposed to begin at eight, continue until noon, break for lunch, and continue for 2 more hours in the afternoon. In the early 1820s, Mikhail Iakovlevich's schedule included 8 weekly hours of Latin (4 on Tuesdays and 2 on Thursdays and Saturdays) and another 12 (not broken down by weekday) of singing, church law, catechism, and Old Church Slavonic. By then he was assisted by another parish-school teacher who taught 6 hours on Mondays, Tuesdays, and Thursdays, and 4 on the remaining three days of the week.

once into the middle to the table. If someone had made noise but knew his lesson and was not underlined [in the record] or standing motionless or kneeling, then he might be sentenced to either of these punishments or be deprived of lunch; otherwise, he would remain at the table to await more painful punishment. Those who had "not read their readings" were almost always sentenced to the rod. If the review of the *notata* showed that someone had been *yerans* or *nontot*, he was made to kneel at his place or by the stove, depending on whether this was the first, second, etc., time he had been "thus noted." Those who were *nessiens* or, especially, *nonprestsens* were mostly sentenced to a caning or deprived of lunch. [. . .] In this way, the first half hour or so was taken up with interrogating and caning culprits. All one heard was pleading, squeaking, squealing, shouting, the hissing of the rods, the words "oh God, I won't, have mercy, I'll try, I won't be lazy; oh, oh, oh, that hurts, oh God, that hurts," and so on. Sometimes, however, the punishments went on well over an hour. [. . .] When the punishments prompted by the review of the *notata* and record were over, Mikhail Iakovlevich started examining those who knew their lessons. If a student recited well, everything was fine, but if he did not, both he and the auditor were in trouble.

We spent a great deal of time on arithmetic. Judging from the way it was taught to us, one might already expect that the students took a long time to learn to solve problems in arithmetic even in a mechanical way. Sometimes, several people would work on a single problem for an hour or more without being able to finish it. In order to write numbers on the board, we stood on a bench. Mikhail Iakovlevich would stand there as well, screaming, cursing, calling a student a sluggard and a bastard, pulling his ear and his hair, hitting him in the back of the head, then making him recite the rule. Often, the boy would recite it perfectly, word for word, and still the problem came no closer to being solved; then the fearsome "the rod!" would be heard. Sometimes, in the heat of the moment, Mikhail Iakovlevich himself would drag the culprit from the bench, hit him, and deliver him into the hands of the holders and the secutioner. Another mathematician would step up to the bench and also be sent to the rod. Arithmetic was especially terrifying for those who, for some reason, were standing by the door, because they were especially likely to be made to work on problems by Mikhail Iakovlevich and to be caned for not solving them to his satisfaction. Finally, we had stretched things out until twelve o'clock, when the bell rang. It was time to leave the classroom, so we recited the prayer "It is Fitting and Virtuous."* But then the elder, an auditor, or even one of the plebeians would sometimes notice somebody who had earned punishment but had not yet been punished, and would say, "Mikhail Iakovlevich! What about so-and-so or so-and-so? They didn't know their lesson. Shouldn't they have to go without lunch?" The verdict was almost always: "All right then, no lunch."

Mikhail Iakovlevich spent the class periods after lunch almost exclusively on writing, that is, he would look over our notebooks, where, on his instructions, we had written a page or two for this class, and he would decide the fate of those who had been deprived of lunch but had still not memorized their lesson. Generally, they were caned. [. . .]

The day we feared most was Saturday. By some ancient custom, we had to prepare for Saturday all the lessons that we had learned during the entire week; these were known collectively as the *subbotiva*.† On most days, many "didn't know their lesson," but how many more were there when, as we put it, "we were examined on the entire *subbotiva*." Even those who had known all the week's lessons individually might now be *yerans* or *nontot*. But they were usually forgiven, or at most they might be made to stand motionless for a while. One who had not known one or two lessons that week, in addition to the *subbotiva*, could also hope for indulgence. But if someone had been written up at least three or four times that week for not knowing his lesson, and especially if he had not been caned for that but only been made to kneel, then he surely faced the rod, even if he knew his *subbotiva*. That is why a rich supply of rods was prepared for Saturdays. [. . .]

It was rare, but it did happen that up to half, even two-thirds of the students squirmed and screamed under the rod that day. However involuntarily, we truly did fulfill literally the beginning of the fifth of Moses' Ten Commandments, i.e., "we remembered the Sabbath day." On that day we usually had already gone to the steam bath at our lodgings, so we would say about each other and ourselves that "you, or I, have now had two steam baths." Indeed, some felt less hot even on the sweating shelf in the bathhouse than on the classroom floor.

This description of Mikhail Iakovlevich's educational work shows that it almost took a miracle for any one of his students not to be caned during a given semester. Not even our elder and our auditors escaped the rod. They even had a privilege that was not particularly

---

* This is a thanksgiving prayer that begins with the words: "It is fitting and virtuous to worship the Father, the Son, and the Holy Ghost." I thank the NIU Press reader for pointing this out to me.

† *Subbotiva* comes from *subbota*, which means both Saturday and Sabbath.

enviable. Since they were big and strong boys, especially the elder, they were always held down by four or even five people. Then Mikhail Iakovlevich would either appoint a secutioner, of course the best one, or take on that office himself. As a result, the elder and the auditors were caned "seldom but hard," as we used to say. In addition, just about half the plebeians had to lie under the rod before the traces of the preceding caning had disappeared, so new designs and ribbons were superimposed on the old ones. There were happy weeks when some lucky fellow had to lie under the rod every day, although they rarely caned anyone twice in one day. Some boys' educational part returned to its natural state only when they were home on vacation, and even then only if their mother and father did not cane them for something. The humane way we were treated was most visible in the summer, when we went in detachments to bathe in the Oka, and it could be seen, by outsiders as well, that few of us were free from traces of the rod. We had nothing to hide from each other, but to avoid being mocked by outsiders, particularly our wicked enemies, the townspeople's boys, we tried to bathe in places where we would be alone.

[Translator's Note: Lest one suspect Rostislavov's account of church-school *(bursa)* life of being eccentric or unrepresentative, consider the following conclusions from a survey of autobiographical writings by priests' sons *(popovichi):* "The vast majority of popovichi, regardless of their political orientation as adults, usually characterized the seminary as a virtual torture chamber, where students were beaten and starved by 'demonic teachers' while living in squalid prisonlike cells. Their descriptions of the horrors of bursa life sometimes bordered on the fantastic. Doctor Sychugov claimed that starvation drove some boys to barter sexual favors with other students for a crust of bread. Kazanskii claimed that rats and mice were occasionally found in his kasha. Another popovich described how many of the students in his bursa were bald, having had their hair torn out by the roots by teachers. In his review of the popovich writer Pomialovskii's infamous exposé on the bursa, Dmitrii Pisarev compared it with Fedor Dostoevskii's *Notes from the House of the Dead*. He concluded that the horrors depicted by Pomialovskii far exceeded those of the prison camp described by Dostoevskii. The bursa represented the ultimate hypocrisy: an educational system designed to encourage morality that instead spawned depravity and corrupted the very souls of its inhabitants."][43]

The Church-School Students

• At the time I entered the school, the best students tended to be orphans and children of sacristans and deacons, whereas the sons of priests very rarely studied well. This seemingly odd phenomenon is due to the fact that, at the time, there were not yet many priests who had graduated from a seminary. Most had about the same education as the sacristans and deacons. Many of the most educated priests stood out for their intellectual arrogance, for they believed that the fact of having studied literature, philosophy, and theology in Latin, and then forgotten almost all of it, made them exceptional thinkers. Naturally, such priests were just as incapable of nurturing their children's intellectual faculties as were the sacristans and deacons. The children of the former inherited only their fathers' arrogance, and since they lived in relative ease and could indulge themselves, they grew accustomed to sloth, wastefulness, and other faults. On the other hand, the children of deacons and sacristans, as well as all orphans, both heard from their kin and sometimes realized on their own that the only way they could achieve anything in life was through education. In addition, they experienced more sorrows and privations and knew fewer joys and comforts than the children of priests, so they were more accustomed to hardship. Also, a priest's son could hope to inherit something from his father, while, as the clergy said, the sacristans' children and orphans in general "had to do without that." A further relevant circumstance was that, in the church's educational institutions, there were far fewer children of living priests than there were orphans and children of sacristans and deacons, since priests made up not quite a quarter of the clergy and many of their children were expelled for mischief or academic failure. In the schools, the majority always gains the upper hand over the minority if the former includes many more bright children than the latter. Therefore, generally speaking, the orphans and the sacristans' and deacons' children formed the dominant party among us; one might say that they set the tone in everything, and the priests' children had to adapt to their spirit or, as the saying has it, "dance to their tune."

It is likewise well known that, then as now, the clergy of a parish almost never got along with their priest, and instead envied and even hated him. That was quite understandable. The priest received more than twice as much income as the entire clergy of the parish, he could oppress them, take away or hide from them some of the revenues, and cause various other problems. Nowadays, most priests are more intelligent and more educated than the other clergy, so the latter can bear their domination and demands a bit more easily. But in the past, as I just said, a priest was as educated as a sacristan, and very often he actually began his career as a sacristan and it was only thanks to favorable circumstances, not his personal qualities, that he was made a priest. So, why should the other clergy like their priest? How could they not harbor envy, hatred, and other hostile feelings toward him? All of this almost inevitably passed on to their children. They heard their father curse the priest, and they believed his words and also started hating the priests, and then the priests' children. Into this they mixed their own childish scores. The priest's son, particularly before he started school, was just as arrogant toward the sacristans' and even the deacons' sons as his father was toward their fathers. The priest's son was almost always better dressed, and the peasant kids did not always dare to insult him, whereas the sacristan's son, especially if he was orphaned, sometimes walked around in rags and was treated with disdain by the peasant children. The parishioners gave the priest's son a two-kopeck or five-kopeck coin, while the sacristan's sons and the orphans were given one kopeck for two or three of them to share. So, how could they possibly like the priest's children? And, how could they not "get even" with them when school presented the opportunity?

Finally, the priests at that time did not exactly live elegantly, like gentlemen, but still better than the deacons and especially the sacristans, whose life of coarseness and poverty was little different from that of the peasants. Consequently, those children entered school with a greater store of coarse instincts and inclinations, cynical habits, and peasant manners than did the priests' children. The latter, of course, also ran around the village barefoot in the summer and with nothing but their shirts on. They, too, were given jackets made from homespun cloth and in general were not dressed like gentlemen, but still, they had boots to wear on holidays. They often got shirts with designs on them—even ones of printed calico—from their mothers, over which they wore a vest. They had a little frock coat of nankeen cotton, a cap, and a little sheepskin coat with a nankeen lining. In these they could look like dandies, especially next to the orphans and sacristans' children, who almost all walked around in bast sandals, simple shirts of heavy coarse linen, sheepskin hats, sheepskin coats with no lining—sometimes even ones made from calves' hides, and jackets and even coats made from very thick homespun cloth. They were used to such poverty and had no possibility or prospect of escaping it, so, following man's natural vanity, they liked to brag about it, showing off their rags and looking with hostility upon those who seemed richer than they. One could naturally expect, therefore, that at school, where they formed the ruling majority, they would—even independently of the teachers—infuse our entire existence with a coarse and cynical attitude of disliking priests' children, envying neatly dressed classmates, and mocking any sort of delicacy of manners. Cynicism and peasant crudeness—that was what the majority liked and what they sought to extend to everything and everyone.

In the school in Kasimov as well, the dominant party consisted of the half-peasant sons of sacristans and was distinguished by its cynicism. Its ringleader in our class was Evsei Petrov. The entire party, and particularly its ringleader, would go after the priests' sons, especially if they had a pretty face, nice clothes and shoes, a gentle voice, and pleasant and genteel manners. Even if they were not sons of priests, the dominant party disliked such people and derided them as "little gentlemen." Life was hard for these supposed little gentlemen, who were despised by *genuine* little gentlemen and called *kuteiniki** by townspeople and peasants. How many times did they have to listen to taunts such as these: "Hey you, little gent, get a move on! Well, priest's boy, what should you want to do that for? You were fed on cheesecake, right? They always had you wearing cotton, right? Sissy!" and so on. An auditor would examine a priest's son much more strictly and pressure him more than the others, and that was calculated. After all, a priest's son had more money and bought special treats more often, and therefore one could extort more bribes from him than from some pauper. He would surely give in—the rod was no one's friend, and once in a while one had to escape it somehow. That is exactly how the elder reasoned and acted, and the others, the plebeians, followed his example. "Give me, give me," they would

---

* An insult for sacristans (derived from *kutia*, a food used in church for ritual purposes).

shout from all sides, "and if you don't, I'll show you, I'll cane the living daylights out of you, I'll hold you so you won't be able to move." If you gave nothing, the threat was carried out, but giving was no use, either. After all, you could not treat everyone, so those whom you had treated were indulgent, but the others would intentionally try to beat them to the duties of secutioner and holder. Besides, as I mentioned earlier, it was impossible to spare anyone during a caning. However, as long as there were no personal hard feelings, they would find some way to be indulgent toward a deacon's son, a poor boy, or an orphan. At least they would not cane him *con amore*, with zest and pleasure. But with a little gentleman they did not hold back. Even if he was willing to lie down on the floor, they would seize his arms and head, brutally shove him and push him down, and in the process they would pinch him or pull his hair or ear as though by accident. When they undressed him, they would either pinch him or scratch him with their nails, so he would sometimes be screaming even before the rod began to strike; that would provoke general laughter because it was attributed to fear, to his being a sissy, and so on. They would press him especially hard against the floor, choose the best rod, strike especially hard, and then taunt him, "So, little gent, little priest's boy, did you like the dinner we served? Were our pancakes hot?" and so on.

It was awful to come into class wearing a nice coat, particularly a new one. Everyone, without exception, got into trouble for that, the priests' children more so only because they had new ones more often, and better ones, than did the others. "Brothers," someone in a greasy jacket or filthy sheepskin coat would shout, "He's got a new coat!" At once they would come running and start "wearing out the seams," that is, punching wildly with their fists. Then they would shout, "We've got to see the lining," i.e., they needed to roll up the skirt of the coat and cane him, and "It's got to sprinkle," i.e., the caning had to draw blood. If the new coat was really nice, you can be certain that, if not on the first day, then certainly during the following days, sometimes with the help of the auditor and the elder, things were arranged so that they would "see the lining" and it would even "sprinkle." It was the greatest triumph, virtually a celebration, when a boy was caned the very day he came to class in a new coat. But independently of that, somebody would try surreptitiously and as though accidentally to soil the new coat with something, even to splash ink on it. [. . .]

I already mentioned that, during the wet and snowy seasons, our classroom floor was covered with a shallow mud that was black, sticky, and viscous. Even in a worn-out sheepskin coat or jacket or in filthy linens, lying down on such a floor was far from pleasant; at the very least, it meant that half of one's person became filthy beyond description. What was it like, then, to do so in clean white linens, soon after a steam bath, in a new nankeen frock coat, or in a sheepskin coat whose nankeen lining was still shiny or that was made from snow-white sheepskin? That is why many of us, when we were supposed to be caned on that dirty floor, begged Mikhail Iakovlevich to let us lie on a bench. Why not allow it? After all, the victim could be held more tightly and caned harder on a bench. Yet Mikhail Iakovlevich never granted the request, and by no means out of kindheartedness, for as I described earlier, he caned us horribly hard. No, you always had to lie down on the disgustingly dirty floor. [. . .] The shirt and long johns directly touched the floor and became dirty; the former was pulled up above the waist, in front and in back, while the latter were pulled down below the knees, so a large part of the victim's body lay in the sticky mud, which was firmly pressed against his body by his fitful movements and by the efforts of the holders to pin him to the floor. Some holders, while not letting the victim go, considered it fun to allow him to turn first onto one side, and then the other, and thereby become even dirtier. Consequently, the victim got up not only with his coat and linens but also his stomach and half of his legs dirty, and as he arranged his linens, he made the inside of them dirty as well. After class he would have to go home in a new coat that was completely soiled in many places. Once he was home, he had to take it off and appear in linens that were more than half soiled in front on both the outside and inside. The landladies and lodgers from other classes of the school almost always already knew what that meant. Sometimes, a kind landlady would at once change his linens and even wash off his dirty body, but most often you just had to walk around like that until the next scheduled bath. What a scarecrow a boy would resemble when he was made so filthy soon after a steam bath! Of course, he might discreetly scrape the mud off his body and even wash it with water, but his linens would stay dirty. Yet most of the spectators loved these occurrences—that is how cynical they were.

However, perhaps the most intense hatred of all was reserved for pantaloons* and pantaloonists, i.e., those who wore them. I already mentioned that the children of most of the clergy at the time were

---

* Tight-fitting, comparatively elegant men's trousers.

sans-culottes.* Only students who came from a town, and those country boys who had close ties to the landowners, had pantaloons. So, how could the entire class fail to become aroused when one of the students appeared in pantaloons? [. . .]

There was no way to complain about all this nonsense. Of course, it was not forbidden to tell Mikhail Iakovlevich that so-and-so had intentionally soiled my sheepskin coat, or pulled my frock coat over my head to examine my pantaloons, but that would have been of little use. To begin with, the accused would most likely have known how to defend himself, and his accomplices would have interceded for him. But even had he been found guilty, it would already have been a lot if they had made him kneel, whereas the one who had turned him in would later have caught it a hundredfold. I never talked about it even at home, and rightly so. Father would, of course, have told the headmaster and the inspector. Those reverends would not have liked to hear that all sorts of disgusting things were going on in their well-ordered school, that it was muddier in their classrooms than in the street, and so on. Maybe, out of respect for my father, they would have said something to Mikhail Iakovlevich, but both he and they would have repaid me with dozens of blows of the rod. No, it was better to remain silent. There was only one means of salvation, and that was to excel in class, because then the dominant party would be afraid that the priest's son might become their auditor or elder. Those individuals could go out in pantaloons and a new coat; in the latter case, of course, a few daredevils would allow themselves to "wear out the seams," but lightly, only for show. On the other hand, both the elder and the auditors could be caned like the others, so it still was best to accommodate oneself to the spirit of the dominant party and live and dress according to its taste. [. . .]

New coats, pantaloons, and nice clothes in general were worn to church, but in class we dressed in old, shabby clothes if we had any. In general, we tried by all means to avoid dressing elegantly. From the circumstances I have described, it was almost inevitable that we should all have adopted the cynical habits and manners of the dominant party. In my own case, at least, I think my deliberately neglectful attitude toward clothing probably began and intensified because of life at school.

---

* *Sans-culottes,* literally "those without breeches," were the lower urban classes in the French Revolution who did not wear the breeches typical of the wealthy and were known for their intense hatred for the rich.

[After completing the two-year Kasimov Parish Ecclesiastical School, Rostislavov graduated to the two-year lower division of the Kasimov Ecclesiastical District School. The teachers were different, but the approach to discipline and academics remained mostly the same as in the parish school, much to the students' disappointment.]

Not liking Mikhail Iakovlevich, we [students in the district school] also did not like the pupils in his parish school. In my *Memoir*, I will repeatedly be pointing out that students of different grade levels did not get along in the ecclesiastical educational institutions. There was one group that liked to assume an air of superiority and look down with arrogance and disdain on their lowly brethren. That second group, humiliated and oppressed, would suffer the insult in silence but wait with concealed anger for the time when they would rise to the same higher position and be able to avenge their own humiliation on others. The third group, which occupied the middle between those two, had no more love for the first group than did the second and would join battle against the first whenever possible, yet they exhibited an attitude that was no less disdainful and hectoring toward those whose status was lower than their own. Such hostile relations were common to all ecclesiastical educational institutions, only in varying degrees. [. . .] Of course, our school in Kasimov was no exception to this rule. While we were in the parish school, the students in the higher class [of the district school] would behave toward us as though they were aristocrats or magnates of some kind. When we would meet, we were required to take off our caps, to which they showed their gratitude by being ready at any moment to pinch us or even pull our hair. As for the students in the lower class, at least the bullies among them, they would come to us on purpose in Mikhail Iakovlevich's absence to hit, kick, or shove us. When we entered the lower division [of the district school], we did not forget the lessons taught by our predecessors, so we looked with disdain on the boys in the parish school and would go up to them during recess to show off how great we were. We even had this expression: "Hey, brother, or brothers," some practical joker would say, "let's go beat up some parish-school kids," and indeed we would head off on such expeditions. If we could not beat them up, at least we consoled ourselves by calling them "the pipsqueak's boys" *(kapsiukovtsy)*. The upper-class students supported and egged us on in all of these stupid tricks, partly with deeds but mostly with words.

CHAPTER SIXTEEN

My Life in Kasimov

[Translator's Note: Despite the central authorities' efforts to provide for them, church-school students often lived in bitter poverty. For
example, for the academic year 1821–1822, imperial regulations provided a limited number of full stipends (80 rubles) and half-stipends
for needy students, on the assumption that the schools would provide
free housing and use the money to buy food at wholesale prices. Based
on estimates submitted by officials in Kasimov, a student on a full
stipend theoretically could hope for a decent supply of candles and a
daily diet of under two pounds of rye flour, one and one-third cup of
groats, one-half cup of peas, one cup of potatoes, two cups of cucumbers, one-third pound of beef, and very small amounts of butter, wheat
flour, cabbage, and fish, with 3 rubles left over for all the year's other
expenses. However, in Kasimov, the headmaster personally occupied
the living space that might have served as a dormitory for at least thirty
people, and Rostislavov claims he embezzled virtually all the money
earmarked for stipends.[44] Without stipends or a dormitory, students
were entirely dependent on parental support for rent, clothing, and
food (at retail, not wholesale, prices), yet their fathers in the parish
clergy typically earned only 25 to 75 rubles a year if they were priests,
and a fraction of that if they were deacons or sacristans.][45]

• [Rostislavov's father believed that once his ten-year-old son entered school in Kasimov in 1819 and was on his own, he would need
an authority figure to guide him in his schoolwork and his personal
life.] As priest, and especially as superintendent, he had long known
the secretary of the Kasimov Ecclesiastical Board, Ivan Efimovich
Beliaev.[46]* It was with him that they decided to have me lodge.
Father's choice may also have been motivated by the fact that three
seminarians were already living there: Pavel Kudriavtsev, in the upper

---

* A district's ecclesiastical board *(dukhovnoe pravlenie),* consisting of one or two abbots, an archpriest,
and clerical staff, formed the administrative link between the diocese and a given district's parishes.

division, the son of the retired priest Iakov from Pogost; Evsei Prud-kov (lower division), the son of Father Ivan Fedotovich, the priest of Prudki; and my cousin and fellow villager Vania, my classmate in the second grade of the parish school.

The actual owner of the house was the old, widowed, childless priest of the Church of the Assumption, Father Fedor, who provided lodging to Beliaev, the husband of his [i.e., Fedor's] niece Anna Iakovlevna; those two were the ones who ran the entire household. The house was large and even had a mezzanine. However, we semi-narians would make an appearance there only on special occasions, by invitation, and instead were lodged with the two workwomen in the very cramped kitchen. [. . .]

The character and moral qualities of the landlords, my fellow lodgers, and the domestic servants were not exactly auspicious for a new student in the parish school.

[Father Fedor was away from home every evening and was a habit-ual drunkard. Beliaev was also a heavy drinker and card player and was eventually fired from his job for alcoholism and for gambling away government money. Anna Iakovlevna was "a very intelligent, kind, and conscientious woman" and sought to prevent young Rostislavov from playing cards or using bad language, but it was difficult for her to im-prove her lodgers' morals when her own husband played cards with them. As for the lodgers, Kudriavtsev and Prudkov were already young men and habitual card players, gamblers, and drinkers when they moved in with Beliaev, and they treated Rostislavov as their personal errand-boy. Both of them subsequently dropped out of the seminary. Kudriavtsev became a clerk in the civil-justice system and soon drank himself to death, while Prudkov became a clerk in the consistory (the board administering church affairs and church courts within a dio-cese) in Riazan, and later in Chernigov, and was always a heavy drinker and bribe-taker. As for Vania, he was a gambler and swindler as well, and died of a fever at the end of 1819.]

[Anna Iakovlevna, in her attempt to discipline Rostislavov and in-flict corporal punishment when necessary,] found a zealous helper in the workwoman Anna. As a cook, she was a smart and honest woman.* But she was also exceptionally nasty. Utterly dependent on

---

* Cooks needed to be skilled in preparing food and had to be trusted with their employers' money to buy food for the household. Since her employers were not noble, Anna was probably a hired domestic, not her employers' serf.

her employers, she was obliging toward them, except that she might be rude if something offended or annoyed her. On the other hand, it was as though she took pleasure in having someone, anyone, on whom she could vent her hostility. [Kudriavtsev and Prudkov were too old, and Vania too savvy, to make for easy targets. That left Rostislavov as the sole victim. His situation was aggravated by the fact that his father had complained to Anna's employers about her, and she avenged herself on him for that remark. She was particularly zealous and energetic in inflicting corporal punishment.]

It is amazing that, living in this household, I did not learn to be a drunkard and card player but also did not become cowardly, down-trodden, and weak-willed. Of course, it was still a bit early for me to be a drunkard, and Anna Iakovlevna would most likely have taken decisive and stern measures against any such proclivity and would have had Anna "beat the nonsense" out of me. However, acquiring a taste for cards was easy, and I was often invited to take part. I admit that I found the game itself quite absorbing and fascinating. Without playing myself, I liked watching others play and would sit with them for hours, even past midnight. Fortunately for me, I knew that, were Father to find out that I played cards, he would have no indulgence for me. When I was still at home, I had heard with what indignation he would always talk about that proclivity, and when there was a chance he would often tell me, "Look here, don't you learn to play cards for money. God help you if I find out something like that— don't expect any mercy from me then."

As regards my character, the reserve, caution, and taciturnity that life at Beliaev's taught me almost bordered on secretiveness, but also forced me, by necessity, to look for sources of strength inside myself. There was no one to whom I could turn for advice, even though I very often found myself in difficult situations, so I was forced to con-sider and weigh the pros and cons of everything myself. It was neces-sity, in fact, that forced me to think intelligently. Reflecting, now that I am old, on my living arrangements back then, I cannot say that they were good; they were actually very burdensome. Yet I also think that I would most likely not have been better off had I been lodged somewhere else.

[Sacristans, and occasionally deacons and priests, poor towns-people, and soldiers were the only landlords willing to take in church-school students as lodgers in Kasimov, and Rostislavov's family had lit-tle money, so renting more comfortable quarters was out of the question. At least Anna Iakovlevna ensured that her lodgers did not live in the "disgusting filth" found in other homes, she ensured that her lodgers were almost alone in the school in not having itch-mites, and she provided plentiful and reasonably good food while many other landlords malnourished their lodgers. Although she could be a harsh disciplinarian, Anna Iakovlevna was kinder than many landlords, and she made a greater effort than many to prevent the older students from encouraging the younger ones to drink, gamble, and swear.]

Anna Iakovlevna had noticed that Kudriavtsev and Evsei [Prudkov] often behaved foolishly and mischievously, and made an attempt to enforce more discipline, but she did not act very resolutely, and besides, it was not easy for her to stand up to these two spoiled, habitually mischievous, and also fairly big gentlemen. When I entered the lower division, both of them moved to Riazan. I alone remained of the previous lodgers, but three more moved in: my fellow villager Andriusha; my uncle Vasilii Martynovich's wife's brother Anton Solov'ev; and my former fellow villager (from Palishchi) Feofilov, the grandson of Evdokim (who was priest there) and son of the sacristan Kuz'ma. Andriusha was a bit younger than I, while Solov'ev and Gorlov were older by a year or a little more.

At the very beginning of the September semester of 1820, Anna Iakovlevna gave a kind of sermon for our edification, in which she advised us to behave ourselves, work hard, and not be naughty or mischievous. If we obeyed, she promised to be kind to us and take care of our needs, but she also threatened us with the birch rod if we did not follow her advice. As someone whom she already knew and who was already in the lower division [of the district school], she made me something of an elder over my three fellow lodgers, who were all still in the parish school, and instructed me to watch over them in her absence and report to her about what they did wrong. Anna listened to all of this and added, "You know, Mother Anna Iakovlevna, you shouldn't give up control over them. Remember all that those other spoiled brats did whom we had before? And this elder we've got now, you've got to be even tougher with him—five blows with the rod might be enough for some, but he's going to need ten." Anna Iakovlevna, of course, followed her own principles rather than Anna's advice, and added, "Mitia, you're already a big boy. For sure, you'll be smarter than they"—she pointed at the parish-school boys—"and won't make us use the rod on you. But watch out, because you won't get away with anything, either."

Anna Iakovlevna not only gave us sermons but took care of us in other ways. As before, our food was good, actually even a little better. She had us beat the dust every other week out of the felt strips on which we slept. The steam bath was heated for us each week instead of every other week. Above all, our solicitous landlady almost always went into the steam bath with us, though she did not take off her shirt in front of us. If she had enough free time, she herself would sit on the bench and wash the head of each of us. Then she would instruct each of us to wash our own body and to rub each other's backs with soapy washcloths. At the same time, she would examine us, as they say, from head to toe, front and back, to see whether we had any itch-mite rashes. In itself, that sort of examination would not have mattered to us, but the trouble was that it also revealed who among us had recently been flogged in class. Then the questions would start—"So, what did you get flogged for?"—and we would be advised to behave and study better and so on.

Since Anna Iakovlevna had given me something like the rank of elder over my fellow lodgers, I began modeling my behavior toward them after the ideal that I had conceived by observing the elders in class. I felt all the more empowered to do this because the fathers of my subordinates had also asked me to look after them, explain their lessons to them, make sure they were not lazy, and so on. The way I saw things at the time, I was essentially a little Mikhail Iakovlevich. And my conduct toward my fellow lodgers was in fact self-important and almost as though I were their commander. I would reprimand them (that is, scold them when they did something wrong) and allow myself to pull their hair and ears, but mainly I would complain to Anna Iakovlevna when they had done something wrong or had dared disobey me, for which Anna Iakovlevna sometimes punished them with the rod. Naturally, I did not win my subordinates' affection with such behavior. But I found ways to aggravate their dislike for me even more by doing other stupid things, such as arguing self-importantly that they, as parish-school boys, were insignificant next to us of the lower division, that we could beat them up whenever we wished, that the teachers did not flog us, and if they did flog us, then not painfully and only with our shirts on, while they, as little kids, would get thrashed almost to death. My subordinates, in turn, began to rebel against me and complained about how I would harass, pinch, and kick them and so on. Anna also took their side: "Mother Anna Iakovlevna, you should give the elder himself a good flogging, 'cause he's really naughty and a bully." Our common commander would reprimand me, even threaten to punish me, too, if I did not give up my pretensions to being the boss, and sometimes she even pulled my hair and ears, and all in front of my subordinates. This hurt my pride and I became even more bitter toward my subordinates.

[On a Saturday at the end of September 1820, Rostislavov had been caned at school and was mortified when his "subordinates" told Anna and she made fun of him. In his determination to avoid the steam bath that night—when all would be able to see the traces of the caning, and he would be questioned about it and would have to listen to a sermon from Anna Iakovlevna—he first lied to Anna Iakovlevna, then ran away to hide in the attic, and finally refused to enter the bath. The result was that Anna Iakovlevna had Andriusha administer a light caning to him, which so enraged him that he later punched another of his housemates and gave him a bloody nose. This caused Anna Iakovlevna's patience to snap, so she strapped him to a bench and gave him a thorough caning.]

The execution was cruel, and when it was over I lay almost completely naked and half-unconscious on the rear bench, and I wept and wept and eventually fell asleep. Andriusha covered me with my dressing gown. Waking up was bitter, for my subordinates had seen me flogged in front of them in a way that they so far had never been flogged; as they say, all my swagger left me. Once she had calmed down, Anna Iakovlevna also felt sorry for me. The next day, she called me into the annex, sat me down on her lap, and said, "Silly you, what were you thinking, being stubborn like that and then starting a fight? Stop this nonsense—now you can see for yourself how you get punished for it." Then she gave me some goodies to eat and let me go. But I had already seen that I had no cause to put on airs in front of my fellow lodgers, so I made peace with them, and Andriusha and I became friends again.

[Rostislavov grew tired of Anna Iakovlevna's authority and occasional floggings and wished to move to a different house where he might enjoy greater liberty. So, in order to obtain his parents' approval, he began to complain to them about life under Anna Iakovlevna.]

However, all of my tales would have accomplished nothing, had it not been for the quarrel between Father and the Beliaevs during my second year in the lower division. At that time, the metrical and ecclesiastical books, that is, the records of births and of who had or had not received communion, were sent to each ecclesiastical board by the clergy of the districts assigned to that board, and from there they were forwarded to the consistory.* Then prelate Sergii decided that the records should all be submitted directly to the consistory. That order was a very good idea. Together with these books, the clergy had always enclosed what people called "Prince Khovanskii's documents," that is, the paper money of the time, as a bribe for the members and secretary of the board. In addition they also had to win over the consistory, which had the right to verify the documents forwarded to it; if you did not win them over, it would cost you more. Under the prelate's new instructions, bribes would have to be paid only to the consistory. The members and secretaries of the ecclesiastical boards were extremely unhappy, even bitter, about this innovation, since it caused significant losses to their bottomless pockets. Whether justly or not, I don't know, but rumor had it that my father, who enjoyed His Grace's favor, had suggested this innovation to him. Of course, the members of the Kasimov Ecclesiastical Board—our headmaster [Polikarp Kistrovskii], [the district-school teacher and inspector] Krasnov, Father Fedor, and especially the secretary, [Ivan Efimovich] Beliaev—began to look askance at my father. At the house, I often had to hear angry complaints about him from Ivan Efimovich, Father Fedor, and Anna Iakovlevna; the latter, it seemed to me, grew harsher toward me than before. Once, when we kitchen-dwellers were all being punished for some mischief or other, she ordered that the others each be given six blows, but when it was my turn, she said, "Give this one ten—you know, his father . . ." and did not complete her sentence, but it was clear that I was getting four extra blows because of my father. I told about that at home, Mother interceded on my behalf, and it was decided that I would be moved to a different residence as of 1822. [. . .]

My new home was right by the St. Nicholas ravine, in the house of some townswoman named Dar'ia. This house consisted of one small wing with three windows along the front. A merchant's clerk and his family occupied almost two-thirds of it, and the remaining space—about twelve feet wide and twenty-three feet long—was home to us

---

* The consistory was the board responsible for the affairs of the entire diocese (in this case, the diocese of Riazan). It supervised the ecclesiastical boards in the diocese's various districts, and these in turn dealt with the affairs of the individual parishes.

seminarians. More than a quarter was taken up by a large "Russian" stove.* Between it and the wall was a passage somewhat over five feet wide, where our coats hung from nails. In the remainder, aside from the benches fixed to the walls, stood a table and a bench. In that room there lived the landlady with her daughter and son, and we eight seminarians, eleven people in total.

[Most of his roommates were from the village of Parakhino, near Tuma: the three Gusev brothers (Iakov, Prokopii, and Dmitrii), sons of the deacon Fedot; Ivan Krylov, the priest Ivan Antonovich's son; and Timofei Gusev, the son of the sacristan Ivan Eliseev. In addition, there were the two brothers Veselkin, whose father Mikhei was sacristan in the village of Kurmon. Rostislavov felt and was treated as an outsider in this group.

Overcrowding and the landlady's poverty meant that the room was always messy, everything became and stayed filthy, and only every other week were linens changed and steam baths taken; even then, the steam bath lacked adequate heat and water. As a result, the linens became extremely dirty. Rostislavov contracted the skin rashes typical of church-school students, and he and his fellow lodgers suffered an onslaught of what were known as "infantry" (lice) and "cavalry" (fleas), though not "artillery" (bedbugs). The food was likewise far worse than at Anna Iakovlevna's. Almost all his fellow lodgers were deacons' and sacristans' sons, hence poor, and brought virtually all their food supplies from home. To supplement their meager diet, the boys would catch crayfish in the Oka.]

Our landlady was not a positively bad woman, and she actually had quite a few good qualities, but her poverty often made her nasty, unfair, and greedy. She and her two young children lived only on the proceeds from the house. I don't remember how much she was paid by the clerk who occupied two-thirds of the house. From each of us she received ten paper rubles a year, but for that she was expected to supply cabbage, kvass, and salt for us at her own expense; her income, you can see, was small. It is therefore not surprising that she liked using our supplies, and no matter how closely we paid attention, she would find ways to steal from us, a little at a time, flour, groats, butter, and even sour cream. When there was meat in the cabbage soup, she would manage to skim off a good portion for her family

---

* A "Russian" stove was made of brick and used for cooking and baking.

and replace it with water; there was no way for us to keep an eye on all of that. Furthermore, she would lose her temper as soon as we damaged or broke anything, or generally if we caused her any sort of loss. [The behavior of the boys involved cards, violence, and the usual crudeness of young church-school students.]

As regards our academic achievements and our conduct, we were considered in general to be good students. Two of us, Dmitrii Gusev and I, graduated from and became ordinary professors* at ecclesiastical academies. Three—the two Veselkins and Krylov—graduated from the seminary, the former two even in the top tier. Our elder, Iakov Gusev, was always one of the top students, but he became sick while in the "philosophical" class† and left to become a monk. Prokopii Gusev was always a very good student but died while in the "rhetorical" class. Only Timofei [Gusev] studied poorly and was soon expelled from the school. As for conduct, if we leave aside the usual schoolboy and childish mischief and foolish pranks, only the elder Veselkin can properly be described as bad. [He became a drinker, card player, and occasional thief while still in the lower division, and his father came to Kasimov to administer a beating to him.] I repeat, with regard to our conduct we were considered to be good, even very good students.[47]‡ And how did things eventually turn out? The seminary education did not bear very good fruit. I alone lived my entire life without being a drunkard.

[Iakov Gusev began drinking as a monk, eventually lost his position as abbot of a monastery near Skopin because of his alcoholism, and currently—in the 1860s—sees devils and hears voices even when sober. Dmitrii Gusev drank moderately while at the St. Petersburg Ecclesiastical Academy but became an alcoholic at the academy in Kazan and also lost his mind to the point that he now "sees the Lord Sabaoth, Jesus Christ, etc." Martinian Veselkin (the older of the two brothers) and Krylov became priests and drank themselves to death. Timofei Gusev became a sacristan in Tuma and is long since retired; "his alcoholism had already caused his hands to shake when he was a little over forty years old." The younger Veselkin left the clergy and "conducted himself better than his older brother," but died a young man.

---

    * As opposed to adjunct professors.

    † The seminary offered a 6-year course of study. Because of the main subject being taught, the third and fourth years were known as "philosophy" and the last two as "rhetoric."

    ‡ School records indicate that Rostislavov himself ranked fourth among the 38 students of the lower division in 1822, with "excellent" academic achievements and "good" conduct.

Rostislavov hoped to move back to Anna Iakovlevna's house. However, his father examined him in Latin and other subjects and was dissatisfied with his progress, even though he was ranked fourth in his class. He may have realized that the instruction in Kasimov was poor, but the marks left by floggings at Mikhail Iakovlevich's hands, the knowledge that his son was often mischievous and lazy, and the realization that he had lied about supposed mistreatment at Anna Iakovlevna's house—all of that convinced Father that his son was not conducting himself well in Kasimov and should be transferred to the church school in Riazan.]

[Translator's Note: After spending the summer of 1822 at home, Rostislavov and his father set out for Riazan on September 7, 1822. The boy would remain there for seven years, taking the last year of the upper-division course in the district school and then the six-year course of the seminary. The following letter, evidently a standard form letter drafted by an official scribe (the kind of routine paperwork for which clerks often needed to be bribed), documents his transfer to Riazan. It reads:

To the Riazan Seminary Administration
From the Priest Ioann Martinov of the Village of Tuma, Kasimov District

A Most Humble Petition:

I have with me my son Dimitrii Rostislavov, who, upon the petition I submitted on September 1 of this year to HIS GRACE,* has been transferred from the Kasimov Ecclesiastical District School to the same in Riazan, and whom, to better his education in scholarship and morals under the supervision of my kinsman, the student of the Seminary's Intermediate Division Aleksei Vikherev, I wish to include among the students who receive a government stipend with disbursement of the appropriate sum.

Whereupon I most humbly petition the Seminary Administration to grant my above-mentioned son Dimitrii Rostislavov a government stipend with disbursement of the appropriate sum, and to give this its gracious attention. September 1822. *[In a different handwriting:]* To this petition Ioann Martinov, priest of the Church of St. Nicholas in the village of Tuma, Kasimov District, affixed his signature.[48]

---

* In official correspondence, the honorific titles of highly placed individuals were always written in capital letters as a mark of deference.

The petition for a stipend was denied, so Rostislavov, like other "self-paying" students, was required to pay 75 to 85 rubles per year for room and board at the school. The church school and seminary in Riazan had many sadly familiar features: squalid housing, disgusting filth, rats and other vermin, repulsive institutional food, intense group rivalries among students, brutal student elders, corporal punishment, capricious and eccentric teachers, a corrupt and authoritarian administration, and a pedagogy that discouraged creative thinking. Compared with Kasimov, however, the intellectual level of the teachers was higher, floggings were less common, and the students were more prone to adult vices such as drunkenness and spying on each other on the administration's behalf.

To ensure that he performed better than in Kasimov, Rostislavov's father followed a common practice by placing his son under the supervision of a tutor responsible for ensuring that Rostislavov was a good student, and empowered to flog him if he was not. As in Kasimov, corporal punishment was also an integral part of the school culture. While the teachers and administration were generally less violent toward the students than in Kasimov, the student tutors regularly inflicted brutal floggings expressly designed to humiliate the victim; Rostislavov devotes lengthy passages to descriptions of these floggings. Students who studied together sometimes even agreed to flog each other for mistakes in their homework. Overall, while he gained a very negative impression of the seminary as an institution and of the social dynamics between administration, teachers, and students, he also found it to be ultimately an academically rewarding and enriching experience.]

CHAPTER SEVENTEEN

Society in Kasimov

• I left the school in Kasimov shortly before turning thirteen, when I was not yet a good observer of the inhabitants of the town. Nonetheless, I do remember things that took place, so to speak, right before my eyes, and I have not forgotten the impression that they made on me. I would now like to discuss those facts and impressions.[*]

Kasimov, at that time, could in no way be considered an aristocratic town and extremely few nobles not in government service lived there, although some of them, including Zasetskii (the landlord of Per'ino), owned large houses. The nobility of the district lived in their hamlets and would come to town to booze or take care of business; even the marshalls of the nobility[†] preferred living in their hamlets rather than in town. Among the government-appointed and elected officials who lived permanently in town, the most important were of course the town police chief, the district judge, the solicitor *(striapchii)*, the land captain, and the treasurer. However, as the Russian proverb says: "In the land of the blind the one-eyed is king," and so the precinct police chief *(chastnyi pristav)*, the secretaries of the district and land courts, and so on also played an appreciable role. The scholarly estate of local society *(uchenoe soslovie)* consisted mainly of our school and the lay district school.[‡] The latter was directed and taught by a headmaster and, I think, three teachers, but they were not much better than ours; they could not punish their students as cruelly as our educators flogged us, but even so, hardly anyone educated at the civil district school avoided making the acquaintance of

---

[*] Via the Oka and the Nizhnii Novgorod road, Kasimov was linked with Moscow and the Volga and Kama Rivers and with trade networks extending as far as China and the Middle East. A major road from Moscow to southeast Russia also passed through Kasimov. Not surprisingly, therefore, Kasimov was a major commercial entrepôt.

[†] The marshall of the nobility was the elected leader of the district's nobles.

[‡] The term "estate" applied to hereditary social strata (e.g., state peasants or nobles), but also to any category of people who shared important sociocultural or economic characteristics.

the rod. The Orthodox clergy should be included partly with the scholarly estate and partly with the service estate of Kasimov. It consisted of twelve priests, ten deacons, and twenty-odd sacristans. The priests were almost all seminary graduates. Some of the deacons had reached the "rhetorical" and even the "philosophical" class. As for the sacristans, they were able of course to read and write, and some had even studied in the lower classes of the seminary, but overall, few among them could be called even half educated.

The priests would each give two or three sermons in the cathedral—in this area, the archpriest [Polikarp Kistrovskii, headmaster of the church school] held, or assigned himself, first place. He would preach the Word of God on certain solemn occasions, for example, on the patronal festival of the cathedral or on some official state holiday. It would become known in advance that His High Benediction was composing a sermon. At those times, he might go for an entire week without visiting anyone, he would moan and sigh and sometimes declaim in his office, and he would even exhibit an unusual indulgence and kindness toward us. Then the recopying of the sermon would begin, for which good scribes from among us or the sacristans were used. They would write in a very large hand, out of concern for the preacher's poor vision and nearsightedness, so it was not surprising that these homilies were huge in terms of the quantities of paper. "You know, the sermon that the archpriest has prepared for Ascension Day fills ten or twelve sheets," we would say with a certain reverence. In church, he would deliver the actual sermons exceedingly loudly, and shout almost as he did when he would greet us with "Hey, you studs"* and so on.

The clergy lived a peculiar kind of life. Within their own parish, of course, like it or not, they would be invited or come on their own to people's homes to perform various rites, but outside their parish they had few acquaintances, except for the archpriest and Krasnov,[49]† for whom doors were opened everywhere. On the other hand, the members of the clergy also were not on very close or harmonious terms with each other; at least, they almost never went to visit one another. Perhaps one reason for this was poverty, because only the Church of

---

* *"Ei vy, kobyliatniki, meriniatniki."* Kistrovskii's tone is evidently crudely jocular. *Kobyliatnik* comes from *kobyla* (mare) and refers to a young man of marriageable age, or a philanderer. *Meriniatnik* comes from *merin* (gelding), but its meaning is unclear.

† Archpriest Ioakim Fedorov Krasnov, born around 1790, taught in the district school and was inspector of the district and parish school, a member of the ecclesiastical board, and priest of the Kazan Nunnery.

the Assumption was considered wealthy in terms of revenues.* In the other churches, the members of the clergy were not starving, but neither could they live in luxury. For example, we were fully aware that tea was not drunk every day, mornings and evenings, in the homes of Gorokhov and Mikhail Iakovlevich.[50] † In addition to poverty, however, the cause for the estrangement between the priests could also be envy, or the petty sense of pride that one notices among them.

The deacons of the town also found reasons to be unhappy with each other. The central issue was their voices. The best bassos were the deacons of the churches of the Annunciation and St. Egor', whereas the cathedral deacons Dmitrii and especially Matvei had a kind of reedy falsetto. However, when joint services were held in the cathedral on state holidays, the order of precedence gave first place to the cathedral deacons, indeed to Matvei. [This discrepancy between status and talent led to a highly public rivalry between the deacons.] There is nothing particular to be said about the sacristans: they rang the bells, sang, drank, walked about the parish—what else could anyone demand of them? Still, there was also a fair number of good people among them.

Towering above the entire clergy, however, was the power of the reverend archpriest [Polikarp Polikarpovich Kistrovskii]. He maintained tight control over everyone, and cleaned them out quite thoroughly, although he did encounter opposition from some people.

[Rostislavov devotes the better part of an earlier chapter (ch. 22 of the Russian original) to the archpriest's lavish lifestyle and the corrupt ways by which he paid for it. One source of income was the local merchants' respect for the church hierarchy and rites: some brought him gifts on holidays; from others he received goods on credit and never paid; with still others he would (without being invited) bless their barges or other operations and expect payment. Another

---

* The Church of the Assumption is located on Cathedral Square and near some of the town's wealthiest homes, which probably belonged to the church's parish.

† Ioakim Fedorov Gorokhov, born around 1792, taught at the district school and was priest at the Church of St. Nicholas. In 1822, the school officially paid the following annual salaries: Kistrovskii, 477.50 rubles; Krasnov, 638.70; Gorokhov, 576.66; Mikhail Iakovlevich Mirtov, 437.20. Though well above the salaries set by official regulations, these sums were very modest. For Mirtov's family, which by the 1830s came to include 2 adults and at least 6 children, this would have represented a measly 44 rubles per person per 42-week school year, i.e., barely over half the sum (80 rubles) that the state budgeted as a stipend to cover food and candles for a single student. Since the teachers were also priests, they could presumably supplement their salaries with fees for performing religious rites, income from "exalting Christ," food from their vegetable gardens, etc.

source was his position as head of the Kasimov Ecclesiastical Board, which allowed him to extort bribes from the lower clergy of the area. Since their correspondence with the consistory had to pass through his office, he could threaten to file damaging reports about them with the consistory. He was responsible for reviewing and approving the sermons that the local priests were required to give in the cathedral, and extorted bribes for not reporting their frequent failure to meet the obligation to preach. At least once a year, he toured the parishes in his jurisdiction to collect "donations," which he also expected from clergy who visited Kasimov; in addition, extraordinary donations were expected if he faced unusual expenditures, such as the weddings and dowries of his son and four daughters.

A third source of money was the church school of which he was the headmaster. Parents who enrolled their son for the first time had to pay him five paper rubles, as well as other payments at least once a year and further payments to ensure that the student did not need to repeat the year. (The students also had to pay for chalk for their classrooms, replace broken school windows, etc.) He also charged double or triple the standard price for required textbooks, which he obtained without ever paying for them from his friend and accomplice, Rector Ieronim of the Riazan seminary. Sometimes the students were told that the money they had paid for their books had "disappeared" altogether and that they would have to pay again. When the Riazan seminary got a new rector and demanded payment for several years' worth of unpaid books, the archpriest made a tour of his district to collect the necessary money from the clergy. Furthermore, as already discussed, he pocketed the money designated for stipends and used the main school building as his personal residence. He also used the school watchmen as his personal servants and embezzled their wages.]

His opponents included: first, Petr, the priest of the coachmen, who was a sort of lawyer, or should I say, a pettifogger.* The archpriest, with his many peccadilloes, was afraid of him. Second, Golenishcha, the priest of the Church of the Annunciation. He would visit the archpriest and also entertain him in return, but he was dangerous because he was an eccentric man who, if he flew into a rage, might start shout-

---

* Russia had no professional attorneys, but amateurs who had sufficient skill, tenacity, and experience could make the slow-moving and corrupt courts work to their advantage. (A pettifogger is a petty, shifty lawyer.) Coachmen (*iamshchiki*) were a hereditary estate of peasants required to provide horses for people traveling on government business and to transport mail and other goods free of charge. They had a separate settlement adjacent to Kasimov.

ing in the middle of the market and reveal all about whoever had offended him. Polikarp Polikarpovich treated him like a vicious dog and did not touch him. Third, the deacon of the Church of the Assumption, an old man rumored to be rich. He lived a very solitary life and refused to mingle with anyone. The archpriest respected him because he could borrow money from the deacon in times of need. And fourth, Isaak, the sacristan of the same Church of the Assumption. He was one of those people who fit the expression "in one ear, out the other." Though only a sacristan, he was able to worm himself into the homes of all the wealthy merchants in town. Touching him would have been dangerous because he would have been able, in a single day, to spread such scandalous rumors that the reverend archpriest would never have recovered, so it was better not to quarrel with him.

The town's real core, one might even say its aristocracy, consisted of merchants, many of them rich people and among whom first place belonged to Ivan Osipovich Alianchikov.[51]* He was a very fat man who had grown rich as a liquor-farmer, conducted almost no trade, and, so to speak, rested on his laurels. His magnificent house was designed in grand style, and almost every day his drawing room was filled with guests, most of whom probably hungered and thirsted when they arrived but could be sure they would be filled by the time they left.† As a result, he was the most honored person in town. Everyone, even the town police chief, bowed first when they met him in the street. When he arrived at the cathedral on state holidays, the precinct police chief made an even greater effort to clear a path through the crowd for him than for the town police chief. Ivan Osipovich would then walk majestically between the two rows of people and graciously acknowledge the deep bows that greeted him from both sides. Facing the iconostasis, he would stand in front of everyone, next to the town police chief. All of this could give you the idea that he was the town's most important person, its leader, and that indeed is what I thought. When I heard that Ivan Osipovich was a merchant, I conceived an exceedingly high opinion of merchants, who stood higher in my eyes than did nobles and officials.

---

* The Alianchikov liquor-farmer dynasty came into being when Osip Samoilovich Alianchikov, Ivan Osipovich's father, first went into the business in 1771. In the 1780s and 1790s, his sons Ivan, Nikolai, and Petr helped expand the family's liquor-farming activities into the neighboring provinces, and they operated on a huge scale in the period 1799–1819 in cooperation with the Iakunchikov family of Kasimov. Since liquor-farmers were required to provide the state with collateral in the form of real estate, the Alianchikovs and Iakunchikovs, as well as G. V. Riumin in Riazan, had enormous mansions built for themselves that still stand today; the Alianchikov mansion is located near the church school.

† Matthew 5:6—"Blessed are they which do hunger and thirst after righteousness: for they shall be filled."

The town's second celebrity was our headmaster, Polikarp Polikarpovich. With his intelligence, his outgoing and cheerful disposition, his lively and engaging conversation, and—when the occasion called for it—his mordant, implacable sarcasm, one could say that he was in command of Kasimov society. People liked him, and respected him, and feared him. When I was already in the "theological" class* and was in Kasimov for New Year's, I thought it my duty as his former student to pay my respects to His High Benediction and spent about two hours at his house right after mass. During that time, every prominent official in Kasimov managed to call on him and wish him a happy new year, and the reverend archpriest received them with a self-important and courteous air that suggested familiarity but also superiority.

Of the other prominent merchants in town, one might mention the Tatar Salekh Burkhaich (I think his last name was Gamza), Dmitrii Sergeevich Barkov, Mikhail Abramovich Iakunchikov, the Kolchins, the Shishkins, and others. Salekh owned large tanneries and carried on an extensive trade in Asian goods.[52]† Although he dressed like a Tatar and lived in the Tatar suburb, he had social relations with Russians, and our archpriest was a close friend of his. Barkov was not very rich yet at that time, but already lived in grand style.

[Barkov was a former serf who had somehow learned medicine—some said that he had served as footman to a physician, others, that his master had sent him to Moscow to study medicine. In any event, he had acquired medical skills (though no license), obtained his freedom, registered as a merchant in Kasimov, and earned a good living with his medical practice and pharmacy. After the period described here, a government-employed physician forced him to give up practicing medicine and become a more conventional merchant. He provided free medical care to the church-school administrators, and they in turn sent their students on frequent, long, unpaid expeditions to the countryside around Kasimov to gather medicinal herbs for him, on pain of floggings if plant-gathering quotas were not met.]

He had a magnificent garden, not only with wonderful trees but also with ponds that had little fish swimming in them, and when I went to him for medical treatment, I loved watching them swim and play in

---

* The last two years of the seminary.

† Salekh Burkhaich (whose surname was Shakulov) was a *sayyid*, that is, a supposed descendant of the Prophet Mohammed, and came from an old Tatar family that had lost its noble status, though not its wealth, and legally become state peasants in the early eighteenth century.

the clear, shallow water. Barkov later became a millionaire in the iron business, but there is something shady about his wealth.[53] Iakunchikov, who had long been Alianchikov's assistant, had at that time already gone up in the world; he grew richer and richer, and when he died during Nicholas I's reign, he left an estate worth seven million silver rubles.* There were also a few other very wealthy merchant families.

Most of the citizens of Kasimov, however, were Orthodox folk who lived by the traditions of the distant past and were not enamored of the latest ideas or the principles of 1789; they ate their fill, slept a lot, went to church on holidays, and so on and so forth, in a word, they prospered and gave glory to Christ. Never again, I think, did I encounter anywhere such a large number of fat people as I saw among the estates of merchants and townspeople in Kasimov. What bigshots they were! Ivan Osipovich Alianchikov, Iakov Petrovich Kurbatov,† the Kolchins, the Shishkins, and so on. I was especially struck by one merchant husband and his wife whose names I have forgotten. They drove the most old-fashioned droshky, with little leather awnings on both sides. They had a big, strong horse but always went at a walk, and in fact it would have been impossible to hurry, because really, each passenger must have weighed at least 360 pounds.

Not many merchant wives had started dressing fashionably yet by that time, with caps and hats, dresses, coats, and so on. The majority wore the traditional tall headdresses *(kokoshnik)*, sleeveless dresses *(sarafan)*, sleeveless fur mantles *(epanechka)*, or tied shawls around their heads. All of these things were very expensive. The headdresses were studded with pearls, the mantles were richly brocaded, and the shawls were embroidered with silver and gold. For some reason, the merchant wives especially loved to show off their finery at communion during Lent. At those times, little boys like us were dazzled, looking at all the gold and silver.

Alas, even back then, the Evil One's presence in Kasimov was revealed through more than just people being turned into swine, for even among the merchantry there were liberals steeped in the ideas of Voltaire and Jean-Jacques Rousseau. Among the chief liberals were Alianchikov's sons Iakov and, especially, Nikolai. They really were widely read people, but, having received no systematic education and hence not knowing what to make of the thoughts that were imprinted in their minds by the books of the French *encyclopédistes,* they

---

* Equivalent to almost 25 million paper rubles.

† See p. 113

merely loved to show off their freethinking and atheism. Old man Alianchikov was very worried about the salvation of his sons' souls, and in hopes of softening their hearts he asked our archpriest to convert them to the true path and charged my father to do the same. "Please," the old man would fret, "go and talk to my Nikolai and my Iakov. My trouble with them is that they don't believe in God, they don't honor the saints, they don't go to church, and they don't want to receive communion." I heard about this apostolic work repeatedly from my father. However, the clergymen's efforts were not enough to shake the convictions of Alianchikov's sons; in this case, Satan the tempter and seducer proved far more powerful than the guardian angel and the clergymen armed with the Word of God.

Throughout the time I lived in Kasimov, the town had temporary residents who formed a distinct group that was feuding almost constantly with the natives. Soon after the end of the War for the Fatherland,* the Izium Hussar Regiment was billeted in Kasimov District. Its troops, who were said to have displayed exceptional bravery during the war, carried their bivouac and campaign habits with them into this peaceful corner of Riazan Province, where they liked to give orders just as they had in enemy territory. The officers were determined to snub even honored citizens and officials, and in the cathedral during prayers for the tsar, to the local residents' great annoyance, they would push all the prominent Kasimov society figures into the background, even the town police chief and Alianchikov. They barely got to know the locals and instead formed a distinct group, and they boozed as befitted hussars of the age of Davydov and Burtsev.†

As much as possible, the colonel and the captains‡ preferred to keep the money that was supposed to pay for the upkeep of the soldiers and horses, and left their hussars to feed themselves in their billets at their hosts' expense. Since they often did not even want to buy hay for the horses, the soldiers sometimes obtained it by foraging. At first, the local inhabitants were unfamiliar with military billeting and felt obligated to satisfy their lodgers' demands. But when it became known that the soldiers were being issued money for both food and

---

* The 1812 war against Napoleon.

† Denis Vasil'evich Davydov (1784–1839) was a dashing hussar officer and partisan leader during the 1812 war, and Ivan Grigor'evich Burtsev (1795–1829) was a native of Riazan Province and veteran of the 1812–1814 campaigns. It was a widespread cliché that hussars were bold warriors and inveterate drinkers and womanizers.

‡ A cavalry regiment was typically commanded by a colonel, and divided into squadrons that were commanded by captains. I thank Mark Conrad for providing me with information on this topic.

fodder and that the inhabitants were required only to provide accommodations, trouble broke out between the military and civilian authorities and between the hussars and their hosts. The hussars did not restrain themselves, and before I started going to school, people were already talking with horror about the excesses perpetrated by a squadron of hussars billeted in the parish of Parakhino. Their way of foraging for hay was especially original. At night, the hussars would ride out on their horses from a number of different stables to a preassigned haystack, tie ropes around the hay to shape it into cylinders, and carry off several *puds* on each horse; sometimes all they left of an entire stack was the rotting hay that formed the top and bottom layers. The peasants began to watch for such outings, so the two hostile parties—one armed with stakes, the other with whips and sabers—would meet by the haystacks or along the way, and if what ensued could not be called a battle, it certainly was a fight. As men who were disciplined and accustomed to combat, the valiant defenders of the fatherland would of course emerge victorious. At least, no one was killed in Parakhino, but in the village of Shost'e the tension between peasants and hussars exploded one holiday, and rumor had it that several peasants were killed in the skirmish. Nor did the hussars forget to steal from people's homes or commit robbery on the roads and streets, so it could be dangerous to walk around Kasimov at night.

What caused an especially great stir, and helped to bring the regiment back under control, was an incident involving the land captain. He was an honest and forceful man who informed peasants and landlords that the hussars were receiving rations as well as money for oats and hay, and that they were supposed to pay if they consumed anything that belonged to their hosts. That cut into the take of the colonel and the captains, so they decided that the land captain needed to be taught a lesson. While returning to town from Gusevskii Pogost, he was surrounded by a mounted hussar detachment, about twenty-five strong. They merely tied up his companions without harming them, but the land captain they beat unconscious with their whips and almost killed him. It was said that the commander of the detachment was an officer, but none of the culprits was ever discovered—that is how cunningly the raid had been planned!

All these disorders finally prompted stern measures against the regimental commanders and caused colonels and captains to be replaced. The colonel mentioned earlier shot himself, and it was rumored that his reason for committing suicide was fear of being demoted. Finally, a regimental commander was sent who used the

Arakcheev method and brought the troublemakers back under control with the help of the cane, the birch rod, and blows with the flat of the saber. Walking past the guardhouse, we would often see such punishment being meted out. Nevertheless, I don't think that this put a stop to the enmity between the local residents and the regiment. On the other hand, the hussars also provided the inhabitants a good deal of pleasure with their drill exercises, the changing of the guards, and the military songs they sang in their stables.

But even on their own, without the hussars' influence, the inhabitants of Kasimov were inclined to warlike exercises. This inclination manifested itself principally in fist fights.* Those who took part were townsmen, coachmen, Tatars, and generally, one might say, the lower class; young merchants of modest means were likewise not averse to beating up others and exposing their own sides to their blows. The solid citizenry, elderly and old people, distinguished merchants and officials, of course did not personally join the ranks of the pugilists, but they did like to egg them on with words, vodka, gifts, and money; as I will shortly explain, this pugilistic patriotism could reach absurd levels of ecstatic intensity. The opposing parties were assembled in various ways. If it was only Russians fighting against Russians, then the coachmen, blacksmiths, and parishioners of St. Egor's Church were on one side, and the remaining folk of the town on the other, although the composition of the battling parties varied and depended on different circumstances. Fights would take place in Cathedral Street. The coachmen would apply their efforts to drive the inhabitants of the town to the cathedral; that was the ultimate disgrace, and the victorious coachmen would call out to them that "you lost the cathedral." When I was lodging with the Beliaevs, I lived near Cathedral Street, which is why I saw these fights. The heat of battle grew so intense that many a combatant would walk away with a black eye, a broken nose, or his chin turned sidewise. There were instances where powerful blows would make eyes pop out of their sockets, to say nothing of blows to the chest and sides. People would even incur consumption. Still, this did not generate that total fervor, and that truly warlike spirit, that were on display when one set of combatants consisted of Tatars and the other set of the entire Russian population.† Those battles almost always took place on what was called "the

---

* A cinematic depiction of such a fight can be seen in the 1998 movie *Sibirskii tsiriul'nik* (The Barber of Siberia), directed by Nikita Mikhalkov.

† As Rostislavov describes in the following chapter, a large part of Kasimov's population were Turkic-speaking Muslim Tatars.

Tatar Side," on the large square near the mosque. The Russian host needed to cross the deep ravine that separated the Tatar quarter from the Russian population. During my time, there were two remarkable battles that all Kasimov talked about for a long time after.

Once, after a long struggle, the Russians had been victorious over the Tatars and pinned them against the house and garden of the rich man Salekh, cutting off any sideways retreat. The protracted battle had inflamed tempers to a high degree, and the victors dealt unmercifully with the defeated. Hoping to benefit from the adage that "you don't kick a man when he's down," the Tatars dropped to the ground. Our Orthodox folk had a sacred regard for tradition but also wanted to beat up the Tatars for their resistance, so they put them back on their feet, two or more would press a Tatar's arms against the wall of the house or against the fence, and another one or two would pound him with their fists, mercilessly and to their hearts' content, in the face or chest. Plenty of Tatars received this kind of beating.

Naturally, they wanted to take revenge on the infidels. In his tanneries and other commercial and manufacturing facilities, Salekh was rumored to have as many as one hundred fifty Tatar workers. It was rare for him to allow them to take part in fist fights, especially all of them at once, but now his Tatar patriotism was aroused. For two or three weeks, a kind of enforced truce prevailed. Finally, one Sunday, the battle—for which the Russians had also done everything to ready themselves—was joined. It lasted a long time, with shifting fortunes, but finally the Tatars started to retreat past the mosque, toward Salekh's house. Flushed with excitement, the Russians pursued their retreating opponents. But when they approached Salekh's house, the gates opened and Salekh's workers, who had not been involved in the affair up to that point, burst forth. Inspired by tribal patriotism, a fresh one hundred to one hundred fifty young fellows threw themselves onto the opponent and gave courage to their coreligionists. The Russians had no reserve force aside from gawkers and devotees (who included respected merchants and officials). As a result, they were unable to resist for long, quickly began retreating down one of the streets, and finally rushed headlong toward the ravine and piled into it any way they could. The Tatars did not hesitate long and descended into the ravine themselves in order to defeat the Russians on their native ground, something they had not done before. The slope coming up to our side was very steep, so the Russians, who had entrenched themselves there, were long able to hold off their enemies.

Alarm spread in the town, and people cried, "The Tatars are coming! They want to take the cathedral! Orthodox folk, at least defend the cathedral!" But nothing helped. The Tatars came down a different street and attacked the Russians from the rear. Of course, caught from two directions, the Russians ran. Urged on by rich merchants, they regrouped near our school in order to defend the cathedral, but on that day, luck or strength was on the side of the worshippers of Mohammed, while the defenders of the Cross, that is, of the cathedral, were utterly defeated and fled in all directions. The Tatars circled the cathedral and, seeing no further resistance, marched back to their suburbs in a dense column, singing Tatar songs. The Russians' patriotism was intensely irritated by this insult, but there was nothing to be done against the law of the fist.

As people who would beat each other up in fist fights, the inhabitants of Kasimov could hardly have failed to enjoy those spectacles at which they had the pleasure of seeing others beaten, and in the most merciless yet lawful way at that.[54]* Scenes where criminals were punished with the lash or the knout were popular with the inhabitants of the town, not only the pugilists but also solid citizens. Suffice it to say that our archpriest would very often come, in his priestly kamelaukion,† to the execution site and stand in the front row. When the drum roll began that preceded the sad procession from the police station to the execution site, how folk of all ages would come running from all sides, form a wide circle around the execution site, and climb the cathedral bell tower or nearby market stalls and so on! It was considered a crime to leave our school during class time, but now, if the teachers were not there yet, we would all run out into the square, and sometimes even our educators would leave their classes. For our part, of course, as we watched the criminals' backs being welted with the knout or lash, we could at least find comfort in the thought that their punishment was incomparably more painful than our floggings. But the reverend archpriest and the teachers—why did they go?

The floggings were carried out in different ways, depending on whether the knout or the lash was used. Scaffolds, which began to appear in the 1840s, were not yet in use. Those who had been sentenced to the lash were usually placed on the bare earth, after first having all their outer clothes and their shirt removed, and then, in

---

* After the abolition of the death penalty in 1744, serious crimes were punished with varying combinations of flogging (often with the knout), branding, mutilation, and Siberian exile. The knout was abolished through the adoption of the new penal code in 1845.

† The headdress of a priest.

nothing but their long johns, they would be flogged on the back. The punishment was carried out either by an executioner or by a police soldier, depending on whether the man who was being punished was being exiled to Siberia for resettlement or returning to his previous place of residence. However, if the punishment was to be carried out with the knout, then a so-called wood-sledge was set up, at an angle and with the runners facing upwards; obviously, the wood-sledge was thus positioned to prevent it from falling during the execution. The executioner would undress the convicted man, not removing his shirt but instead tearing it off, and then make him lie down between the runners of the sledge and bind him to it tightly with straps. Before each blow he would take a few steps back from the sledge, raise up the knout and, as people said, strike a running blow at the unfortunate man's back. During the reign of Alexander I and in the first half of Nicholas I's reign, at least, the prescribed number of blows with the knout was low; I heard that there were instances when they limited themselves to one or two blows, and they did not go beyond fifty or, later, even twenty-five. However, under Catherine, Paul, and at first under Alexander I, they would count them out to some people by the hundreds, and my grandfather himself witnessed punishment by three hundred blows of the knout. In the 1840s, when scaffolds were introduced and the knout was abolished and replaced with the lash (which now had three tails instead of the earlier two), the maximum number of blows was raised to one hundred, though now they no longer flogged the back but instead, as they delicately phrased it, the soft parts of the body. The three-tailed lash inspired a witticism in Petersburg. Its introduction coincided with the adoption of silver as the basis for the currency.* Now, it is well known that the silver ruble's value exceeds the paper ruble's three and a half times. Ignoring the fraction when speaking of the replacement of the one-tailed knout by the three-tailed lash, wits would add that Perovskii† had converted the knout from paper to silver. Perovskii was the wits' target here because, as minister of internal affairs at the time, he supposedly insisted more than others on the introduction of the three-tailed lash.

---

* Prior to July 1839, prices, salaries, and so on were calculated in paper rubles; from that date on the silver ruble became the official standard.

† Count Lev Alekseevich Perovskii.

CHAPTER EIGHTEEN

The Tatars of Kasimov

[Translator's Note: By the Late Middle Ages, the region around Moscow was mostly Slavic and Orthodox, while the Volga valley to the east had a largely Muslim, Turkic-speaking population whom the Russians called Tatars and who dominated Russia politically from the thirteenth to the fifteenth century. Ivan the Terrible conquered these areas in the sixteenth century, and Orthodox Russians began settling there. Kasimov, linked to the Volga by the Oka River, was a western outpost of this historically Tatar region.]

• I have more than once mentioned the Kasimov Tatars on the side, so to speak. I would now like to provide somewhat more detailed information about them than I have so far. They lived not only in Kasimov, but also in many nearby hamlets. In the town itself they made up probably a quarter, if not a third, of the inhabitants, and were sharply distinguished from the Russian population by their appearance and dress. While not very tall, they were broad-shouldered, stocky and thickset, with a slightly pointed chin and prominent cheekbones, a bold gaze, a proud gait, and a somewhat majestic bearing. One could still glimpse a few traits in them that recalled the past age when they had ruled the Russian land. It is worth noting that even Russians, if they have friendly relations with them, will call an adult Tatar man "prince" *(kniaz')* out of courtesy. The only Tatars who lived in town were merchants and townspeople, but in the hamlets one encountered not only peasants, but also noble landlords. The nobles would sometimes elect one or another of them to various offices. I remember a Tatar who was land captain (Devlesh-Kindeev, I think), and an assessor of the land court; people found this land captain far more honest than many Russian officials.

The male costume of the Tatars consisted mainly of robes, boots of morocco leather over which they would wear galoshes, and skullcaps that no Tatar would remove from his head no matter where he found himself. In hot weather, Tatars of modest means, just like our peasants, wore only their shirt and did not put on any garment over it. But even in this they differed from us. Their shirts were much longer than ours and descended below the knees, and also the Tatars never put on a belt, whereas our common people considered it almost sinful to be without a belt. In Kasimov District at least, if one Orthodox man saw another without a belt, he would usually say to him, "How come you're not wearing a belt? What, have you turned into a Tatar?" The Tatar women of Kasimov never covered their faces with muslin or any other material, as is customary among Muslim women in Turkey or Persia. However, their costume, especially the headdress, did not at all resemble the Russian clothing of the time. As a special adornment, they made use of pierced silver coins that they would normally weave into their braids or thread onto strings that they arranged on their heads. I have to say that these adornments were not lacking in taste. Polygamy was almost unknown among Kasimov Tatars, with only a few rich men having two or three wives.

One could not say that the relations between Russians and Tatars were entirely pacific. As God-fearing Orthodox folk, we looked with disdain upon people who believed in someone named Mohammed and who even ate horsemeat yet never touched pork or suckling pig. For that reason, most Russians considered the Tatars unbelievers, heathens, accursed, etc., and called them thus. If a Tatar man or woman appeared in Russian streets, then not only little boys, but adults as well—not always, of course, but also not rarely—would shout to him, "Hey, you damned infidel," or "You unclean horsemeat eater," or "You can go stuff your Mohammed," and so on, or "How about a little pork? Come over here, eat some suckling pig," and they would shape a corner of the skirt of their coat into something resembling a pig's ear and show it to him. The public that was standing about, of course, was happy to sympathize with these displays of pseudoreligious zeal. Unfortunately, I have to say that our clergy often aroused and supported the enmity of the Orthodox toward the Tatars. Vysheleskii, my brother-in-law from Sinulitsy, even now speaks of the Tatars with the deepest contempt as being infidels, calling them heathens and not listening to or understanding anything said in their defense. "A heathen's a heathen, what else is there to say?" I have to say, to the Tatars' credit, that it was exceedingly rare for them to return the abuse or, as they say, to bite back. It was almost only gibes about Mohammed that would sometimes make them lose their temper. As for a Russian who walked on their streets, he could be certain that no one would bother him as long as he himself did not insult anyone. The Tatars also were probably more honest than the Russians. At least, many among the latter thought it better in Kasimov to buy various goods from Tatar rather than from Russian merchants, a rule that my sister Mar'ia still follows today.

The Tatars were aware of the disdain, mockery, and outright hostility that the surrounding Russian population harbored toward them, so their common interest forced them to pull together and form a tightly knit community whose members would support each other. If a Russian should offend a Tatar, the latter's coreligionists would be certain to stand up for him. How many times did I have to see some policeman drag a Russian peasant or townsman to the police station and give him one kick after another, with hardly anyone ever putting in a word for his brother Russian. The Tatars, on the other hand, would come running in case of such an arrest, an entire crowd would form, they would make a ruckus, escort the arrested man to the police station, and there demand justice, so that the Kasimov authorities of the time had to act cautiously in such cases and treated Tatars much better than Russians.

The Russian common people had good reason to be envious of the wealth and resultant well-being of their Tatar counterparts. Generally speaking, the Tatars lived in greater prosperity than the Russians. You very rarely met beggars among them, and then only women. It is worth noting that these beggars would also come for charity to Russian homes, where people could not pass up the opportunity to taunt the infidels. The Tatar women usually begged for alms for God's sake, not Christ's sake [as Russian beggars did], but often they were either turned down or told to "take this, for Christ's sake." In that case, the Tatars would never accept the alms and instead ask again for God's sake, and if the almsgiver refused to give in, they would leave without taking anything. On the other hand, from what I heard, Russian beggars would receive alms in Tatar homes without anyone indulging in comparable mockery—no Tatar would offer them charity for Mohammed's sake.

There are many reasons why the Tatars of Kasimov were generally richer than the Russians: first, they formed a separate corporation, so to speak, and sought to support one another in economic matters. Their common interests required this, because the fewer paupers and the more rich people there were among them, the more strength and importance the entire corporation would have, since money can accomplish anything in Holy Russia. It should be said, though, that Muslim religious motivations also played a role here. Second, it seems that none of the Tatars who lived in Kasimov District were serfs, and probably all of them belonged to the free estates of society, whereas the vast majority of Kasimov's Russian peasantry were enslaved and suffered ruin at the hands of their landlords.

Third, our chronicles attribute to Grand Prince Vladimir the famous dictum that "drinking is the joy of the Rus'."[55]* Down to this day, in good times and bad, the Russian loves to drink. Mohammed, on the other hand, forbade his followers to consume liquor. Of course, not all Tatars observe this commandment, for living among Russians gives them, too, the opportunity to get to know the bottle. I myself have seen Tatars drunk, and I know from my sister Mar'ia that, on patronal and other important holidays in the villages of the vicinity, Tatars tour the homes of the clergy and peasants whom they know, wish them a happy holiday, and not only will not decline a drink but will actually ask for one if the host does not have the sense to offer his guest some liquor. There are even liberals among them who, when they hear someone say, "How can you drink vodka when Mohammed forbade you to do so?" will answer, "No, Father, Mohammed only commanded us not to drink grape wine, but he didn't say anything about your vodka." But even so, drunkenness was very rare among the Tatars of Kasimov. Since they work instead of supporting taverns and suffering hangovers, is it any surprise that they save their kopecks better than do the Russians?

Fourth, intellectually as well, the Tatars at that time were ahead of the Russian peasants and townspeople, for they had schools in the hamlets as well as in Kasimov, and these stood under the authority of their clergy. Of course, they were taught to read and write in Tatar, but at least they were taught something, at least their minds were stimulated, and there were very few completely illiterate men among them. We would very often walk past the Kasimov Tatar school in the summer on our way to the little river Babenka to gather herbs [for Barkov's pharmacy], and almost every time we would see the students taking a break in the street, in front of the building, wearing only their linens and the skullcap on their heads. If we left them alone,

---

* According to the medieval *Primary Chronicle*, this was the reply that Vladimir (Grand Prince of Kiev, 978–1015) gave to Bulgar emissaries who urged him to adopt the teetotaling Islamic faith. He instead decreed that his people, the Rus' (ancestors of today's Russians, Ukrainians, and Belarussians), convert to Orthodoxy.

they would never in any way offend us or pursue us with the gibes that our coreligionists gave out so generously, and they would allow us to come into their school and show us their alphabet.* But we could not help displaying our Orthodox spirit, and so we might show them a pig's ear or make rude allusions to Mohammed, but in that case we needed to be as far away from them as possible, or else our ribs might have to pay the price for our gibes.

Fifth, communal ties with each other, sobriety, and a degree of education gave the Tatars the ability to make money through commerce and other occupations, not only in Kasimov, but also in other places, even Petersburg. Many of their merchants had commercial ties to Kazan, Astrakhan, Orenburg, and even Khiva and Bukhara— rumor attributed the latter to Salekh.[56]† I knew several Tatar stores in Petersburg and bought dressing-gowns in one of them, on Nevskii Prospekt near Nikolaevskaia Street. In Petersburg, it was especially popular (because of their sobriety) to hire Tatars from Kasimov as custodians *(dvorniki)*, coachmen, and servers in confectioner's shops; in those cases, their clergy allowed them to take off their national costume and wear the Russian one instead.[57]‡

I will not enumerate additional factors, but what I have said should be adequate to make clear why the Tatars of Kasimov were richer and enjoyed greater well-being than did the Russian common people. However, the inhabitants of Kasimov saw things differently: many times I heard them attribute the Tatars' well-being to the aid of the Evil One, who was very solicitous of these damned infidels. But they usually comforted themselves with the prospect that "they" surely would catch it in the fires of Hell in the next world, while we would enjoy heavenly bliss as reward for our faith in the crucified Christ.

---

* The Tatar language was written with Arabic letters.

† Cultural, ethnic, and family ties linked the Tatars with vast regions to the southeast. From Kasimov, one could travel down the Oka to the Volga and on to Kazan. The population of Kazan Province was one-quarter Tatar. From there a trade route led east to the frontier outpost of Orenburg—the eponymous province was 40 percent Tatar, Bashkir, or Chuvash—and on through the Kazakh steppes and the deserts of Central Asia to the independent Uzbek khanates of Khiva and Bukhara, which had long been important stations along the "silk road" that linked China, India, and the Middle East. Astrakhan, where the Volga flows into the Caspian Sea, is another gateway to the Middle East. The Tatars of Kasimov were linked to all these peoples—Tatars, Bashkirs, Chuvashes, Kazakhs, Uzbeks—by the similarity of their Turkic languages and Islamic faith (except for the Christian Chuvashes), though the Tatars were more sedentary, secularized, literate, and orthodox in their Islamic beliefs than were some of these other peoples.

‡ Like coffeehouses in Western Europe, these upscale, often Swiss-owned establishments in St. Petersburg and Moscow offered their patrons waiter service and the opportunity to peruse recent Russian and foreign journals.

Their wealth, or at least prosperity, made it possible for the Tatars not only to be independent of the surrounding Russian population but even to have power over it. Not in one Russian house in or near Kasimov does one meet a Tatar workman, while there are many Russians, especially female servants, in Tatar houses. Were a Tatar man or woman to live in a Russian family as a permanent hired workman or workwoman, what mockery they would have to endure, not only from the children but also from the adults: they would hear "damned infidel" and "heathen horsemeat eater"; they would be shown not only the semblance of a pig's ear formed out of the corner of the skirt of a coat, but also a real pig's ear; there would be relentless attempts to serve them ham, and pork, and suckling pig; and things would even be arranged so that they would eat some forbidden morsel that was slipped into their food. Needless to say, any housewife would reject with pious indignation their request to cook or roast a piece of horsemeat in the common oven—such an act would be seen as defiling the entire house. I know for certain, however, that Russian servants in a Tatar family will not see or hear anything offensive to their religious sensibilities; if, perhaps, some spoiled little boy does something foolish out of spite, his father and mother will not neglect to scold or punish him. The servants can be assured that no one will mock them by feeding or even offering them horsemeat. If the employers' lunch or dinner consists only of that, then a separate meal will be prepared for the Russian workman or workwoman.

One can often hear a rather strange complaint from Russian servants who work in Tatar households. "So, what's it like for you, living with the Tatars?" you ask. "Nothing that would offend the good Lord, honey," they reply, "it's a good life, we never see or hear any insults, the little ones are friendly and sweet, the master doesn't argue with us, not even the mistress gets mad, but it's so clean and neat that we really can't stand it anymore." Here is what that means. I have already spoken of the slovenliness that not only exists, but virtually rages, in the cabins of most Russian peasants. Not to mention the courtyard— unless it is on an incline from which the water runs off by itself, it is literally impossible to walk across it in rainy weather without sinking into the mud, and undemanding though the peasants might be in matters of comfort, they sometimes find it necessary to lay down boards of some sort so they can walk across without getting stuck in the mud. Naturally, it follows that the carts and domesticated animals have no fixed places and are left anywhere that is the least bit dry, even if it is right next to the entrance to the house. The Tatars, on the other hand, love cleanliness and order in those things. Their court-yard is usually paved and even swept clean, with separate sites for carts and animals, and the owner expects everything to be in its place. Not to mention the cabin, which even the Tatar peasant keeps cleaner and tidier than some Russian priests. In light of all this, it makes sense that Russian servants who, at home, are often used to living and sleeping in the same accommodations with swine, calves, and so on, who are accustomed to utter disorder in how they do things and where they put or even throw or shove things—that they would say they really can't stand how clean and neat it is in a Tatar household.

During the so-called working season, the number of Russian hired hands in Tatar households increases still more. In the hamlets, the Tatars own a far greater quantity of plowland than do the Russian peasants, and while they work it themselves, they and their families are not able to reap all the grain. So, Russians, especially women, come to work for them in entire parties and are hired to reap and thresh the grain, bring in the hay, and so on. During that time, many manage, as they say, to make a pretty kopeck. But even outside of the working season, Tatar traders provide much lucrative work for the surrounding Russian female population. They import various kinds of wool and "goat's fluff"* from the eastern provinces, especially Orenburg, and give it to the women for opening and loosening. Not only peasant women, but also women of the clergy take on this work. My sister Mar'ia often did it with her daughters. Unfortunately, this work is not without danger, for it has long been observed that Oren-burg "goat's fluff" and wool sometimes infect people in Kasimov with the Siberian sore.†

Lastly, I must say something about the Tatars in a religious respect.[58]‡ They have a fair number of mosques in the hamlets. I have seen three mosques near the village of Sinulitsy, low wooden build-ings with a little tower or something resembling a small turret on

---

* A particularly soft, delicate wool.

† I.e., malignant anthrax.

‡ Faced with the challenge of integrating the Muslim peoples along Russia's southeastern frontier into the empire, Catherine II and Alexander I sought to promote the practice of Islam in ways that encouraged loyalty to Russia. As part of this policy, they supported building or—as in Kasimov—restoring mosques and religious schools, and Muslim clerics, unlike their Orthodox counterparts, sometimes received government salaries. To counteract the influence of traditional centers of Islamic culture in Central Asia that lay beyond Russia's borders, a Muslim Spiritual Assembly, headed by a mufti, was established near Russia's frontier with Central Asia (its seat alternated between the towns of Orenburg and Ufa) to which all Muslim communities in the Russian Empire, with the exception of those in the Crimea, were administratively subordinated.

them. But the mosque in Kasimov, as I already said, is made of stone and is architecturally impressive. I particularly liked its tall minaret, which seemed more beautiful and better made than many church towers in Kasimov at the time. The clerics who formed Kasimov's Muslim hierarchy bore various titles; the ones I remember are *akhun,* mullah, *abyz,* and muezzin. A mullah is equivalent to our priest. An akhun is higher, somewhat like our archpriest. A muezzin takes the place of our bells and uses his voice to call the faithful to the mosque to pray; what the abyz's function is, I don't know.* Within the hierarchy, the akhun and the mullah were subordinate to the mufti of Orenburg, to whom, so I heard, they would travel either to receive instructions or for something resembling examinations and training for their duties. I must admit that I have not been able properly to verify this information regarding the Muslim clergy. However, I did often see the akhun and mullahs both on the streets and in Russian homes. They were easy to distinguish by the turban they always wore. I was struck by their sense of personal dignity and the special air of respectability and solemnity in their conversation, gaze, and gait. These were no Russian priests, now groveling and full of activity before the powerful, now arrogant and inaccessible toward the poor. I will not presume to elucidate the causes that make this contrast so unfavorable to us, because I have not had the opportunity to observe for myself the way of life and the degree of learning of the mullahs.

I don't know whether the Tatars of Kasimov performed all the daily ablutions and at-home prayers, so to speak, that are prescribed by Mohammed, but every Friday at the mosque there was always a religious service for which the faithful came together. During our excursions, we would sometimes hear the muezzin summon the faithful to prayer. He was a blind, vigorous, elderly but not yet old man. He would walk around the square near the mosque, alone, without escort, talking to himself, perhaps reciting prayers. He would find the rock near the mosque, put down his cane, step up onto the rock, cover his ears, and, in a loud voice, start not just saying but almost chanting something, all the while turning round and bowing in all four directions. On certain occasions however, I don't know which ones, he would ascend the minaret, and his strong and

---

* Dal's dictionary (1:5) gives the following definition for abyz: "Local usage in Riazan and Tambov provinces: Mullah, Tatar priest." However, in what may be a symptom of the anti-Muslim sentiment that Rostislavov mentions, Dal' also cites two further meanings: "Pejor. Infidel, impious person. Local usage in Iaroslavl' and Perm' provinces: scoundrel, insolent fellow," etc.

euphonious voice would resound from the platform and be audible in almost all the streets of the town. When the muezzin called out, so we noticed, all the Tatars in the streets would stop and wait until the end of his summons.

The worshippers would leave their galoshes, lined up in rows, at the entrance to the mosque. They did not stand in the mosque, but rather sat, in the Asian manner, on the rugs with which the floor was covered. They not only did not talk during the service, as is common in our churches, but they would not even turn around, and all their attention (at least externally) was focused on praying and listening to what the mullah was reading. During that time, you could have done anything you wished in the entrance or the lobby and not one of the faithful would have turned his head. There, again, the Russians could not help being mischievous and downright nasty. They would stand in the entrance and mix up the galoshes that had been left there, or even take away the odd pair; I remember how some strapping fellows of ours boasted of having gotten themselves "boots," that is, galoshes, in the *mizgit* (that is what they called the mosque). One time, some miscreants even dragged a dead piglet into the lobby. I don't know why the Tatars at the time did not have a guard by the entrance to the mosque.

Governor-General Balashov

• While we students were at home with our parents during the summer vacation of 1824, two locally noteworthy events occurred in Riazan: the death of Archbishop Sergii and the three-day visit of Emperor Alexander I to Riazan. [. . .] By way of introduction, I should talk about two celebrities of the time, Governor-General Balashov and the landowner and rich Riazanian, Riumin. Rumor had it at the time that these two celebrities were, in some sense, rivals. One was a man who stood close to the emperor, was actually his protégé, and had immense power in five provinces. The other also enjoyed the sovereign's favor, and though he had no official power, his immense fortune and mastery of the art of living allowed him to exert extensive influence in Riazan. People said at the time that Alexander had come to Riazan for Balashov's sake, but that it had been his personal decision, taken against Balashov's wishes, to stay at Riumin's house.

General of the Infantry Aleksandr (Dmitrievich, I think) Balashov had been the police chief in Petersburg in 1812 and had taken part in the intrigue that forced Speranskii into exile from the capital.[59]* Subsequently, he was minister of police for some time, and then, I don't remember in what year, he was made governor-general of Riazan. Apparently, that reassignment should not be taken as a sign that he had somehow fallen out of favor with the emperor. While he had lost the title of minister of police, the fact that the title of governor-general

---

* Aleksandr Dmitrievich Balashov (1770–1837), son of a senior official at Catherine II's court, was a cultivated, cosmopolitan member of the political and social elite. After spending the early part of his career in various provincial military commands, he was made police chief of Moscow in 1804, police chief of St. Petersburg—a very politically sensitive post—in 1808, and in 1810, minister of police. Having spent the 1812–1814 campaigns against Napoleon as a trusted member of Alexander I's personal suite, he was sent on diplomatic missions after the war. Upon his return to Russia in 1818, he helped implement a plan to reorganize provincial government by grouping clusters of provinces into governor-generalships. Riazan and several other provinces were selected as a test case, and Balashov was named governor-general on November 4, 1819, the same day he ceased to be minister of police—

placed five provinces (Riazan, Tula, Kaluga, Orel, and Voronezh) under his authority made him quite a substantial little tsar who was stronger, in terms of the number of his subjects, than any member of the German Confederation at that time except the Austrian emperor and the Prussian king; and indeed, he was jokingly, sometimes also mockingly, called "the little tsar of Riazan."[60]*

Of course, as a student in Riazan, I heard and actually saw a great deal of how this famous protégé of Alexander I's lived and acted in Riazan, but I learned far more still from the former Riazanian merchant Andrei Mikhailovich Shenn and the former chairman of the Riazanian chamber of the criminal court, Evgraf Ivanovich Stromilov. [Shenn] had been a wealthy and enterprising merchant under Balashov. The governor-general liked Shenn very much for the skillful way he carried out government contracts, so Shenn enjoyed the favor of Balashov and his entourage. I lived in his apartment for about four years, at a time when Shenn (whose other last name was Gladkoi) was almost a hundred years old. He was living in a fashion that was definitely no longer rich, almost poor, and he enjoyed reminiscing about the time under Balashov when he had been an important figure in Riazan whom even governors would come to visit. As for Stromilov, I got to know him on my father's recommendation as soon as I moved to Riazan in 1852, and I enjoyed his friendship right up until his death in 1868. As someone who had lived and served in Riazan almost without interruption, he also knew Balashov well, although Balashov apparently did not know him.

I don't know why Balashov took it into his head to settle in Riazan, which—then as now—was less attractive than Orel, Tula, Voronezh, and Kaluga. Once he had settled in Riazan though, he lived as befitted a famous Russian grandee and administrator. He took over a huge house on the best street in town. A military guard of two soldiers was always posted outside the entrance to his quarters. Wherever he drove

---

the ministry being disbanded. Balashov remained in that position until 1828, when the death of his wife and his own ill health caused him to resign.

Mikhail Mikhailovich Speranskii (1772–1839), whose early life must have been much like Rostislavov's—both were sons of priests, born about 37 years and 60 miles apart, and graduates of the St. Petersburg Ecclesiastical Academy—was Alexander I's most influential domestic-policy adviser in the years 1808–1812 and the author of far-reaching, but ultimately unrealized, liberal reform plans. Under pressure from conservatives, Alexander abruptly dismissed him in March 1812 and sent him into internal exile in eastern European Russia. Beginning in 1816, he again occupied various senior governmental positions, though none as significant as in 1808–1812.

* In 1811, the five provinces reportedly had 5,597,800 inhabitants. By contrast, in 1816, Bavaria—the most populous German state other than Prussia and Austria—had 3,560,000.

in town, he was escorted by a mounted gendarme,[61]* and on festive occasions, such as the so-called imperial holidays—when he drove to the cathedral for services—he had two gendarmes galloping behind him and the town police chief sitting with him in his carriage or sleigh. It goes without saying that the residents of Riazan—whether out of respect for the governor-general or fear of ending up at the police station for alleged disrespect toward the authorities—would take off their hats and bow before His High Excellency.

It goes without saying that all sorts of officials came to him every day with reports and memoranda. On all holidays, something akin to [both] grand and minor palace receptions took place in his quarters. The late Shenn told me that it was usual for all individuals who were more or less prominent, not only officials but also noble landowners and merchants, to feel obligated to make an appearance in the governor-general's receiving hall around noon, after mass. There they would wait, sometimes for a good hour or more, for the prince of Riazan to appear. When he finally made his entrance, all would line up and bow. Then the ritual began: this one would enjoy the favor of a conversation; that one, a handshake; some would find that, after they had bowed, they received in reply something that likewise resembled a bow; another would be passed by with merely a gaze, or without even being glanced at. There also, necessarily, were more overt expressions of the authorities' dissatisfaction: reprimands were issued, and instances of carelessness were pointed out. If someone had not been very diligent about appearing at these receptions, he would be reminded that it seemed to have been quite a while since he had last been seen. The effect of all this was that most individuals who had both the right and the duty to appear at this court made an effort to please their commander and, if they did not appear every holiday, at least they did not dare miss many holidays in a row. On the imperial holidays, Easter, New Year's, and so on, these gatherings involved very many people. I don't know why and when, but the gatherings took place both before mass and afterwards. We little boys would make a point of walking to Cathedral

---

* Under Alexander I, the term "gendarme" could refer either to the military police, or—more likely in this context—to members of "gendarme divisions" that carried out police duties among the general population and were locally under the command of either (civilian) police chiefs or (military) garrison commanders. When, under Nicholas I, the Third Section of His Imperial Majesty's Own Chancellery was established in 1826 with the mission of monitoring and combating domestic subversion, it took control of the gendarmerie, which henceforth became associated with political repression and efforts by the central government to intervene in local affairs.

Street to see how the governor-general, racing to the cathedral for services in the company of his two gendarmes, was followed at the same speed and at various intervals by droshkies, coaches, carriages, sleighs, and so on, in which sat various officials with embroidered collars.* When mass was over, the same convoy would sometimes race to the governor-general's house. Even the coach of His Grace,† drawn by four horses harnessed in pairs, soon also set out to visit the tsar's representative.

Since he was governing five provinces, sending out a great many instructions, and receiving all sorts of reports in far greater numbers still, Balashov needed a large administrative staff. The staff was housed in a separate building that in earlier times had served as the governor's quarters. Just like on a ministerial staff, the chief of staff when I was studying in Riazan was a high-ranking official, one Kavelin. I think he was an actual state councillor; at least, he had a very large house for his quarters.‡ There were many who wished to join the staff—so-called mommy's boys§ even came from Petersburg for this purpose, and residents of Riazan considered it an honor to be accepted as a member. Overall, though, the team of officials on the staff seems to have been good. People were interested in this assignment not only because it offered a better salary than did the offices of the provincial government, but also because the governor-general liked to give these officials—as individuals known personally to him or at least to his chief of staff—positions in government offices at both the provincial and the district level. [. . .]

Balashov himself seems to have been an honest man while he was in Riazan. He had already made quite a fortune as police chief of Petersburg, so in Riazan he could afford to be, or at least appear to be, honest. But not all of his associates were indifferent to the lure of money. Shenn told me a characteristic story about the provincial police chief, whose (probably not disinterested) favor he enjoyed. A certain town police chief had made some sort of important mistake and was supposed to come to Riazan to explain himself to the provincial chief. Before appearing in front of this fearsome judge, he thought it best to predispose him in his favor with an appropriate little bribe, so he came to Shenn for advice. After discussing the matter,

---

* Embroidered collars were a part of the uniform of civilian government officials.

† I.e., the archbishop.

‡ An official in class four on the fourteen-level Table of Ranks, an actual state councillor was the civilian equivalent of a major general. Balashov himself, as a general of the infantry, was in class two.

§ I.e., spoiled and capricious young men.

they decided to try to appease the wrathful judge with a gift befitting his status. Shenn went to negotiate. He appeared before the provincial chief and said, "You know, this little bird (by which he meant the guilty town police chief) has flown here, and now it doesn't know how to come before you, with one wing or two" (a "wing" meant one hundred rubles). "Well, isn't that something," the provincial chief replied, "how is a little bird supposed to fly with one wing! What is this bird, anyway, that you found with just one wing?" However, this high-ranking zoologist preferred that the wings be brought to him by Shenn, not by the little bird itself. After the ceremony had been performed, the town police chief appeared and was given the appropriate oral reprimand and dismissed to return in peace to his God-fearing community to compensate himself for the losses he had sustained as a little bird. Of course, my kind landlord Shenn also did not go unrewarded for his role as "righteous intermediary."[62]*

Balashov tried to introduce what he thought were improvements in the provinces entrusted to his authority. In Riazan, his improvements mainly concerned the streets. Before he arrived, they were unpaved (with two or three exceptions), and sidewalks were either nonexistent or such that walking on them was quite inconvenient. As a result, even though many people walked and drove on the unpaved streets of old, they were almost impassable. I personally saw carriages turn from Cathedral Street onto Seminary Street (which was unpaved), advance a few dozen sazhens, and come to a halt, even though four horses might be harnessed to them.† Despite the tireless application of the coachmen's and postilions' whips, the horses simply would not move any farther. Lanky footmen would then open the carriage doors and carry their mistresses to the pavement or sidewalk on Cathedral Street, while people would be asked and ropes be brought on to help the horses rescue the carriage from the mud, and after intense joint effort and even more intense shouting they would somehow pull the carriage out.

---

* A local police chief's entire annual salary in 1796 (and salaries were little altered in the following years) was 300 rubles. Therefore, this official's willingness to offer a 200-ruble bribe to his superior suggests that his official salary constituted only a small part of his overall income, much of which presumably came from bribes. This was typical of conditions at almost all levels of Russian officialdom.

† Cathedral Street is wide, straight, and runs for about two-thirds of a mile from the seventeenth-century Cathedral of the Assumption (in the Riazan Kremlin) to the New Market Square and the beginning of the Moscow road. It forms the northern side of a quadrangle that comprised most of the town and that was redeveloped on a grid pattern under plans approved by the imperial government in 1780. The yellow, neoclassical seminary building (which presently houses airborne forces of the Russian army) was near the edge of town, one block north of Cathedral Street on Seminary Street.

In this regard, Balashov really did much that was good for Riazan. Of course, down to this day about a third of the streets still have no pavement, but almost all the streets that are paved became so under Balashov, and it was also under him that sidewalks were built almost everywhere. Of course, they were not, so to speak, completely "mudless" in bad weather, but at least you could mostly walk on them without having to worry about getting stuck in the mud or leaving your boots behind. To facilitate the construction of pavement for the town, Balashov used his authority to establish a special tax on everyone— meaning, naturally, the peasants—who entered Riazan. Everyone was required to turn in at least three small cobblestones at the city gates, or pay so-and-so many kopecks. That is why there were good-sized piles of cobblestones at the time at the Moscow and Astrakhan gates, where the fee-collectors were posted who took in the tax. I don't know whether the two-kopeck pieces added up to large piles, though; rather than showing those off, they slipped them into their pockets.

Despite the exceedingly obvious usefulness of the sidewalks, Riazanian homeowners were very unhappy about the governor-general's orders. Not only the sidewalks, but I surmise the pavement as well, were installed at the homeowners' expense; [I know that,] at least, despite all its pleas, the seminary had to spend its own money, not the town's, to pave the street in front of its building and courtyard. But even if the pavement in front of the houses of private owners was built at town expense, the necessary money, a previously unprecedented expenditure, was still taken out of the homeowners' pockets in the form of a special tax. Then they began lighting the town with lanterns on many streets, and again money was needed. Finally, in the more prominent streets, both the sidewalks and the pavement had to be swept every day, for which a custodian had to be hired. Obviously, the homeowners' pockets suffered again.

This was aggravated by a further misfortune. Balashov tried to eliminate fraud and profiteering in commerce, so he gave orders to supervise weights and measures, make sure that the merchants did not harass the peasants who conducted business out of their carts on market days, and so on. Riazan's merchant profiteers would either have to give up their traditions of fraud and profiteering, or spend money to pay off the police. But even the latter did not always help. Like Harun al-Rashid,* the governor-general liked to walk about the town and the market in civilian clothes and often had the opportu-

---

* Eighth-century A.D. caliph of Baghdad, a protagonist in the *Arabian Nights*.

nity to see for himself the tricks of the merchants. That, of course, got the police into trouble, and they, in turn, took it out on the merchants. In a word, Riazanian homeowners and merchant profiteers had plenty of reasons to dislike the governor-general. Sometimes they even cursed him out loud.

Once, a townsman found an opportunity to make a stinging remark to him that the people of Riazan later took pleasure in repeating. Under Balashov, a new jail was built in Riazan that looked like a kind of knight's castle, with four towers at the corners, a high wall around the courtyard, and an iron gate.* Balashov came in civilian clothes to inspect the construction site, saw a crowd of gawkers, walked up to them, and said, "Well, folks, how do you like that little house?" "Pretty nice," answered the folks, who either really did not recognize the governor-general or only pretended not to recognize him. But he continued, "And did you folks realize that this house is being built for you?" Then a townsman, who, so they said at the time, was only pretending not to know the governor-general, replied with a smile, "Come on, milord, stop making fun of us—how could we ever live in a house like that? If only you, sir, were so lucky as to spend some time there." Of course, Balashov did not pursue the conversation.

Riazan owes him a special debt of gratitude for improving the fire department, which had of course existed before he arrived but had been of very little help when fires actually occurred. As former police chief of Petersburg, Balashov truly organized it very well, and under him fires were never permitted to destroy [too] many houses.†

Riazan's merchant profiteers and homeowners were not the only ones who did not like Balashov—senior and middling officials hated him almost more than did the people of the town. The provincial governor, the chairmen and councillors of the chambers,‡ and other top officials at the provincial level found themselves exposed to constant oversight by His High Excellency, eternally having to "stand at attention," constantly having to worry that some peasant's or townsperson's complaint might place them in the disagreeable position of having to provide explanations to higher authorities regarding a delay or

---

* The prison, located near the Moscow road (barely outside of town in Balashov's time), still remains in use today.

† In Russian towns and villages, with their mostly wooden buildings, catastrophic fires were a constant danger. Fire safety was one of the many responsibilities of the police, who in general had a mandate for regulating and enforcing public order and safety that extended far beyond that of modern police forces.

‡ I.e., the treasury and the law courts.

incorrect decision in some case. Less important officials might experience the same kind of trouble, and not only with the highest authorities but also with their immediate superiors. In addition, had there not been a governor-general in Riazan, all of the lesser officials could have nursed the hope of obtaining a more advantageous post in the provincial administration, or at least becoming a district-court secretary in some district capital. Instead, the governor-general's staff was an inexhaustible breeding ground for officials who received most of the appointments to positions of any importance.

Like its counterpart in town, the population in the countryside was very unhappy with the governor-general and had good reasons to complain about him. Balashov wanted to repair at least the so-called main roads in the provinces entrusted to him. The roads truly were in poor condition: in many places they were almost impassable during the muddy season, the bridges over brooks and rivulets had rotted, and in autumn and especially in spring, the wooden logs that had been laid across the Meshchora's numerous marshes would be floating on the water. My uncle Vasilii Martynovich told us, when he returned to Tuma from the seminary at Easter in 1818, that he and his companions had crossed the marshes in the so-called Forty (the forty-verst distance between the hamlets of Vlaskovo and Ershovo, which at the time was covered with dense forests) in the following manner. The logs were floating, and the smaller ones would usually sink into the water when someone stood on them, but at various intervals between them were fairly thick logs that could support a person. Consequently, one at a time, the seminarians would run across the less muddy logs, hoping to be on them as briefly as possible, and then stop for rest on the thick ones. A light log would often sink before the person who had stepped onto it had the time to get off, and sometimes even thick ones would turn over or also sink under the weight of two or three people; the result was that the seminarians would sometimes end up waist-deep in the water. In addition, the verst-posts, that mark of privilege reserved for our main roads, which seem to have been set up back under Catherine, had rotted and were still visible only here and there, like survivals of years long gone by. Lastly, for some reason the versts themselves in many places were marked as seven hundred sazhens long instead of five hundred.*

Balashov's improvements began with having the roads newly surveyed, but the surveying was not done everywhere with great precision.

---

* One verst was equal to 500 sazhens.

My father once asked a Riazanian land captain whom he knew, why it was that the versts were not all the same in the so-called Forty Forest. "You know, Father," the land captain replied, "it was hot when we were surveying the road and we often had to take breaks, so we would try to find dry, shady places where we could settle down comfortably. Out of gratitude, that's where we would set up a verst-post. Also, sometimes we would have had to set it up right in the marsh, where, of course, it would soon have rotted, so we tried to find it a spot that was drier. At least, one way or another, the verst-posts did get set up."

Furthermore, the width of the roads was set at 210 feet or even more,[63]* despite the fact that there were roads on which you could go for several versts without meeting anyone, so there was plenty of space! Drainage ditches at least two feet deep were dug on both sides of the road, not only in low-lying or flat areas, but even on knolls where water would not be able to gather anyway. Then, along both sides of each ditch, a strip ten to fourteen feet wide was raised seven inches or a little more above the rest of the road, so that it looked almost like a little terrace. The soil that was used to make this terrace was taken from the surface of the road, while the soil taken from the ditches was deposited in a narrow, rampartlike rise along the outside of the road. They would try to give the road itself the same shape as a cobbled city street, that is, the middle was supposed to be slightly elevated, and the road was supposed to slope from the middle toward the terraces on both sides and allow the water to run off toward the terraces. The terraces themselves were planted with two rows of trees, either birch trees or white willows, about fourteen or so feet apart.

And so, the trees were planted. A white willow, of course, is not very demanding and easily takes root if a branch or even a stick covered with bark is driven into the ground. For a birch tree, however, you need to choose the correct season and apply at least a little knowhow. However, since the peasants who planted them were not particularly skilled in this area, what they planted did not take root, and even the ones that did take root were broken, gnawed at, and dug up by the domestic animals grazing in the fields where the road lay. The following year, the planting needed to be done again, and to shield them against animals, orders were given to build a protective fence of

---

* This figure—30 sazhens, a standard width confirmed by other sources—is wider than a 17-lane U.S. interstate highway. In fact, imperial regulations established another category of roads that were supposed to be twice that width. In Siberia, there apparently still exist unpaved roads that are made enormously wide to ensure that at least a few lanes remain useable even when rain, mud, and vehicle traffic render most of the road's surface impassable. I thank Matthew Payne for that information.

willow twigs around each tree. These fences were shaped like inverted, truncated cones, and people referred to them as "baskets." Under their protection, the trees began to take root, but the sides of the baskets hindered the growth of their branches; and so, I think after about two years, orders were given to discard the baskets and instead drive four stakes into the ground by each tree and tie them together at the top and bottom with bunches of birch or willow twigs.

All the jobs I have described might be considered easy if they had been performed by peasants from the hamlets closest to this or that segment of the road. However, our wise administration, which has been looking after us since time immemorial and down to this day, divided the roads of each district among all the peasants in such a way that only a very few lucky hamlets were assigned segments that lay on their own fields or nearby. No, the peasants were required to travel twenty to thirty versts and more to their segments. Living close to their segments would have permitted them to do the work and still sleep and have lunch and dinner at home, and take the necessary trees for free from their own woods. Instead, they were required to go twenty to thirty and more versts, pay for lodging or else camp like gypsies in the middle of the road, bring their food supplies with them, and then obtain the trees themselves in the neighboring hamlets at greater or lesser cost. That was the first year. The following year, the difficulties increased, because in addition to the trees, the baskets were now needed as well. Then, after another two or so years, they had to come back again and buy four stakes for each tree.

Meanwhile, His High Excellency would have either seen for himself, or found out from his trusted officials and acquaintances, that the rows of trees on the terraces were growing poorly, that those lazy peasants did not know how to protect the trees against their sheep and swine or how to use a spirit level to even a road, and that the land captains were not dealing properly with this publicly useful and absolutely indispensable project. And so, reprimands would be sent out to the land captains, who in turn would rake the assessors* over the coals (there were no district police officers [*stanovye pristava*] yet at the time), and in the end it was the peasant's purse, the peasant's face, the peasant's hair, and the soft parts of the peasant's rear or else his back, that were held liable, and the consumption of birch or willow switches increased.

---

* The assessors were members of the land court, the district-level law enforcement unit headed by the land captain.

Improving the roads also resulted in other hardships for the peasants, in addition to the ones I have described. Bridges had to be built along the roads, of course in places where they were necessary and where they were in fact built, but also in places where they were not needed. In a word, I saw bridges that almost no one ever crossed, because there was almost never any water under them, either. In the summer heat, sheep and swine would usually take shelter under them to enjoy the shade. The reason for this excessive zeal was the fact that the construction of bridges was not assigned to the peasants of this or that hamlet, but instead was funded with money that was supposed to be collected from the peasants of the entire district. The plans for the bridges were made, and the competition for the contract to build the bridges was conducted, by officials in the towns. However, our architects have long had a knack for producing estimates that are two or even three times above what a construction job should cost, and the officials know how to conduct the competition in such a way that the contractors discount their estimate a little and then share the abundant profits with their benefactors—one hand washes the other. For example, in the Meshchora, the peasants themselves were also carpenters and at the time had plenty of forest, so all they would have needed was to cut the trees and haul them to a certain place, sometimes two or three or even fewer versts away. In that way, the bridge would have cost the peasants only a few workdays. However, the wise administration awarded all the contracts to its well-known protégés at prices almost identical to their original estimates, which is why they paid a thousand or even two thousand rubles for a bridge that could have cost a hundred, and [they paid] a hundred fifty or two hundred rubles for a bridge that would not have required ten to twenty to build. Of course, the peasants would have had no reason to be upset about this if the officials had paid with their own money. But the problem was that the money was collected from the entire district and then generously given away by the officials to the contractors, and also ended up in the pockets of the officials themselves. In settlements where there were postal stations,* the station houses were built in exactly the same way. Of course, the houses turned out to be very comfortable and pretty, and even now the station houses are better in Balashov's former governor-generalcy than in other provinces, except for the ones built by the imperial government along paved highways. But the cost of those houses and

---

* These were stations where travelers on official business could obtain fresh horses for their carriages.

bridges! As a former contractor on many such construction jobs, Shenn could not speak about them without becoming especially animated. "Those sure were times, Dmitrii Ivanovich! You could both make a pretty kopeck for yourself and be of service to others. Thousands would fall into your pocket, just like that."

Now that the saplings that were planted along the main roads have grown into fifty-year-old trees and, in many places, come close to forming shady alleys, there are many who admire them and extol Balashov. But the peasant of Balashov's provinces in the twenties had no reason to be enthusiastic about them. He had to leave home for several days, travel twenty to thirty or more versts, live under the open sky, seek shelter from the rain in his cart, bast mat, or homespun coat, sometimes get soaked to the skin, catch fevers and rheumatism, eat nothing but bread, and when he was out at work, he had to go to the nearest settlement for bread or even rusks from the priest, which he would obtain either for money or as alms, and he would dig ditches, often in the rain and in the mud. The next year, he would have go back again to set up the baskets, and later, to drive the stakes into the ground and tie them. As reward for these labors, he would be slapped in the face, punched in the jaw, and sometimes made to lie under the birch rods. Then, he had to give rubles from his own pocket for the bridges and postal stations. He might only be a peasant, but still, he understood that the roads did not need to be lined with trees, that the bridges and stations could be built at a price that was ten times cheaper, and that they could have assigned him a segment of road near his own hamlet instead of sending him someplace almost thrice-nine lands away.

Along main roads, the worst mud is found not in the fields but in settlements. I remember very many villages and hamlets whose streets would dry out only in the hottest summers, including Tuma, my home. Balashov had resolved to drain the settlements as well, but without success. For that purpose, he ordered that ditches be dug along the streets, near the houses, and that they be fenced off from the middle of the street by a balustrade made of little posts that rose two feet above the ground and were connected to each other with two bars at the top and bottom. In addition, trees were ordered to be planted in front of the houses, so that here, too, something like a tree-lined street would take shape. It was absurd to watch how these ditches and balustrades were installed everywhere, even in places where the settlement stood on a hillside and the water would drain off anyway to low-lying areas. Where the ditches were dug, they only caused problems and made the streets even muddier. In Tuma, for example, the clergy considered themselves a privileged estate and did not want to dig ditches in front of their houses. Even where ditches were dug throughout an entire settlement, nothing was done to drain the water to a place behind the houses or into a field, so the ditches not only filled up with water but actually overflowed. First the bars between the posts and the posts themselves would get broken, and then, especially at night, passing vehicles would fall right into the ditches and the horses would be unable to pull the wheels back out. There was no choice but to ask the local residents for assistance, and they were often not averse to selling their assistance at a high price,[64*] not to mention adding such helpful comments as, "What the hell got into you? Where the devil were you going? What, are you blind? What, there's no road here?" and so on. The trees that were planted took root almost nowhere.

---

* General staff officers found 30 years later that peasants in the area still earned tidy sums helping to free carriages stuck in the mud.

CHAPTER TWENTY

The Merchant Riumin

• Before Balashov, and after Balashov, and under Balashov, there lived in Riazan a native, one might say a natural and unrefined, celebrity: the state councillor Gavriil Vasil'evich Riumin, about whom even now, more than forty years after his death, quasi-mythical stories are told. Even though he was already over seventy in 1824, there were still in Riazan a few old men his age who had seen his childhood and knew his former occupations. By birth, Riumin was a townsman, and in his childhood and youth he had earned his keep hawking fritters, pancakes and pies, and pursuing various sorts of petty trade. Of course, he was very poor and survived from day to day any way he could, sometimes having enough to eat, other times going hungry.* Not long before 1824, there lived in Riazan a poor townsman named Kharin whom Riumin had once owed three half-kopecks for fritters or pancakes. Kharin was in the habit, when he had been drinking, of going up to the house of his former comrade in poverty who had now become rich, and shouting to him from the street, "Hey, Gavriushka, why won't you give me back my three half-kopecks that you took from me God knows when? I'm telling you, give them back, or I'll never leave you alone!" More than once he was given, not half-kopecks, but ruble coins and banknotes,† yet even as he took them he would keep saying, "That's not it, no, you have to give me three half-kopecks like the ones they used to have back then, just like you got three half-kopecks' worth of fritters from me." Of course, the drunkard would catch it both from the police and from Riumin's domestics, but nevertheless he loved reminding the rich man about his three half-kopecks.

---

* Even in Russia's largest cities, most retail trade until the early nineteenth century was conducted at markets and out of makeshift stalls rather than in shops. Prepared foods were sold mainly by street vendors, not inns or restaurants. Riumin's early career was typical of a townsman who was successful enough to have a ramshackle business that traded in odds and ends (rather than having to hire himself out as a laborer) but who lacked the wherewithal to establish a permanent, settled business.

† Banknotes existed only in denominations from 5 to 100 rubles.

Various rumors circulated about how Riumin had become rich, but they all concurred that he gave up fritters, pies, pancakes, and other objects of petty trade and, as the expression went at the time, "went into" the tavern business. He first got a position as "drinks server" *(podnoschik)*, that is, assistant to the liquor-farmer's sworn official, and then became a sworn official himself. That is when he attracted the notice of the rich Riazanian liquor-farmer Mal'shin, who made him his representative, his assistant, and so on. People even said that Riumin was able to enrich himself through his benefactor in ways that were less than honest, but, be that as it may, he soon became a liquor-farmer himself and enrolled, of course, in the first merchant guild.[65]* From here it was not far to the title of commercial councillor, and after he had spent several years in the rank of commercial councillor, even though he might have offered absolutely no counsel regarding Russian commerce, he was able to obtain the rank of court councillor.[†] In addition, Riumin made many significant donations to public causes; it was said, in particular, that he had donated up to a million for the war effort in 1812. All of this brought him medals, ranks, and celebrity.

[Translator's Note: Members of the merchant estate belonged to one of three "guilds," in accordance with their wealth and the nature of their business. To enroll in a guild, an individual needed to declare that he owned capital worth no less than a certain sum, which for the first guild was fixed at 10,000 rubles in 1775 and gradually raised to 50,000 by 1807. The annual tax that a merchant of any guild was required to pay was equivalent to 1 percent of the capital he had declared, e.g., 100 rubles for a first-guild merchant in 1775. (By comparison, third-guild merchants' minimum required capital grew from 500 to 8,000 rubles over the same period.) Above even the first-guild merchants stood the exclusive category of "honored citizens," which a businessman might join if his capital exceeded a minimum that was already set at a staggering 50,000 rubles as early as 1785. Given that even the 5-ruble tax for the third guild in 1775 was beyond the means

---

* Riumin (1751–1827) and Petr A. Mal'shin (1752–1821) are known to have operated together as liquor-farmers in three districts of Riazan Province by the 1780s. Both were subsequently by far the richest men in Riazan, competed in business, cooperated in donating money to the church, served as heads of the municipal government *(gorodskoi golova)*, and were ultimately ennobled.

† Commercial councillor was an honorific rank granted to some merchants. On a par with a class-seven title in the Table of Ranks, it theoretically made its holder the equal of a lieutenant colonel. Court councillor was also a class-seven rank but entailed a substantive role in government.

of most townspeople, one can appreciate the spectacular nature of Riumin's social ascent from his days as a street peddler who had to borrow half-kopeck coins: by 1790, Riazan (a town of several thousand inhabitants) had 196 merchants in the third guild, 2 in the second, 4 in the first, and—at the very top of the pyramid—only 2 "honored citizens," the former partners Riumin and Mal'shin. In Russia overall, the entire merchantry was outnumbered 17 to 3 by the even poorer estate of the townspeople. Membership in the guilds offered exemptions from military service and corporal punishment, the right to engage in particular types of business, visible and greatly prized symbols of social status (such as the right to drive certain types of carriages), and other valuable privileges.[66]

Riumin had an astonishing career—not discussed by Rostislavov in detail—that exemplifies the close connection between government patronage, business success, and advancement from merchant to noble status in eighteenth- and early nineteenth-century Russia.[67] Though Riumin apparently started out poor, other branches of his clan had been prominent Riazan merchants throughout the eighteenth century; around 1800, no fewer than five Riumin families were registered in the Riazan merchantry. After he had grown rich in the liquor trade, his promotion to court councillor in 1799 automatically gave him and his descendants membership in the nobility and reflected the government's appreciation for his valuable contribution to the state budget as a liquor-farmer. Over the next two decades, he occupied senior positions in Riazan town government and in imperial economic management. When he retired from state service in 1824, he held the rank of state councillor and was thus equal in status to the governor of Riazan Province; rank dictated the use of honorific titles, seating arrangements at formal dinners, and other symbolic matters that were important anyway in Imperial Russia but held special significance for social climbers who wished to shed the stigma of their humble origins. Medals (*ordena*) awarded by the tsar were coveted for the same reason. Riumin's sons studied at Moscow University and became civil servants and army officers, thereby demonstrating what the ultimate goal of upwardly mobile Russian merchants was: to leave the merchantry, join the nobility, and enter government service, thereby exchanging the merchant's humble status and precarious position (since maintaining merchant status depended on continuing financial success) for the social recognition, status security, and right to acquire serfs that membership in the hereditary nobility conferred.][68]

The late Emperor Alexander I heard about him, met him, came to like him and became the godfather of one or several of his children, and whenever he came to Riazan, he would always stay at Riumin's house. Balashov was once unhappy with Riumin over something and prepared lodgings for the sovereign in some other house. But when the sovereign was taken to the lodgings that had been set aside for him, he said, "What is this? I want to stay at Riumin's," and ordered that he be taken there. The old man had been prepared, just in case, and so the emperor found his previous lodgings looking just as they had on his earlier visits.

Rewarded with ranks and medals, Riumin nevertheless did not forget what had allowed him to obtain them—money. He had lived and made his fortune as a clever and resourceful liquor-farmer, and now that he had become a nobleman, he began buying peasants with the money he had amassed. At his death (which occurred, I think, in 1827), it turned out that he bequeathed to his children, according to what people said, more than ten thousand peasant souls and up to fifteen million rubles in cash.[69]* Even after he had become a state councillor and a rich man, and had the sovereign as his children's godfather, this former pancake-man and drinks server apparently did not forget his earlier poverty and was a very good landlord to his peasants. He imposed on them very moderate dues *(obrok)*, twenty or thirty rubles per assessment unit,[70]† supplied his peasants with land in quantities that were more than adequate, and above all, his name provided them protection against harassment by officials. The land captain, the assessor, the solicitor, even the entire temporary unit established to conduct some investigation or other, all were wary of pressing one of Riumin's peasants, except perhaps that they liked to visit Riumin's bailiffs to have tea, eat, and drink. It therefore is not surprising that Riumin's peasants lived well, and beggars were rare among them. In and around Tuma, Riumin's peasants were the most affluent.

As the clergy put it, he also did not neglect the churches of God. In Riazan, he built the second story of the cathedral bell tower and

---

* A "soul" meant one male peasant, so the number needs to be doubled to calculate the total number of individuals. By the late 1850s, only 1 percent of Riazan Province's 5,595 landlords owned more than 1,000 souls, while 80 percent owned 100 or fewer (51 percent owned 20 or fewer), and it was reported by spokesmen for the nobility that "one-fourth of all the noble households of that province were so poor that 'together with their peasants they form one family, eat at one table and live in one hut.'" Riumin was thus an unimaginably rich serf owner even by noble standards, and his wealth in cash was similarly breathtaking.

† An assessment unit *(tiaglo)* was often, though not always, one household.

arranged for the cathedral to be heated.[71]* Furthermore, priests whose parishes included peasants of Riumin's could boldly go to the peasants' master; there was almost no instance of his refusing assistance to a petitioner when a church's needs were explained to him, and usually he gave substantial sums. My father went to see him a number of times in connection with the construction of the stone church and other matters. He told me that he was received in the most polite manner, and it even happened that Riumin would attend only to Father, hear him out about his needs, and then ask him to stay for a while and have tea, and would talk with him for an hour or two, even if it meant abandoning his guests.

Twice Father had the opportunity to see his treasury. This is how he described one of these instances. After listening to the account of the Tuma church's needs, Riumin called for his housekeeper and asked my father, "Would the reverend archpriest come into my storeroom?" His storeroom was set up in a windowless corner of his house. First there was, I think, a red wooden door, and then an iron one with several locks. When both doors were open, Father, who had followed the housekeeper and Riumin into the storeroom, saw a large iron chest that was attached with chains from all sides. Riumin first tested the padlocks, then ordered the housekeeper to open the chest, and when the lid had opened with the aid of some sort of mechanism, he quickly examined the inside of the chest, where Father noticed piles of banknotes and sacks of coins.

The old man said to his housekeeper, "Take the thousand rubles in that corner over there." Riumin then took them in his hands, ordered her to close the chest, and tested every lock after the housekeeper had closed it. He did the same with the locks on the doors. When they had reached one of the rooms, he ordered the housekeeper to put the bunch of keys back into the same drawer in the chest from where she had earlier taken it, and the key to the drawer he put into his own pocket. After giving Father the money and asking him to be sure to count it, he said, "I don't keep much money in this chest of drawers, Father. Instead, I always go myself to get it from the storeroom; it's safer that way."

[Riumin did not socialize much with merchants, but nobles and officials had easy access to him and were frequent visitors to his

---

* Riumin gave 30,000 rubles to renovate the Cathedral of the Nativity of Christ the Savior in Riazan, as well as 10,000 to restore the crumbling Cathedral of the Assumption and 40,000 for its bell tower. This was in addition to 27,000 donated to institutions to aid the poor and orphans in Riazan.

house.] Riumin provided various amusements to the other inhabitants of Riazan as well. For several years, he maintained at his own expense a theater in Riazan that contemporary rumor said caused him up to ten thousand rubles in pure losses. I never attended any performances at that theater myself, but heard with what enthusiasm the students in the theological and philosophical classes talked about what they had seen and heard there. They especially praised some opera called *The Water Nymph (Rusalka)*.[72]* Furthermore, all residents of the town—if they were properly dressed, of course—had access the whole summer long to Riumin's country estate. It is located near town and even now is almost the only place where you can breathe the fresh air of the fields while being able to take shelter beneath shady trees and amble along smooth, level paths. It was maintained far better under the older Riumin than under his son and grandson, for at the time, a small hamlet of serfs had as its only obligation to keep the grove in clean condition. Annually at that country house, on the occasion of various family celebrations, Riumin would arrange to have very nice fireworks. These were especially magnificent at the weddings of his two daughters, one of whom, incidentally, married General Pavlenko, who later commanded the Riazan militia in the Crimean War.

Balashov sought to compete with Riumin by likewise arranging fireworks on his wife's name day, but in Riazan itself, in the middle of town so to speak, on vacant land near the secondary-school *(gimnaziia)* building. But those fireworks were far less impressive than Riumin's, not to mention that a stray rocket could have set fire to the best streets in town, and they soon ended owing to the death of the governor-general's wife. That death gave Riazanians the opportunity to see what was, for their town, a most grandiose funeral. Not only was the funeral service held in the cathedral and did the entire Riazanian clergy, led by the prelate himself, participate in the ceremony, but the funeral procession was escorted from the cathedral to the Moscow Gate by literally thousands of onlookers of all estates (a tomb had been prepared for the deceased somewhere away from Riazan). I don't know why, but we had no classes that day, so we too gazed in astonishment at the canopy that covered the hearse on which the coffin lay, the funeral attire of the horses and people, the burning torches, and so on.

---

* Perhaps a reference to *Lesta, dneprovskaia rusalka* (1803) or *Rusalka* (1804), operas by Stepan I. Davydov that apparently were based on the German composer Ferdinand Kauer's *Das Donauweibchen*.

Soon, one after the other, the two rivals not only parted company with each other but also left Riazan forever. As I already said, Balashov left for Petersburg to be a member of the State Council. Then it was Riumin's turn, but he left by that road by which all people must leave sooner or later. Most likely, some time in the past, once he had become rich, he had not wanted to content himself with our green liquor,* even though it had given him wealth, public esteem, and even a touch of aristocracy. I suppose that he took up champagne and other wines of Western provenance, for which he received Bacchus's punishment by contracting the rich man's disease. Long before I moved to Riazan I heard that Riumin's body was all swollen, that his legs and arms were covered with sores, that each day they would cover him with plaster, that the fingers on his hands were thick from swelling and plastering and that he always wore gloves to hide them when he met with people. That is how popular rumor described the gout that the Lucullus of Riazan suffered, apparently for decades, in his feet and hands. Rumor also had it that he did not treat himself with plasters alone, but that he also followed the example of King David. How accurate that is, I cannot say. However, I had the opportunity personally to judge how gout in his feet and hands affected this old Céladon when he would come to our so-called public examinations.†

Although he signed even his own name very poorly and was not able to read well, and all he read were promissory notes, contracts, and so on, especially great care was shown to invite him to the seminary for examinations, so that his keen liquor-farmer's eye might evaluate our scholarly work and so the honor of his attention might stimulate us to pursue further learning. How tense everyone would become when he arrived! He would still be straining to climb with difficulty out of his carriage with the aid of two strong footmen, slowly lowering his feet from one step to the next, only barely managing to drag them even across the level sidewalk, yet in the room it was already being said out loud that "Gavrila Vasil'evich is here, Gavrila Vasil'evich is here!" The examination would come to a halt. The rector and the inspector would rush to meet their honored benefactor. The others would stare at the door, and even the archbishop seemed to sense the arrival of a new luminary who was about to eclipse him.

---

* I.e., grain alcohol.

† Lucullus was an ancient Roman known for his ostentatious elegance. Céladon—the name of a shepherd in the novel *L'Astrée* by Honoré d'Urfé—was, according to the 1835 edition of the *Dictionnaire de l'Académie française*, an ironic term for "a delicate and passionate lover." Given this context, the reference to King David may concern his illicit affair with Bathsheba.

At last, the luminary arrived in the room. All would rise. Barely moving, he would accept the other luminary's blessing, and, without kissing the hand that blessed him, give his own hand to those whom he considered worthy of the honor, while bowing his head to others. He would take a seat next to the archbishop and receive from the rector himself a written overview of the subjects that the examination was supposed to cover. Finally, they would remember us, and with a movement of the head, eyelash, or hand, command us to be seated. Little by little, all would become quiet and the interrupted examination would resume. And, surprise! One's surroundings do certainly have a magical effect. This former seller of fritters and pancakes, this drinks server and liquor-farmer, would also ask questions that were listened to and discussed with the attention that was due, if not to his mind, then at least to his purse. In those situations, we would "be all eyes."

However, neither Riazanian medicine with its plasters, nor the Davidian compresses, could save the Lucullus of Riazan from the bony old woman with her scythe. As I already said, Riumin passed away in 1827. On that occasion, his children and heirs took the trouble to provide the inhabitants of Riazan a spectacle that was not exactly common. The deceased lay in one of the large rooms of his enormous house, on an elevated catafalque, in a magnificent casket that was covered with the richest brocade and surrounded with candlesticks holding the thickest candles. Riazan's high society was invited to the memorial services that were held twice a day by the casket, with the clergy jointly singing "With the Saints Give Rest"* and "Eternal Memory." The remaining middling and lower society were permitted to honor the memory of the deceased by paying their respects during the memorial services. The doors to the house were open to anyone who wished to enter; one merely had to wipe one's feet before coming in. The casket was somewhere far away from the anteroom, so one had to pass through a long series of rooms where the servants were posted in the appropriate funeral attire. Then visitors reached the catafalque and the casket, where they were permitted to pause briefly, pay their respects to the deceased, and proceed onward, but through different rooms; as a result, they had the opportunity to admire just about all the rooms on the second floor of the palace of the deceased. The actual transfer of the body from the house to the Trinity Monastery and the funeral service there were

---

* "With the Saints give rest, O Christ, to the soul of your servant, where there is no toil, nor grief, nor sighing, but everlasting life."

not very majestic. Of course, the hearse, the canopy, the horses and coachmen in funeral attire, the torches and spruce branches—those were all as they should be. Although the prelate, who was then living in Petersburg, could not attend the funeral, there nonetheless were plenty of clergymen, under the solicitous leadership of our rector, and the choristers sang "Holy God" with the deepest devotion. Behind the casket, in proper funeral attire, walked the four sons of the deceased, without caps despite the cold weather and the three-verst distance between the house and the monastery. But not very many people turned out to escort the casket. Everywhere, in the streets, there stood a fair number of gawkers, but they did not join the melancholy ceremony in which only about two hundred people walked behind the casket.

Since our rector and inspector were taking part in the ceremony, some of us, including myself, had the opportunity to leave the seminary and join the funeral procession. We decided to do this because rumor had it that the rector [Iliodor] would give a sermon. So, we listened to it. I have had many occasions to hear graveside orations; they were particularly in fashion at that time, especially at seminaries. Even for a boy of fourteen or sixteen, speeches, sermons, even verses would be composed and would be delivered in church over the casket or at the cemetery when it was lowered into the grave. Of course, they did not hold back with pompously vacuous phrases, since it was difficult to find thoughts that were truly meaningful for such all-too-common occasions. But Iliodor's funeral sermon was truly a model of empty, pointless seminary verbiage. The basest flattery for the deceased, overblown praise for his virtues, an abundance of ecclesiastical and biblical words that were combined into turgid phrases, banal reflections on the vanity of the world and the transitory nature of earthly happiness and so on—even we seminarians, who had almost no literary taste, found all of this too farfetched and unbearably phony.

I will say a few words about the children and heirs of the Lucullus of Riazan. I have already said that his daughters were married, but there remained four sons: Nikolai, Aleksandr, Vasilii, and Ivan. It was among them that the father's rich inheritance was divided, since the daughters had earlier been provided with dowries.

Nikolai was a worthy son of his father and had a love and a knack for saving and acquiring money, and it is probably in recognition of that knack that his father rewarded him more than his other sons. According to the rumors of the time, the peasants were supposedly divided evenly among the sons, with each one inheriting about three thousand souls or so. However, Nikolai inherited just about all or at least most of the money, and he sought to bring it quickly under his direct control. When his father was still alive, he was already living in his own house virtually across the street from his father's palace. While his father's body lay in the house, the money chest remained in the storeroom. As soon as the body had been solemnly seen off to the Trinity Monastery, however, people acting on Nikolai Gavrilovich's authority transferred the chest to his house with almost even greater solemnity, and, of course, with all the bundles and sacks that were stored in it.

The second son, Aleksandr, for some reason was considered to be a fool. I don't know whether that is true, but I did notice that he wept the most of any of the children both during the transference of their father's body and during the funeral. Vasilii and Ivan were youths of twenty or a little older. Aleksandr soon died, so I cannot say anything about him, but Vasilii inherited the hamlets of the parish of Tuma and the environs of that village. In his dealings with the peasants, he was probably the best of Riumin's sons. A few years after his father's death, he resolved himself to an act that was rare during the time of serfdom—emancipating his peasants to become free agriculturalists.[73]* This act deserves all the more praise because his older brother Nikolai would have given him a far greater sum than what the peasants were required to pay for their emancipation. This magnanimous man did not live long. Ivan lived in Petersburg. All I know about him is that he was a member of that city's prison committee and that he, too, did not live long.[74]† None of these three brothers had any offspring, and in fact they probably never even married.

Nikolai alone was to perpetuate his family tradition. Having received millions of rubles and thousands of peasant souls into his possession, he followed in his papa's footsteps, became one of our esteemed liquor-farmers and, so people said for a long time, acquired an immense fortune. For about thirty years or more, the

---

* The 1803 Law on Free Agriculturalists "permitted the emancipation of serfs, singly or in groups, if they could come to mutually satisfactory terms with their masters. Because of bureaucratic obstacles in the execution of the law and the indifference of the majority of nobles, only 37,000 male serfs out of 10 million were freed under the terms of this act" by 1825.

† The Society for the Supervision of Prisons was a philanthropic organization with close ties to the Russian government and to British social reformers. Established in 1819 to bring religion and better material conditions to prison inmates, it was typical of the Protestant-inspired social, educational, and religious policies pursued by Alexander I after 1815.

Riazan nobility continually elected him honorary curator of their secondary school. In that capacity, he really did render the school enormous services. Not to mention the fact that, after buying his father's palace from one of his brothers—Vasilii, I think—he donated it for a boarding school for noble children, but he also annually made more or less substantial donations whose total amount exceeded a hundred thousand rubles. Yet when liquor-farming was abolished, this rich man attempted a variety of unsuccessful, speculative business ventures, and while of course he did not become poor, he nonetheless ceased to be a rich man and did not leave his only son God knows what kind of fortune. That son has a gaunt, emaciated, prematurely aged sort of physiognomy, and his own only son also does not promise to be healthy. It would therefore be no surprise at all if the posterity of our rich man were to come to an end after the fourth generation.[75]*

---

* Nikolai Gavrilovich Riumin (1793–1870) achieved the high government rank of privy councillor (class three) and had twelve children, of whom five survived to adulthood: four daughters, and one son, Fedor, who married a princess from the blue-blooded Golitsyn clan and in turn had one son—also named Fedor—who died childless.

CHAPTER TWENTY-ONE

The Death of the Tsar

• In Riazan, just as in almost all of Russia, the announcement of Emperor Alexander I's death came as unexpected news.* I remember how, at the end of November or the beginning of December, we were joking and laughing amongst ourselves, carefree, when suddenly the great cathedral bell rang.

"Hey, brothers, the prelate must have died," someone said cheerfully. Then it rang a second time, and a third time, and so on. Everyone was perplexed. Soon, however, the news spread that an imperial edict had been received regarding the death of the sovereign and the oath of loyalty to the new tsar. Discipline was temporarily forgotten, and all who wanted hurried into town. I managed somehow to slip into the cathedral, where the people were already flocking in droves. The church bells continued ringing for about an hour and a half as officials with their embroidered collars, the merchantry, the nobility, and so on crowded into the cathedral. [The new archbishop] Filaret† also appeared, with an expression on his face that befitted the sadness of the news. Once he was robed in his funeral chasuble,‡ the archdeacon read the manifesto on the death of the previous emperor and the accession to the throne of the new sovereign Konstantin Pavlovich.

We were incredulous at the death of Alexander, the very one who had covered himself with glory by his victories over Napoleon. After the manifesto, they began celebrating the memorial service. Who was the first to weep, I don't know—probably many did so. As though they were contagious, tears began to appear in the eyes of all the people who were assembled in the cathedral, especially after they had seen Filaret, who was barely moving around the cathedral to incense the icons and who was all in tears during the verses that begin with the refrain "Blessed are you, O Lord, teach me your statutes." That

---

* Alexander I died in Taganrog, on the Sea of Azov (near the Crimea), on November 19, 1825, at the age of 48.

† Filaret later went on to be metropolitan of Kiev.

‡ A vestment worn by the celebrant at mass.

made everyone feel even more like crying. I, too, cried along with the others. But the setting truly was mournful and solemn. The wax candles that everyone had been given and that were lit, the doleful physiognomies, the funeral dirges sung by the choristers, and so forth, had a powerful effect even on people who felt indifferent. And when the archdeacon finally said and the choristers sang "Eternal Memory," there were not many in the cathedral who were not weeping.

The next day, we too were rounded up for the oath, as they said back then, with all the students of both the seminary and the church school gathering in the seminary church and our signatures then being taken that we had indeed sworn the oath. I don't know whose idea it was, but even little boys of nine or ten years were rounded up for the oath. Truth be told, though, it made us very proud, and we assumed that surely we were important individuals if it was thought necessary to have us take the oath of loyalty to the new tsar.

By the time we broke for the holidays, nothing had been heard yet in Riazan about the Fourteenth of December and the replacement of Konstantin with Nicholas.* When I arrived home, my father, who had returned from a tour of his superintendency, said confidentially that there had been a mutiny in Petersburg and yet another emperor had mounted the throne. A day later, during the night, an assessor † came galloping into the village with an edict regarding both events. At once they began ringing the large bell, people came running to the church, and the edict about Nicholas's mounting the throne and so on was read out; then they also read the oath. However, only the clergy and townspeople took the oath, while the peasants, both state or economic peasants as well as serfs, were not considered worthy of this honor.

The mutineers, that is, the Decembrists, were regarded at the time as the progeny of Hell, the children of Satan. The nobles were quite disconcerted that their brothers should have wanted to topple the tsars from their throne and establish a republic that would have taken their peasants away from them.

---

* Initially, it was assumed that the childless Alexander's brother Konstantin would succeed him. After some confusion, it became clear that Alexander and Konstantin had earlier agreed that the heir would actually be their younger brother Nicholas. With Konstantin in Warsaw (from where he governed Russian Poland), and Nicholas in St. Petersburg, it took several weeks to clear up the matter. Amidst the confusion, on December 14, a group of noble officers (subsequently known as Decembrists) attempted to stage a coup in St. Petersburg, ostensibly to defend Konstantin's rights against the "usurper" Nicholas, but actually to take power themselves and carry out liberal reforms.

† A representative of the land captain.

Endnotes

1. Rostislavov, "Peterburgskaia dukhovnaia akademiia" (September 1883), 238; *Allgemeine deutsche Biographie,* ed. R. von Liliencron, 56 vols. (Leipzig: Duncker & Humblot, 1875), 2:156; Titlinov, 1:145, 150.

2. GARO, *f.* 129 (Riazanskaia kazennaia palata), *op.* 19, *d.* 49, "Svedeniia o prikhodakh," *l.* 387; *Rospisanie gorodskikh i sel'skikh prikhodov,* no pagination; Freeze, *Russian Levites,* 115.

3. GARO, *f.* 129, *op.* 1, *d.* 29, *l.* 367 *ob.*

4. *Spiski arkhiereev ierarkhii vserossiiskoi i arkhiereiskikh kafedr so vremeni uchrezhdeniia sviateishago pravitel'stvuiushchago sinoda (1721–1895)* (St. Petersburg: Sinodal'naia tipografiia, 1896), 13.

5. GARO, *f.* 129, *op.* 7, *d.* 67 ("1795 god. Revizskie skazki sviashchennosluzhitelei Kasimovskogo uezda"), *l.* 809, and *op.* 19, *d.* 49 *l.* 425; Baranovich, 458–79.

6. Tikhon Vozdvizhenskii, *Istoricheskoe obozrenie Riazanskoi ierarkhii i vsekh tserkovnykh del seia eparkhii ot uchrezhdeniia eia do nyneshniago vremeni* (Moscow: V Tipografii S. Selivanovskago, 1820).

7. RGIA, *f.* 802, *op.* 1, *d.* 138, *ll.* 18, 96, 98 *ob.*

8. Freeze, *Parish Clergy,* 53.

9. Baranovich, 458–79.

10. GARO, *f.* 129, *op.* 19, *d.* 49, *l.* 416 *ob.*

11. *Voyages en Europe, 1829–1855,* reprinted in *Le Voyage en Russie: Anthologie des voyageurs français aux XVIIIe et XIXe siècles,* ed. Claude de Grève (Paris: Robert Laffont, 1990), 641.

12. Bernhard Grzimek, ed., *Grzimek's Animal Life Encyclopedia,* 8 vols. (New York, 1972–75), 8:406, 416.

13. For a description of peasant homes, see *The Peasant in Nineteenth-Century Russia,* ed.Wayne S. Vucinich (Stanford: Stanford University Press, 1968), 4–8.

14. GARO, *f.* 129, *op.* 19, *d.* 60, "Okladnaia kniga 7-i revizii. Goroda Kasimova i [ego] Uezda. 1816," *l.* 103 *ob.*

15. GARO, *f.* 129, *op.* 19, *d.* 49, *l.* 416 *ob*–417, and *op.* 43, *d.* 222a, *l.* 113 *ob.*

16. I. A. Chistovich, *Rukovodiashchie deiateli dukhovnago prosveshcheniia v Rossii v pervoi polovine tekushchago stoletiia* (St. Petersburg: Sinodal'naia tipografiia, 1894), 29–35, 39–42, 84, 111.

17. GARO, *f.* 129, *op.* 19, *d.* 49, *ll.* 425 *ob*–426; *op.* 32, *d.* 222a, *l.* 115 *ob.*

18. Ibid., *op.* 19, *d.* 49, *ll.* 425 *ob*–426; *op.* 32, *d.* 222a, *l.* 113 *ob.*

19. Ibid., *op.* 32, *d.* 106, *l.* 374 *ob.*

20. Benedikt Franz Johann Hermann, *Statistische Schilderung von Rußland* (St. Petersburg: Bey Christian Tornow und Compagnie; Leipzig: In Commission bey Friedrich Gotthold Jacobäer, 1790), 467–68; Friedrich Raupach, *Reise von St. Petersburg nach dem Gesundbrunnen zu Lipezk am Don* (Breslau: Bei Wilhelm Gottlieb Korn, 1809), 89–90, 238; *Russkii biograficheskii slovar',* 19:219; Aleksandr Turgenev, *La Russie et les Russes,* 3 vols. (Paris: Au comptoir des imprimeurs-unis, 1847), 2:396–432; Jerome Blum, *Lord and Peasant in Russia: From the Ninth to the Nineteenth Century* (Princeton: Princeton University Press, 1961), 464, 470; V.I. Semevskii, "Sel'skii sviashchennik vo vtoroi polovine XVIII veka," *Russkaia Starina* 19 (May–August 1877): 501–38, 520.

21. *Russkii biograficheskii slovar',* 19:218.

22. Baranovich, 458–79.

23. GARO, *f.* 4, *op.* 47, *t.* 9, *d.* 6768, "Posluzhnoi spisok Kasimovskago zemskago suda Oprisudstvuiushchikh Sekretare iprikazno Sluzhiteliakh," *ll.* 27 *ob*–28; *f.* 98 (Riazanskoe gubernskoe dvorianskoe deputatskoe sobranie), *op.* 38, *d.* 28, "Delo o dvorianstve roda artillerii-porutchika Karla Vasil'evicha fon-Kronshteina," *ll.* 2, 4, 5 *ob.*, 19; *f.* 129, *op.* 19, *d.* 60, *ll.* 265 *ob.*, 395.

24. Walter M. Pintner, *Russian Economic Policy Under Nicholas I* (Ithaca: Cornell University Press, 1967), 76–81.

25. Georg von Reinbeck, *Flüchtige Bemerkungen auf einer Reise von St. Petersburg über Moskau, Grodno, Warschau, Breslau nach Deutschland im Jahre 1805,* 2 vols. (Leipzig: Bei Wilhelm Rein und Comp., 1806), 1:252.

26. GARO, *f.* 129, *op.* 32, *d.* 106, *l.* 468 *ob.* Baranovich, 458–79.

27. GARO, *f.* 129, *op.* 32, *d.* 222a, *l.* 107 *ob.*

28. Dal', 2:491.

29. Ibid., 4:840.

30. Elise Kimerling Wirtschafter, *Social Identity in Imperial Russia* (DeKalb: Northern Illinois University Press, 1997), 43–44.

31. M. Zabylin, *Russkii narod: ego obychai, obriady, predaniia, sueveriia i poeziia* (Moscow: Izdanie knigoprodavtsa M. Berezina, 1880; reprint, Moscow: Sovmestnoe sovetsko-kanadskoe predpriiatie "Kniga Printshop," 1990), 218.

32. *Entsiklopedicheskii slovar',* eds. F.A. Brokgauz, I.A. Efron, 41 vols. (St. Petersburg, 1890–1905), 9: 358–59.

33. Boris N. Mironov, *Russkii gorod v 1740–1760e gody: Demograficheskoe, sotsial'noe i ekonomicheskoe razvitie* (Leningrad: Izdatel'stvo Nauka, 1990),143.

34. GARO, *f.* 626 (Kasimovskoe dukhovnoe uchilishche), *op.* 1, *d.* 3, *ll.* 109 *ob*–110, "Perechnevaia vedomost' o uchashchikhsia v Kasimovskom Dukhovnom uezdnom i prikhodskom uchilishchakh."

35. Ibid.

36. Titlinov, v. 1, passim.

37. GARO, *f.* 626, *op.* 1, *d.* 2, "Kasimovskoe uezdnoe dukhovnoe

uchilishche," *ll* . 234 *ob*–235; Evgenii V. Mikhailovskii, Irina V. Il'enko, *Riazan', Kasimov* (Moscow: Izdatel'stvo "Iskusstvo," 1969), 203–23; Protoierei Vladimir Pravdoliubov, *Religioznaia istoriia Kasimova* (Kasimov: Izdanie Uspenskoi tserkvi g. Kasimova, 1998), 23–24; Nikolai I. Shishkin, *Istoriia goroda Kasimova s drevneishikh vremen* (Riazan: Tipo-Litografiia N.D. Malashkina, 1891; reprint, Riazan: Izdanie gazety "Blagovest'," 1999), 160–64.

38. GARO, *f.* 1280 (Riazanskaia dukhovnaia seminariia), *op.* 1, *d.* 36, *t.* 2, *ll.* 480 *ob*–481; *f.* 626, *op.* 1, *d.* 7, *sviazka* 3, no *list* numbers.

39. GARO, *f.* 626, *op.* 1, *d.* 3, *l.* 32.

40. Titlinov, 1:298–99; GARO, *f.* 626, *op.* 1, *d.* 3, *ll.* 13–14.

41. GARO, *f.* 129, *op.* 22, *d.* 222a, "Kazanskii zhenskii monastyr'," *ll.* 52–53; *f.* 1280, *op.* 1, *d.* 36, *t.* 2, "Vedomost' o Smotritele i uchiteliakh Kasimovskago Dukhovnago uezdnago i prikhodskago uchilishch za 1822 god," *ll.* 480–84; *f.* 626, *op.* 1, *d.* 7, *sviazka* 3, no *list* number (personnel files of 1826); *d.* 37, *ll.* 245–245 *ob,* "Rospisanie chasov Gospod uchitelei."

42. GARO, *f.* 1280, *op.* 1, *d.* 37, *l.* 245 *ob.*

43. Laurie Manchester, "The Secularization of the Search for Salvation: The Self-Fashioning of Orthodox Clergymen's Sons in Late Imperial Russia," *Slavic Review* 57, no. 1 (Spring 1998): 50–76, 67.

44. Chapter 22, p. 94 of the original.

45. Manchester, "Secular Ascetics," 271; Titlinov, 1:95, 314, 351, 353, 374; Freeze, *Russian Levites,* 135–36; GARO, *f.* 1280, *op.* 1, *d.* 28, no *list* number.

46. Freeze, *Russian Levites,* 53–54.

47. GARO, *f.* 1280, *op.* 1, *d.* 36, *t.* 1, *l.* 270 *ob.*

48. Ibid., *t.* 2, *l.* 365.

49. Ibid., *l.* 482.

50. GARO, *f.* 626, *op.* 1, *d.* 3, "Kasimovskoe uezdnoe dukhovnoe uchilishche," *ll.* 13–14; *f.* 1280, *op.* 1, *d.* 28, no *list* numbers; *f.* 1280, *op.* 1, *d.* 36, *t.* 2, *l.* 482 *ob.*

51. D.Iu. Filippov, "Kasimovskie otkupshchiki," *Riazanskie Vedomosti* (24 June 2000).

52. Andrei Azovtsev, "Sud'ba potomkov proroka v Rossii," *Riazanskie Vedomosti* (24 June 2000).

53. On D.S. Barkov (1772–1837) and the long-lived merchant dynasty he founded, see D.Iu. Filippov, "Torgovyi dom Kasimovskikh kuptsov Barkovykh: K istorii predprinimatel'skikh dinastii Rossii," in *Otechestvennaia istoriia: Liudi. Sobytiia. Mysl'. Sbornik nauchnykh trudov kafedry Otechestvennoi istorii* (Riazan: Riazanskii gosudarstvennyi pedagogicheskii universitet im. S.A. Esenina, 1998), 163–75. Rostislavov discusses him in ch. 22 of the original.

54. See Abby M. Schrader, "Containing the Spectacle of Punishment: The Russian Autocracy and the Abolition of the Knout, 1817–1845," *Slavic Review* 56, no. 4 (Winter 1997): 613–44.

55. Thomas Riha, ed., *Readings in Russian Civilization,* 3 vols. (Chicago: University of Chicago Press, 1969), 1:1–11.

56. Vladimir M. Kabuzan, *Narody Rossii v XVIII veke: Chislennost' i etnicheskii*

sostav (Moscow: Izdatel'stvo "Nauka," 1990), 43–45, 237–46; *Entsiklopedicheskii slovar': Rossiia*, 148–50.

57. Jean-Geoffroy Rohr, *Un missionnaire républicain en Russie* and Jean-Baptiste May, *Saint-Pétersbourg et la Russie en 1829*, quoted in *Le voyage en Russie*, 824, 978.

58. Vishlenkova, 125–30; Shishkin, 181–82.

59. *Russkii biograficheskii slovar'*, 2:443–44.

60. Adol'f G. Rashin, *Naselenie Rossii za 100 let (1811–1913 gg.): Statisticheskie ocherki* (Moscow: Gosudarstvennoe statisticheskoe izdatel'stvo, 1956), 28–29; Nipperdey, 103.

61. Isaak M. Trotskii, *III Otdelenie pri Nikolae I; Zhizn' Shervuda-Vernogo* (Leningrad: Lenizdat, 1990), 13–14.

62. *Rossiiskaia Imperiia razdelennaia v gubernii v 1796 i 1797: Prezhde byvshie staty gubernskie, koi nyne peremeneny. 1776 do 1796* (n.p., n.d.).

63. *Entsiklopedicheskii slovar'*, 11:54; *Voenno-statisticheskoe obozrenie*, 14; Baranovich, 72.

64. Baranovich, 69.

65. Kusova, 61, 75–76, 78, 85.

66. Mironov, *Russkii gorod*, 163–64; Kusova, 31–32.

67. Manfred Hildermeier, *Bürgertum und Stadt in Rußland 1760–1870: Rechtliche Lage und soziale Struktur* (Cologne: Böhlau Verlag, 1986), 110–19.

68. *Russkii biograficheskii slovar'*, 17: 757; Kusova, 27, 40.

69. Blum, 376, 368; *Russkii biograficheskii slovar'*, 17: 757; *Dva veka riazanskoi istorii*, 22.

70. Blum, 444.

71. *Russkii biograficheskii slovar'*, 17: 758.

72. Ibid., 6:32; *Entsiklopedicheskii slovar'*, 28:768.

73. Allen McConnell, *Tsar Alexander I: Paternalistic Reformer* (New York: Thomas Y. Crowell, 1970), 35.

74. Judith C. Zacek, "A Case Study in Russian Philanthropy: The Prison Reform Movement in the Reign of Alexander I," *Canadian Slavic Studies* 1, no. 2 (Summer 1967), 196–211; Barry Hollingsworth, "John Venning and Prison Reform in Russia, 1819–1830," *Slavonic and East European Review* 48, no. 113 (October 1970), 537–56.

75. *Russkii biograficheskii slovar'*, 17:762–63.

Bibliography

WORKS BY DMITRII I. ROSTISLAVOV

Nachal'naia algebra. Moscow: Tipografiia Gacheva i Komp., 1868.
O pravoslavnom belom i chornom dukhovenstve v Rossii. 2 vols. Leipzig, 1866.
Ob ustroistve dukhovnykh uchilishch v Rossii. 2 vols. Leipzig, 1863.
Opyt izsledovaniia ob imushchestvakh i dokhodakh nashikh monastyrei. St. Petersburg: Tipografiia Morskago Ministerstva, 1876.
"Peterburgskaia dukhovnaia akademiia do grafa Protasova. Vospominaniia."
    Vestnik Evropy 7 (July 1872): 219–43; (August 1872): 664–706; (September 1872): 152–207.
"Peterburgskaia dukhovnaia akademiia pri grafe Protasove 1836–1855 gg."
    Vestnik Evropy 18 (July 1883): 121–87; (August 1883): 581–611; (September 1883): 200–48.

WORKS CITED

Archival Sources

Gosudarstvennyi Arkhiv Riazanskoi Oblasti (State Archive of Riazan Province), fondy 4; 98 (Riazanskoe gubernskoe dvorianskoe deputatskoe sobranie); 129 (Riazanskaia kazennaia palata); 626 (Kasimovskoe dukhovnoe uchilishche); 1280 (Riazanskaia dukhovnaia seminariia).
Gosudarstvennyi Arkhiv Rossiiskoi Federatsii (State Archive of the Russian Federation), fond 1395 (III otdelenie "sobstvennoi ego imperatorskogo velichestva" kantseliarii [sekretnyi arkhiv]).
Rossiiskii Gosudarstvennyi Istoricheskii Arkhiv (Russian State Historical Archive), fond 802 (Komissiia dukhovnykh uchilishch).

Printed Sources

Aksakov, Sergei. *A Russian Gentleman.* Oxford: Oxford University Press, 1994.
Akul'shin, P.V. "Riazanskii general-gubernator A.D. Balashov (reformatorskie plany Aleksandra I i Riazanskii krai)." In *Iz proshlogo i nastoiashchego Riazanskogo kraia. Sbornik nauchnykh trudov.* Riazan, 1995.

Allgemeine deutsche Biographie. Edited by R. von Liliencron. 56 vols. Leipzig: Duncker & Humblot, 1875.

Azovtsev, Andrei. "Sud'ba potomkov proroka v Rossii." *Riazanskie Vedomosti,* 24 June 2000.

Baranovich, M. *Materialy dlia geografii i statistiki Rossii, sobrannye ofitserami general'nago shtaba: Riazanskaia guberniia.* St. Petersburg: Tipografiia Tovarishchestva "Obshchestvennaia Pol'za," 1860.

Belliustin, I. S. *Description of the Clergy in Rural Russia: The Memoir of a Nineteenth-Century Parish Priest.* Translated and with an interpretive essay by Gregory L. Freeze. Ithaca, N.Y.: Cornell University Press, 1985.

Bibliograficheskii slovar' pisatelei, uchenykh i khudozhnikov, urozhentsev (preimushchestvenno) Riazanskoi gubernii. Edited by I. V. Dobroliubov and S.D. Iakhontov. Riazan: Gubernskaia Tipografiia, 1910. Reprint, Riazan: Izdatel'stvo Riazanskogo gosudarstvennogo pedagogicheskogo universiteta, 1995.

Biograficheskii slovar' studentov pervykh XXVIII–mi kursov S.-Peterburgskoi Dukhovnoi Akademii: 1814–1869 gg. (K 100-letiiu S.-Peterburgskoi Dukhovnoi Akademii). St. Petersburg: Tipografiia I.V. Leont'eva, 1907.

Blum, Jerome. *Lord and Peasant in Russia: From the Ninth to the Nineteenth Century.* Princeton: Princeton University Press, 1961.

Chistovich, I. A. *Rukovodiashchie deiateli dukhovnago prosveshcheniia v Rossii v pervoi polovine tekushchago stoletiia.* St. Petersburg: Sinodal'naia tipografiia, 1894.

Clyman, Toby W., and Judith Vowles, eds. *Russia Through Women's Eyes: Autobiographies from Tsarist Russia.* New Haven: Yale University Press, 1996.

"D.I. Rostislavov (po povodu 30 letiia so dnia konchiny)." *S.-Peterburgskiia Vedomosti,* 18 February 1907, 3.

Dal', Vladimir I. *Tolkovyi slovar' zhivogo velikorusskogo iazyka.* 4 vols. Moscow, St. Petersburg: Tovarishchestvo M.O. Vol'f, 1903–9. Reprint, Moscow: Izdatel'skaia gruppa "Progress," "Univers," 1994.

Dülmen, Richard van. *Kultur und Alltag in der Frühen Neuzeit.* 3 vols. Munich: Verlag C.H. Beck, 1999.

Dva veka riazanskoi istorii (XVIII v.–mart 1917 g.). Edited by I. P. Popov, E. S. Stepanova, E. G. Tarabrin, and Iu. F. Fulin. Riazan: Riazanskoe otdelenie Sovetskogo fonda kul'tury, 1991.

Entsiklopedicheskii slovar'. Edited by F. A. Brokgauz and I. A. Efron. 41 vols. St. Petersburg, 1890–1905.

Faggionato, Raffaella. "From a Society of the Enlightened to the Enlightenment of Society: The Russian Bible Society and Rosicrucianism in the Age of Alexander I." *Slavonic and East European Review* 79 (July 2001)

Filippov, Dmitrii Iu. "'Epokhi kupecheskikh dinastii' v zhizni provintsial'nogo goroda XVIII–XIX vekov." In *III Konferentsiia "Goroda Podmoskov'ia v istorii rossiiskogo predprinimatel'stva i kul'tury" (Serpukhov. 3–4 dekabria 1999 g. Doklady, soobshcheniia, tezisy)."* Serpukhov, 1999.

———. "Kasimovskie otkupshchiki." *Riazanskie Vedomosti,* 24 June 2000.

————. "Kupechestvo goroda Kasimova kontsa XVIII–nachala XX v." Avtoreferat dissertatsii na soiskanie uchenoi stepeni kandidata istoricheskikh nauk. Voronezh, 1998.

————. "Torgovyi dom Kasimovskikh kuptsov Barkovykh: K istorii predprinimatel'skikh dinastii Rossii." In *Otechestvennaia istoriia: Liudi. Sobytiia. Mysl'. Sbornik nauchnykh trudov kafedry Otechestvennoi istorii.* Riazan: Riazanskii gosudarstvennyi pedagogicheskii universitet im. S.A. Esenina, 1998.

Freeze, Gregory L. *The Parish Clergy in Nineteenth-Century Russia: Crisis, Reform, Counter-Reform.* Princeton: Princeton University Press, 1983.

————. *The Russian Levites: Parish Clergy in the Eighteenth Century.* Cambridge: Harvard University Press, 1977.

Gleason, Abbott. *Young Russia: The Genesis of Russian Radicalism in the 1860s.* New York: Viking Press, 1980.

Grzimek's Animal Life Encyclopedia. Edited by Bernhard Grzimek. 8 vols. New York, 1972–75.

Hermann, Benedikt Franz Johann. *Statistische Schilderung von Rußland.* St. Petersburg: Bey Christian Tornow und Compagnie; Leipzig: In Commission bey Friedrich Gotthold Jacobäer, 1790.

Hildermeier, Manfred. *Bürgertum und Stadt in Rußland 1760–1870: Rechtliche Lage und soziale Struktur.* Cologne: Böhlau Verlag, 1986.

Hollingsworth, Barry. "John Venning and Prison Reform in Russia, 1819–1830." *Slavonic and East European Review* 48, no. 113 (October 1970): 537–56.

Kabuzan, Vladimir M. *Narody Rossii v XVIII veke: Chislennost' i etnicheskii sostav.* Moscow: Izdatel'stvo "Nauka," 1990.

Kusova, Irina G. *Riazanskoe kupechestvo: Ocherki istorii XVI–nachala XX veka.* Riazan: "Mart," 1996.

Le Goff, Jacques. *Medieval Civilization.* Translated by Julia Barrow. Oxford: Basil Blackwell, 1988.

Le Voyage en Russie: Anthologie des voyageurs français aux XVIIIe et XIXe siècles. Edited by Claude de Grève. Paris: Robert Laffont, 1990.

Manchester, Laurie. "Secular Ascetics: The Mentality of Orthodox Clergymen's Sons in Late Imperial Russia." Ph.D. diss., Columbia University, 1995.

————. "The Secularization of the Search for Salvation: The Self-Fashioning of Orthodox Clergymen's Sons in Late Imperial Russia." *Slavic Review* 57, no. 1 (Spring 1998): 50–76.

Martin, Alexander M. *Romantics, Reformers, Reactionaries: Russian Conservative Thought and Politics in the Reign of Alexander I.* DeKalb: Northern Illinois University Press, 1997.

McConnell, Allen. *Tsar Alexander I: Paternalistic Reformer.* New York: Thomas Y. Crowell, 1970.

Mikhailovskii, Evgenii V., and Irina V. Il'enko. *Riazan', Kasimov.* Moscow: Izdatel'stvo "Iskusstvo," 1969.

Mironov, Boris N. *Russkii gorod v 1740–1760e gody: Demograficheskoe, sotsial'noe i ekonomicheskoe razvitie*. Leningrad: Izdatel'stvo Nauka, 1990.

———. *Sotsial'naia istoriia Rossii perioda Imperii (XVIII–nachalo XX v.): Genezis lichnosti, demokraticheskoi sem'i, grazhdanskogo obshchestva i pravovogo gosudarstva*. 2 vols. St. Petersburg: Izdatel'stvo "Dmitrii Bulanin," 1999.

Nipperdey, Thomas. *Deutsche Geschichte 1800–1866: Bürgerwelt und starker Staat*. Munich: Verlag C.H. Beck, 1987.

The Peasant in Nineteenth-Century Russia. Edited by Wayne S. Vucinich. Stanford: Stanford University Press, 1968.

Pintner, Walter M. *Russian Economic Policy Under Nicholas I*. Ithaca, N.Y.: Cornell University Press, 1967.

Pomyalovsky, N. G. *Seminary Sketches*. Translated and with an introduction and notes by Alfred Kuhn. Ithaca: Cornell University Press, 1973.

Pravdoliubov, Vladimir (Protoierei). *Religioznaia istoriia Kasimova*. Kasimov: Izdanie Uspenskoi tserkvi g. Kasimova, 1998.

Rashin, Adol'f G. *Naselenie Rossii za 100 let (1811–1913 gg.): Statisticheskie ocherki*. Moscow: Gosudarstvennoe statisticheskoe izdatel'stvo, 1956.

Raupach, Friedrich. *Reise von St. Petersburg nach dem Gesundbrunnen zu Lipezk am Don*. Breslau: Bei Wilhelm Gottlieb Korn, 1809.

Readings in Russian Civilization. 3 vols. Edited by Thomas Riha. Chicago: University of Chicago Press, 1969.

Reinbeck, Georg von. *Flüchtige Bemerkungen auf einer Reise von St. Petersburg über Moskau, Grodno, Warschau, Breslau nach Deutschland im Jahre 1805*. 2 vols. Leipzig: Bei Wilhelm Rein und Comp., 1806.

Riasanovsky, Nicholas V. *A History of Russia*. 3rd ed. New York: Oxford University Press, 1977.

Rospisanie gorodskikh i sel'skikh prikhodov, tserkvei i prichtov Riazanskoi eparkhii. N.p., n.d.

Rossiia: Entsiklopedicheskii slovar'. Leningrad: Lenizdat, 1992.

Rossiiskaia Imperiia razdelennaia v gubernii v 1796 i 1797: Prezhde byvshie staty gubernskie, koi nyne peremeneny. 1776 do 1796. N.pl., n.d.

Russkii biograficheskii slovar'. Edited by A.A. Polovtsov. 25 vols. St. Petersburg: 1896–1911. Reprint, New York: Kraus, 1962.

Schrader, Abby M. "Containing the Spectacle of Punishment: The Russian Autocracy and the Abolition of the Knout, 1817–1845." *Slavic Review* 56, no. 4 (Winter 1997): 613–44.

Semevskii, V.I. "Sel'skii sviashchennik vo vtoroi polovine XVIII veka." *Russkaia Starina* 19 (May–August 1877): 501–38, 520.

Shchukinskii Sbornik, vyp. 5. Moscow: Tovarishchestvo tipografii A.I. Mamontova, 1906.

Shepelev, Leonid E. *Chinovnyi mir Rossii. XVIII-nachalo XX v.* St. Petersburg: "Iskusstvo-SPB," 1999.

Shishkin, Nikolai I. *Istoriia goroda Kasimova s drevneishikh vremen*. Riazan: Tipo-Litografiia N.D. Malashkina, 1891. Reprint, Riazan: Izdanie gazety "Blagovest'," 1999.

Spiski arkhiereev ierarkhii vserossiiskoi i arkhiereiskikh kafedr so vremeni uchrezh-deniia sviateishago pravitel'stvuiushchago sinoda (1721–1895). St. Petersburg: Sinodal'naia tipografiia, 1896.

Tappe, August Wilhelm. *Neue theoretisch-praktische Russische Sprachlehre für Deutsche.* 2nd ed. St. Petersburg: in der deutschen Hauptschule zu St. Petri; Riga: bei Hartmann, Meinshausen, Deubner und Treuy, 1812.

Titlinov, B.V. *Dukhovnaia shkola v Rossii v XIX stoletii.* 2 vols. Vilna: Tipografiia "Russkii Pochin," 1908–9.

Trotskii, Isaak M. *III Otdelenie pri Nikolae I; Zhizn' Shervuda-Vernogo.* Leningrad: Lenizdat, 1990.

Turgenev, Aleksandr I. *La Russie et les Russes.* 3 vols. Paris: Au comptoir des imprimeurs-unis, 1847.

Vishlenkova, Elena A. *Dukhovnaia shkola v Rossii v pervoi chetverti XIX veka.* Kazan: Izdatel'stvo Kazanskogo Universiteta, 1998.

Voenno-statisticheskoe obozrenie Rossiiskoi Imperii. Izdavaemoe po Vysochaishemu poveleniiu pri 1-m Otdelenii Departamenta General'nago Shtaba. Tom 6, chast' 3. *Riazanskaia guberniia.* St. Petersburg: V Tipografii Departamenta General'nago Shtaba, 1848.

Vozdvizhenskii, Tikhon. *Istoricheskoe obozrenie Riazanskoi ierarkhii i vsekh tserkovnykh del seia eparkhii ot uchrezhdeniia eia do nyneshniago vremeni.* Moscow: V Tipografii S. Selivanovskago, 1820.

Wirtschafter, Elise Kimerling. *Social Identity in Imperial Russia.* DeKalb: Northern Illinois University Press, 1997.

Worobec, Christine D. *Peasant Russia: Family and Community in the Post-Emancipation Period.* DeKalb: Northern Illinois University Press, 1995.

Zabylin, M. *Russkii narod: ego obychai, obriady, predaniia, sueveriia i poeziia.* Moscow: Izdanie knigoprodavtsa M. Berezina, 1880. Reprint, Moscow: Sovmestnoe sovetsko-kanadskoe predpriiatie "Kniga Printshop," 1990.

Zacek, Judith C. "A Case Study in Russian Philanthropy: The Prison Reform Movement in the Reign of Alexander I." *Canadian Slavic Studies* 1, no. 2 (Summer 1967): 196–211.

Websites Used

Bible concordances:
  "Bibliia" (www.serve.com/irr-tv/Russian/Bible/index.html)
  "The Bible Gateway" (bible.gospelcom.net/bible?)
  "Project Elizaveta" (Old Church Slavonic Bible) (elisaveta.hypermart.net/text.html)
Dates of Orthodox holidays in the nineteenth century calculated by thinktime.tripod.com/cgi-bin/calendar/thinktime.cgi.
Dictionnaire de l'Académie française, 1835 edition: "Project for American and French Research on the Treasury of the French Language, University of Chicago" (www.lib.uchicago.edu/efts/ARTFL/projects/dicos/ACADEMIE/SIXIEME/sixieme.fr.html)

Orthodox search engine: "Tserkovnost: An Eastern Orthodox Resource
    Centre" (www.tserkovnost.org)
Texts of funeral rites:
    "Otpevanie mirian," published by the Holy Protection Russian Orthodox
        Church, Los Angeles (In Russian) (www.fatheralexander.org/booklets/
        russian/otpevanie.htm)
    "Anastasis, the Home Page of the Monastery of Saint Andrew the First
        Called Manchester, England" (in English) (web.ukonline.co.uk/
        ephrem/funeral.htm)
United States Census Bureau:
    "Population: 1790–1990" (www.census.gov/population/censusdata/
        table-16.pdf)
    Gibson, Campbell. "Population of the 100 Largest Cities and Other Urban
        Places in the United States: 1790 to 1990." U.S. Census Bureau, Popu-
        lation Division Working Paper No. 27 (www.census.gov/population/
        www/documentation/twps0027.html)

Index

DATE DUE

Demco, Inc. 38-293